PRAISE FOR ADRIAN HAVILL'S BOOKS

THE SPY WHO STAYED OUT IN THE COLD

"Mr. Havill did his homework—going beyond the headlines to provide an exhaustive picture of Mr. Hanssen by recreating detailed scenes from throughout his life and pointing to where the FBI went wrong."   —*Dallas Morning News*

"Compelling . . . Mr. Havill pieces together more than 100 interviews of the veteran FBI agent's friends, colleagues, co-workers and family members—along with information from several confidential sources—to answer the important questions of why and how he did it . . . a meticulous portrait."   —*The Washington Times*

"*The Spy Who Stayed Out in the Cold* is much like reading a well-written mystery. This one, however, happens to be true.
                                                       —*Tulsa World*

"A fascinating portrait . . . well-written and carefully researched."
                                                  —*The Indianapolis Star*

"A timely biography . . . numerous interviews with Hanssen's friends, neighbors, and acquaintances . . . The most fascinating aspect here—and what perhaps most reveals the man's true nature—are the samplings of correspondences exchanged over the years."
                                                      —*Kirkus Reviews*

"Havill's chronicle of the Hanssen–KGB relationship reads like a John le Carré novel, full of codes and secret signals . . . fascinating . . . an intriguing, unsettling portrait of a man whose poor finances and personal frustration drove him to betray his country."
                                                    —*Publishers Weekly*

"*The Spy Who Stayed Out in the Cold* presents the elaborate process by which the espionage was carried out."   —*The Weekly Standard*

MORE . . .

"A meticulous researcher, Havill generally paints on a larger canvas than the other accounts, adding fuller historical and diplomatic context. His intriguing speculation of how a Russian diplomat likely sold Hanssen's file to the FBI is unmatched in . . . other books."
—SunSpot.net

THE MOTHER, THE SON, AND THE SOCIALITE

"An instant true-crime classic! Gritty and riveting."
—*New York Post*

"Crime journalism at its best! Well-written, carefully researched."
—Jack Olson, bestselling author of *Salt of the Earth*

"The book's catalog of doctored passports and errant blood drops [offers] an engrossing account."
—*Time Magazine*

WHILE INNOCENTS SLEPT

"Written with compelling detail, *While Innocents Slept* plunges readers into the murky world of Sudden Infant Death Syndrome. Adrian Havill's fair-minded reporting keeps you guessing about a syndrome that can easily destroy an innocent parent's reputation or serve as a perfect mask for the cruelest of murders. Havill's thoroughly written account is a scientific spellbinder—a heart-beating mystery that is even more frightening because it is true."
—Pete Earley, Edgar Award–winning author of
Confessions of a Spy and *The Hot House*

"In *While Innocents Slept*, Adrian Havill offers up one of the most chilling and evil characters in the long, dark history of true-crime writing. People will be talking about this book for some time—as well they should!"
—Carlton Stowers, Edgar Award–winning author of
To The Last Breath

THE SPY WHO STAYED OUT IN THE COLD

The Secret Life of FBI Double Agent Robert Hanssen

ADRIAN HAVILL

St. Martin's Paperbacks

This book is for Jane and Miriam.

THE SPY WHO STAYED OUT IN THE COLD

Copyright © 2001 by Adrian Havill.

Cover photo © Nonstock.

ISBN: 0-312-98629-7

Printed in the United States of America

St. Martin's Press hardcover edition published 2001
St. Martin's Paperbacks edition / November 2002

St. Martin's Paperbacks are published by St. Martin's Press, 175 Fifth Avenue, New York, NY 10010.

10 9 8 7 6 5 4 3 2 1

CONTENTS

PREFACE

You are about to read the first inside account of the life of Robert Philip Hanssen. Government officials believe he has damaged U.S. security and revealed prized secrets on a level not seen since Julius and Ethel Rosenberg gave away America's nuclear exclusivity half a century ago.

I have lived six miles from Robert Hanssen for more than a dozen years. We have attended the same church, shopped in the same stores, and visited the same parks. I cheered on my son when he ran cross-country at high school meets in Nottoway Park in Fairfax County. According to the FBI, it was Bob Hanssen's favorite "dead drop" site, intelligence language for a hidden location where one deposits documents or money for pickup at a later date. I have never met Bob, but our paths have undoubtedly crossed. We have friends in common and have belonged to the same community swimming pool. Certainly, knowing the local terrain was of great help to me in writing this account of his life.

Northern Virginia, where both our families live, is populated in great numbers by those who work for covert government agencies. The most notorious double agent prior to Robert Hanssen was Aldrich Ames, who once lived within walking distance from my home. The U.S. Central Intelligence Agency's headquarters, where Rick Ames worked, is a seven-mile drive. Many of the people I see socially either are foreign diplomats or work for the CIA or the FBI. This book could not have been written without their help.

While many have asked me to omit them from this acknowledgment section, I do want to thank retired FBI agent Larry Cordell, former ambassador to Suriname, Dennis Hays, and Peter C. Murray of the FBI's Washington field office, who helped to steer me through the labyrinth that is the American intelligence community.

Krista J. Box was invaluable in helping to find Bob Hanssen's college classmates. Chase Culeman-Beckman and Betsy Beckman were my eyes and ears for New York, and I'm very grateful for the help of Amanda Beeler, Alan Schmidt, and Ruth Kremske in Chicago.

The number of people who were willing to speak to me about Bob Hanssen or otherwise help me in researching this account number more than one hundred. A few that I have to thank must begin with Bob Hanssen's mother, Vivian. That she chose to speak to me at all under difficult circumstances will always be remembered. Also, Fran Wauck, Bonnie's mother, answered factual questions despite her pain. Keith Higginbotham, Ph.D., Marj Lane, Connie Slack, Robert Brodsky, Kimberly Lichtenberg, Pete Earley, John L. Sullivan Jr., Tom Grubisich, Neil Knolle, Larry Butler, Jeffrey Davee, Jerald Takesono, Robert Lauren, Ron Sanderson, Victor Sheymov, Kay Kuciak, Martin Ziegner, John Hargrave, Crissy Mueller, Momcilo Rosic, Jack Drescher, Bill Sessoms, Ernie Rizzo, Brenda Atkins, Paul D. Moore, Ches Lain, and Pat Camden, all gave of their time unselfishly.

My photojournalist wife, Georgiana, was there to offer criticism and editing support throughout this project. I couldn't have done it without her.

Thanks also to my agent, Jane Dystel, who has represented me with energy and zeal for more than a decade. It has been an interesting journey.

My editor at St. Martin's, Charles E. Spicer, and his two assistants, Joe Cleemann and Anderson Bailey, did yeoman work in transforming the text from manuscript to type rapidly. This book is as much theirs as it is mine.

Robert Hanssen's letters to his handlers have been reproduced exactly as provided by the FBI. No changes were made to the punctuation, grammar, or spelling.

A final note. Though confidential sources are never cited, no poetic licenses were taken in the writing of this account. For example, if I describe a KGB agent as sweltering in ninety-degree heat on a certain summer day, the reader can be assured that the temperature for that time was checked. Or when the number of litters a rabbit produces in a year is mentioned, the reader should know that a park naturalist was interviewed.

Adrian Havill
Reston, Virginia
July 2001

INTRODUCTION

Spying has been called the world's second-oldest profession. Prostitution, of course, is the first. If you think about it, the two occupations are not that dissimilar. A member of a brothel plies her trade, first for the money, and then for the interesting type of labor that is required and the thrills it sometimes offers. In the twenty-first century the thrill often comes first for someone who chooses to spy either for or against his country. Compensation can be secondary, a way of measuring one's skills and worth to an employer. Ideology, the decision to risk one's life for a political belief, is now a distant third.

The two careers can be illegal or legal. Prostitution's legality is determined by the jurisdiction in which the prostitute works. In the world of espionage, legality depends upon one's employer. Spy for your country and you are a quiet, unsung hero. Spy for another nation and you are a traitor, a monster. Getting caught while working for the wrong side can mean death.

Robert Philip Hanssen, the subject of this account, has done as much damage to his country and its intelligence secrets as anyone since the aforementioned Rosenbergs. Julius and Ethel Rosenberg gave away nuclear secrets to the

Russians because they believed fervently in the Soviet form of socialism; with Robert Hanssen, political ideology was largely absent. Bob Hanssen did what he did partly for the thrills the game of espionage provided him and partly for the hundreds of thousands in dollars, diamonds, and Rolex watches he received from his KGB/SVR handlers. At times he would tell them he couldn't spend all they were giving him without drawing attention to himself and urged that they pay him less. The political policies of his employers seemed irrelevant to him. He began working for what became the Russian Federation in 1985 when it was still the Soviet Union and beginning to dismantle its communist government. Soon after that it segued into a republic where the worst aspects of capitalism raged and ran rampant, at times out of control. Bob Hanssen continued to live frugally, spending portions of the fortune he received on private schooling for his children and home improvements. He lived in a brown, wood-and-brick, split-level house in the Washington suburbs with far-from-new cars and an old minivan in the driveway. Church and family activities seemed to take up most of his time away from his work as a highly regarded senior FBI agent with a Top Secret clearance. He specialized in counterintelligence.

But it wasn't only for thrills and cash. As we shall see, the mysticism inherent in facets of the Catholic religion may have driven him and his genuinely disturbed mind into believing what he was doing was ordained.

Men may have been sent to their deaths because of Robert Hanssen. He knew their names and maybe their families. It can be argued that they were only his counterparts—agents of another nationality who knew the risks. Did he view them as one does soldiers killed in battle? When espionage agents are executed, spies on both sides usually pause, shudder, shrug their shoulders, and continue their work. They are, after all, largely unseen foes. That families and children may be attached to the fallen is forgotten. This is necessary. Such is the nature of a life spent as a spy.

*   *   *

"Gentlemen do not read each other's mail," U.S. secretary of state Henry Stimson said in 1929. America had intercepted a coded message from a foreign government, and Stimson would have none of it. His sentiments were not behind the times; they were naive. Spying is a profession that traces its roots to the Bible and into prehistory. Espionage has employed gentlemen, gentlewomen, prostitutes, and barflies. The socially prominent are ideally suited for the profession. They have access to the highest echelons of power—generals and politicians—people who dictate policy and know secrets. They have access to each other's mail. And, unlike Secretary of State Stimson, they read it.

George Washington and Benjamin Franklin sanctioned, organized, and operated spy rings during the American Revolution. During the Civil War, a wily and aristocratic Southern belle named Rose Greenhow ran one of the most prominent salons in Washington. As hostess, she seduced politicians and military officers alike, extracted from them whatever useful information they had, and sent it straight to her Confederate handlers. Her actions cost the Union the lives of more than fifty thousand soldiers.

By the last decades of the nineteenth century both the army and navy each had its own intelligence network. Still, the U.S. government continued to activate agents as the need arose, and then informally. Private citizens could be counted on to obtain technological secrets from rival nations. That was certainly the case in 1889 when Alfred Du Pont stole France's recipe for a new and better gunpowder by posing as a factory worker and putting in a few months at a plant where it was manufactured. Only in the first decade of the twentieth century—still a good twenty-one years before Henry Stimson's sanctimony got the better of him—did a centralized espionage network begin to take shape.

*   *   *

The Federal Bureau of Investigation had its genesis in 1908, calling itself at first the Bureau of Investigation. Its origin was humble. A single agent had the mission of "detecting and prosecuting crime" for an entire nation. (Today there are roughly twenty-five thousand men and women working both in Washington and operating from field offices in every large U.S. city with one- and two-man satellites in the suburbs.)

The Bureau began its counterintelligence actions in 1917. Following America's entry into World War I, the agency was assigned to enforce newly passed federal laws on foreign espionage and sabotage. Some seven years later, a young attorney named J. Edgar Hoover became the Bureau's sixth director, heading a group of agents that had multiplied to six hundred men. (Women would wait several more decades before being allowed the same status.) Hoover would head the FBI for nearly half a century, increasing his power and the Bureau's size as each year passed. At times his stature would rival and even surpass that of the president. His success resulted from a formidable publicity machine that controlled popular radio and television programs that chronicled the FBI. The Bureau's hunting of organized-crime members and bank robbers made those criminals household names. Who hasn't heard of John Dillinger, Pretty Boy Floyd, Baby Face Nelson, and Machine Gun Kelly, all captured or killed by faceless FBI agents?

Though today's image of Hoover is of a pudgy man who lived with his chief assistant and sometimes wore dresses— none of these allegations were ever conclusively proven— he established standards that partly endure. New agents were required to have university degrees, undergo arduous physical training, and abide by standards that were set down in a manual that became known as "the bible." Hoover insisted that every agent wear a suit, white shirt, and tie. (Following his death, colored and striped shirts were permitted, and today the code is simply "dress appropriately.")

The files of the FBI were said to detail the aberrant sexual activities of celebrities and politicians, as well as other Americans whose behavior had offended the Bureau. Fingerprints of virtually every American were cataloged. The FBI's forensic capabilities became known as the finest in the world. Soon, local police departments would begin to rely heavily on the Bureau's lab to solve cases.

The FBI was not always successful, though its biggest mistakes were suppressed. In the 1930s, it spent so much time cultivating its G-man image and tracking down gangsters that its counterintelligence divisions missed a huge spy ring operating in Hawaii. The group, known as the Kuhn organization, had spent years developing intelligence for the Japanese. The Kuhn group provided much of the information that led to Japan's successful attack on Pearl Harbor in December of 1941.

While the Bureau would claim that its intelligence division distinguished itself in World War II, many of its successes were due more to the ineptitude of the enemy spies themselves. Dropping off Germans by submarine for sabotage missions sounded daring and even possible. But not when many of them couldn't speak English and when double agents were often among them. Their thick accents made them easy prey with the FBI scooping them up and trumpeting the arrests.

Military intelligence reached new heights during World War II. Ingenious new methods included the use of Native Americans to communicate messages with one another in their tribal language, translating the words of signal officers who wanted to talk to one another securely over phone lines. (For example, the Comanche phrase for "crazy white man" was the code name of Adolf Hitler.) An armed services cryptology team deciphered what the Japanese had thought was a foolproof secret language of forty-five-thousand words. Each word was a sequence of five different numbers. Cracking the code, partly by using the fledgling science of computer programming, enabled the United States to intercept Japan's planned attack on Midway Island. The American victory in the battle changed the course of the war in the Pacific.

The advent of the Cold War followed total victory in Europe and the Pacific. Hoover fought the Soviet threat by authorizing illegal burglaries of both foreign embassies and domestic organizations that he thought might have communist leanings. In all, the Bureau would later admit to 238 such covert break-ins between 1942 and 1966. The results helped it to apprehend some of the last of the ideological spies, including Ethel and Julius Rosenberg.

President Harry S. Truman took notice of the worldwide spying tactics of the Soviet Union and in 1947 had Congress pass the National Security Act. The bill helped to create the U.S. Central Intelligence Agency out of what had been the Office of Strategic Services. The OSS had been a World War II intelligence service of thirteen thousand men and women who specialized in conducting daring feats in Europe such as parachuting behind enemy lines and aiding resistance groups. The CIA would be much different.

The CIA would become the favorite of American presidents for intelligence, much to the consternation of the FBI. The new agency had been opposed by Hoover from the beginning. He claimed it would only duplicate the Bureau, but foresaw that the creation of the CIA would usurp his power and cause his authority to erode. It did.

From the very beginning, the CIA and FBI were at odds. The CIA appeared to look down its nose at the "brick pounders" of the Bureau. *Let the Bureau be physical; we'll be the brains of the intelligence community* was the unspoken philosophy of the Agency. Jogging in groups on CIA grounds was at first discouraged because it looked too paramilitary. The Agency men saw their roles as more professorial. Most of its leaders came not just from colleges, but the Ivy League, predominantly Yale. Former CIA chiefs George Bush (class of 1948) and R. James Woolsey (class of 1968) were both Yale men, as was its legendary counterintelligence chief, James Jesus Angleton (class of 1941).

A Yale rowing coach, Allen "Skip" Waltz, was a paid CIA recruiter for fourteen years. As the Yale *Banner* would recount in its review of the 1962 school year: "When Ian Fleming's *Dr. No* came to the New Haven screen during the year, it mattered little whether our hero was James Bond or Frank Merriwell . . . we worshipped the essence of what it was to be a Yale man."

Robert Philip Hanssen, a senior at Chicago's William Howard Taft High School in 1962, also saw the first James Bond movie that year. It was the height of the Cold War, with the Cuban missile crisis about to bring the world to the very edge of nuclear destruction. Perhaps it was whistling in the dark, but international intrigue was about to become a pop phenomenon.

Dr. No was followed by another Bond movie, *From Russia with Love,* a year later. Of all the Bond films, that one was his favorite. Nearly forty years later he would confirm it with a vote for the title on the James Bond Internet Web site. On that day he also named Sean Connery as the best Bond ever. It should come as no surprise then that, in executing search warrants after Bob Hanssen's arrest, the FBI found fourteen weapons in his home, including not one but two German-made Walther PPK handguns—James Bond's weapon of choice. (In *Dr. No,* Bond was handed the six-shot PPK by an armorer from the British Secret Intelligence Service, better known as MI6. The technician assured him that the small pistol "has a delivery like a brick through a plate-glass window.")

Oleg A. Gordievsky, the former head of the KGB's or Komitet Gosudarstvanoy Bezopasnosti's London offices, defected in 1985. He once explained that the KGB used to study James Bond movies. The reason? To come up with memos for the Kremlin that forecast what the West's new espionage gimmicks would be for the year ahead. According to Gordievsky, the Soviets believed that the technology in the Bond films was predictive of the new gadgets the

CIA or MI6—his employer—would next invent.

By the time Bob Hanssen reached twenty-one, a life as an espionage agent had replaced becoming an astronaut as a fantasy career for young men. After the success of the first Bond movie, prime-time television became filled with variations on the theme. In the mid-1960s, Bill Cosby and Robert Culp took up an hour of prime time with *I Spy,* while Robert Vaughn and David McCallum played Napoleon Solo and Illya Kuryakin in *The Man from U.N.C.L.E.* At the time, a series depicting an American and a Russian teaming up to seek world peace defied credulity, but perhaps that's why it was a huge hit. *Mission: Impossible* and others followed. Mel Brooks even mocked the genre by creating *Get Smart,* a sitcom where its star, Don Adams, took off his shoe—it was a disguised telephone—to call his superiors.

Spying was our new national pastime. Espionage was a game—and seemingly a glamorous one at that. Football coaches, starting at the high school level, had no qualms about sending an assistant to spy for them at the practices of upcoming opponents to steal their plays. Sportswriters have said many times that one reason the NFL's Washington Redskins failed to go to the Super Bowl in 2001—they were favored to do so—was because they set a precedent and opened their preseason practices to anyone willing to pay $10. NFL teams immediately sent spies to take notes on Redskin players and their season became a disaster. The experiment was not repeated.

Corporations relished sending agents into rival factories under the guise of assembly-line workers. The world became an intelligence free-for-all with few morals or rules. Honor—once the code of those who called themselves gentlemen—was dead.

By 1962, nearly one hundred thousand men and women were in the various U.S. intelligence agencies. The last organization to be formed, the National Security Agency, would have nearly forty-thousand employees by the late 1990s. Its mission was to steal the codes of foreign nations, develop new ones for the American side, and listen in electronically to conversations around the world. And as you shall learn in this account, the NSA was Bob Hanssen's first choice for a career with a U.S. intelligence organization.

The NSA had received the first hints that the Soviet Union was stockpiling Cuba with short-range nuclear missiles. NSA listening devices had overheard conversations in Spanish on a Czechoslovakian airfield. Further investigation showed that Cubans were supervising the shipments of missiles to their Caribbean nation.

By now, one needed only do the math. With one hundred thousand people working in the American intelligence community, if just one-tenth of 1 percent of them became double agents, one hundred traitors would be working within the government. Yet, with almost blissful innocence, the hierarchies of the various spy units continued to do little to protect themselves. *These are our guys,* the spymasters seemed to be saying. *We won't embarrass them with undue scrutiny.* A policy of sporadic credit checks administered by a rookie case officer was enough. A young man or woman was supposed to come into an agent's neighborhood every five years—they were usually two or three years behind and it was more like seven—to ask the people who lived next door questions about the character of the sanctioned spy. And if you were forced to take a polygraph test and you flunked a couple of questions, so what?

The CIA mole Aldrich Ames, who was arrested and charged with spying in February of 1994, was listed as "deceptive" on two polygraph exams taken five years apart. He dismissed them as "witch-doctory" and was allowed to continue working at his highly sensitive job despite an alarming display of instant wealth that included a wine-red XJ6 Jaguar, newly capped teeth, and Italian silk suits. But Rick Ames couldn't be a spy. He was a second-generation

CIA career employee whose own father had been station chief in Rangoon, Burma. Outsiders may have faced a high bar to enter the service of a government intelligence agency, but once ensconced in a department, they were virtually home-free. Insiders had a cakewalk, particularly if their father—like that of Rick Ames—had also worked for the organization.

For two decades Bob Hanssen was a perfect spy. He was never once asked to take a polygraph test, and when the case agents did come around to his leafy New York or Virginia neighborhoods, he appeared to be living almost on the edge of poverty. Like Ames's, Bob's father, Howard, was a thirty-year veteran in law enforcement. Bob Hanssen had also been a cop—in intelligence—before joining the FBI. He was one of their own even before being hired.

Bob Hanssen impressed virtually everyone who met him as being a quiet, religious family man, though his actions were devastating to his country and destroying other men's lives. Those who knew him a bit better saw a disturbed, dogmatic man. Still, he appeared to be harmless, albeit eccentric and quirky, but then one could ask, are not all brilliant men? In hindsight, his life shows a startling dichotomy that at first glance defies explanation.

Let me try.

PART ONE

Man is the creation of an all-powerful, all-good, and all-seeing God. What is sin, the conception of which arises from the consciousness of man's freedom? That is a question for theology.

The actions of men are subject to general immutable laws expressed in statistics. What is man's responsibility to society, the conception of which results from the conception of freedom? That is a question for jurisprudence.

Man's actions proceed from his innate character and the motives acting upon him. What is conscience and the perception of right and wrong in actions that follows from the consciousness of freedom? That is a question for ethics.

—LEO TOLSTOY,
War and Peace

Prologue

Foxstone Park isn't much of one. The long, narrow stretch of Northern Virginia woods is in reality a fourteen-acre floodplain that forms small lakes each time it rains. Casual strollers have to step gingerly at those times or risk returning home with wet feet. And today, February 18, 2001, Foxstone is not just a sea of puddles and ponds. It is in total disarray.

Broken branches are strewn over the black asphalt path that runs northwesterly nearly two miles from the corner of East Street and Ayr Hill Avenue. At the end it culminates in a small basketball court and a tot lot of swings and slides. Midway, the park is broken up by Creek Crossing Road, which one has to cross if walking Foxstone's full length. But traffic is light on this suburban thoroughfare. Mothers and children out for a Sunday stroll have rarely had problems traversing its two narrow lanes.

To the left of the asphalt path is a small stream some twenty feet wide. On February 18 it is littered with raggedy strands of indestructible plastic, blue and gold cans of cheap beer labeled Busch Bavarian and Milwaukee's Best, and old, graying paper coffee cups. The beer containers have been tossed there by teens seeking the still-forbidden taste of alcohol.

The blue and gold beer cans seem impervious to fading or rusting. They glitter in the water. The empty cans and the polyethylene remnants clinging to the barbed vines at the water's edge will have to wait. The county's cleanup crew isn't scheduled to arrive for a month. Then they will remove the trash along with the twigs and branches that have been blown to the ground by the winds. In the parks of the county, the garbage collectors are among the first heralds of spring.

The stream is named Wolf Trap, an ubiquitous name in these parts that has been tacked onto roads, subdivisions, and even delicatessens. The best-known Wolf Trap is a nearby hundred-acre performing arts center that boasts a 6,800-seat covered amphitheater and draws pop performers ranging from Tony Bennett to Willie Nelson. Wolf Trap runs into a larger creek called Difficult Run, which meanders for miles before emptying into the Potomac River. The Potomac separates Washington from Virginia as it flows east, emptying toward and into the great Chesapeake Bay.

Foxstone Park is inside the Vienna town limits. This Vienna is not the Austrian city of music and intrigue, but a self-governed village inside Fairfax County, some thirteen miles west of the White House in Washington. Its residents are, for the most part, government workers. Vienna's main street, called Maple Avenue, is really a state highway, Route 123, and if you drive north five miles from the center of Vienna, the road runs directly by the entrance to the headquarters of the CIA.

At noon on this day Foxstone Park is a stage, set for optimism. Perhaps it is the bright sun. Warmer weather is only weeks away, and although it will likely snow again, somehow you can feel the warmth coming. At midday the temperature hovers near thirty degrees Fahrenheit in the woods, and after dark it is predicted to be back in the low twenties. But spring is coming, and after a colder-than-normal winter, the season will be welcome. The tulip poplar trees, so prevalent in the park, will flower, and what are now bare patches of honeysuckle and blackberry vines will turn green with leaves that hide their thorns. You can already see buds forming on the forsythia bushes and the green shoots of jonquils starting to spike upward between the trees.

Rabbits eat this greenery, and their numbers have grown so large the children and their mothers have begun calling Foxstone "the bunny park." The rabbits breed two or three times each year, the mothers birthing between five and seven bunnies each time. You can walk through the woods in the springtime and be virtually assured of seeing at least one hare, usually lying so still it seems you could reach out and touch the animal before it feels your presence and darts away.

Their predators are red foxes, horned owls, and hawks, who swoop down from the sky to eat the younger rabbits. Still, there are just too many of the furry creatures. The foxes breed only once a year, and their maximum litter is three kits. Foxes have to face automobiles in the suburbs, and their street crossings are often poorly timed. It is common to see them dead on a road, their carcasses becoming flatter with each passing car. Rabbits prefer to stay in the park; they won't go near a street. So the birds of prey and the foxes feast, but they can't keep up with what seems to be an endless buffet provided by Mother Nature.

A country club's golf course runs along one side of the park between the East Street entrance and the Creek Crossing break. On the other side a walker can see the backyards of brick and vinyl-sided suburban mini-manses whose most distinctive features are their mansard roofs. In this part of the park you can see dimpled white balls half-buried in the mud of the stream looking a bit like duck eggs, the product of cold-weather duffers whose drives have gone wrong.

You have to cross four bridges to get from one end of the park to the other, such is the serpentine shape of the Wolf Trap stream. The bridges have rusty metal sides with a flooring of wooden planks. The structures are not hand-made but rather have been manufactured on an assembly line. If you look closely, you will notice a small metal plaque warning that the bridge is for pedestrian traffic only. MAXIMUM LOAD, FIVE TONS, the tiny sign reads, and below that, MADE BY BILTOLAST PRODUCTS, FORT PAYNE, ALABAMA. American corporate efficiency is alive and well in Foxstone Park, Virginia. The joggers and dog walkers who comprise the bulk of the visitors to the park in winter rarely notice these details. But, come at the right time, and you might find another of the park's regular visitors, a man who notices all the details. He was once rail-thin but has become soft and fleshy with age. He is tall, six-foot-two or -three, with a long, pointy nose. If you were to see him from the side, you might notice his old man's paunch that speaks of south Florida, white belts, and early-bird buffet dinners.

His brown eyes dart everywhere, even though he knows the park like the back of his hand. Just like the trios of white-tailed deer who live here, he too sometimes looks like an apparition, appearing seemingly out of nowhere, either at dawn, dusk, or in the dead of night. He is not always alone, often showing up with a dog, a mixed black Lab. The man tries to enter the park differently each time. He strolls in where the path begins at the corner of East Street and Ayr Hill Avenue. On another day he will park a silver 1997 Taurus just off Creek Crossing Road next to the Vienna water-pumping station and enter the path there. At other times he might drive slowly by an entrance, come to a rolling stop, and then speed away. There is a third entrance too, just off Talisman Drive and less than a mile from the man's house. It may be his favorite.

The man lives on that street, and when he bought his house in 1987, at 9414 Talisman Drive, he thought the name a fortunate omen. A talisman is a good-luck charm, and back then, when he made his down payment on the home and moved in with a loving wife and six beautiful children, he knew there would be times when he would need all the luck in the world to survive the course he had chosen. It will turn out that even all the luck in the universe won't be enough to save him.

ONE

The Last Days of Ramon Garcia

The man's name is Robert Philip Hanssen, and today—February 18, 2001—is to be his retirement ceremony. Perhaps it should be called a sabbatical. He won't be getting a gold watch, although the $50,000 in new and used non-sequentially numbered hundred-dollar bills he is about to retrieve isn't a bad parting gift. The money will see him through the year. Bob Hanssen will also be retiring from the FBI in five weeks. He has been with the Bureau for twenty-five years.

The way retirement worked, he told his wife, Bonnie, you got 2.5 percent of your salary per year. That was for the first twenty years, and then you got 2 percent per year after that. So he would be taking home a 60 percent pension, or close to $68,452 a year. He was making $114,088. All Bureau employees were required to retire at age fifty-five, and here he was already fifty-six. The Bureau had been willing to give him a waiver on the extra year.

Bob was going to ground. Again. It was time to let things cool. Maybe somewhere down the line he could return to playing the game. Just before daybreak, alone in the gloom of his locked basement office, he tapped out a letter while still wearing his pajamas. They were black pajamas. Black was virtually the only color—though sometimes he would wear midnight blue—that he could bring himself to put on his body.

Bob could feel something or somebody getting close and had begun to believe his Taurus might be bugged. The radio was making strange, crackling sounds. It was. He didn't know it yet, but a tracking device had been hidden in his car that used the global positioning system and satellites. He had once revealed the technology to his Russian handlers, so it was a bit ironic that he was being shadowed with the same system.

Bob wrote the memo on an IBM ThinkPad 365E laptop. He encrypted it, then put his words on a disc and added it to the package he would be delivering late that afternoon.

Dear Friends:

I thank you for your assistance these many years. It seems, however, that my greatest utility to you has come to an end, and it is time to seclude myself from active service.

Since communicating last, and one wonders if because of it, I have been promoted to a higher do-nothing Senior Executive job outside of regular access to informaiton [sic] within the counterintelligence program. It is as if I am being isolated. Furthermore, I believe I have detected repeated bursting radio signal emanations from my vehicle. I have not found their source, but as you wisely do, I will leave this alone, for knowledge of their existence is sufficient. Amusing the games children play. In this, however, I strongly suspect you should have concerns for the integrity of your compartment concerning knowledge of my efforts on your behalf. Something has aroused the sleeping tiger. Perhaps you know better than I.

Life is full of its ups and downs.

My hope is that, if you respond to this constant-conditions-of-connection message, you will have provided some sufficient means of re-contact besides it. If not, I will be in contact next year, same time, same place. Perhaps the correlation of forces and circumstance then will have improved.

Your friend,
Ramon Garcia

Ramon Garcia was Bob Hanssen. The name was as far away from his real name as one could conjure up. He had borrowed the alias from a Central American exchange student he'd once known at a parochial school back in the late 1980s. Bob's boys had traveled more than thirty miles into Maryland just to attend the conservative Catholic institution. The Latino boy was not taking life seriously, Bob had lectured his sons. Bob didn't have much respect for a teenager like that.

After writing his letter, Bob scanned his Sunday *Washington Times*. The paper was by far the more conservative voice among the two major newspapers in Washington, and even though it was largely owned by the Unification Church and some people said it was a propaganda instrument for the Reverend Sun Myung Moon, the *Times* was the only daily paper Bob would read. Still, it was a good paper and he had subscribed to it for more than a decade. Bob Hanssen wouldn't allow the competition, the *Washington Post,* into the house, despite its eight-to-one circulation advantage, bigger sports section, and a reputation as one of the best newspapers in the country. To Bob Hanssen, the *Post* was the liberal rag that preached pro-abortion values. *Doonesbury* alone was enough to make anyone vomit, he had once told a neighbor.

Bob's week was heavily structured. The Catholic Church, family, the FBI. Especially Opus Dei, an organization within the church. Just two weeks prior he had attended one of their retreats. Daily mass and weekly confession were parts of the Opus Dei regimen. Still, not a bad life. Six children. Three boys, three girls. Everyone was healthy. Bob had gone on camping trips with the family; they had all marched in pro-life rallies together; he liked to attend gun shows. Even the name of the family dog, a black mixed Lab called Sunday, sounded sanctified. It was conservative values all the way for Bob's family. No New Age nonsense was allowed in this house, he had said.

And their side had won! No more Clinton and his abortion-rights liberal swill! Bob's eldest son, Jack, with his *Elect Bush* bumper sticker on the backside of his little red Jeep, had worked hard to get the Texan into the White House.

There were a few exceptions to this rigid, yet idyllic life. Bob would disappear from the house for an hour or two, and then his spouse, Bonnie, would worry. It was all part of being an FBI wife, she told herself. The brief interlude where he had worked for the other side was twenty years past. That had been an aberration, and he had promised her it would not happen again. His abrupt comings and goings were part of his job. Bonnie told herself that story so many times that she believed the tale to be true.

Bob had a houseguest that morning, a retired army lieutenant colonel, Jack Hoschouer. He was one of Bob's few friends from Chicago, Bob and Bonnie's hometown. Hoschouer had gone to the same high school and the same Lutheran church as Bob, and they had graduated together in 1962. Then Hoschouer's parents had sent him off to Saint Olaf's, a Lutheran school in Northfield, Minnesota, while Bob took advantage of a scholarship to Knox College in Galesburg, Illinois. The two had stayed close though, enough for Bob to invite him to stay at the house after learning he would be in town for the weekend. Hoschouer had to attend a conference as part of his job. He was the Bonn, Germany, correspondent for *Defense News,* a magazine that was part of the military publishing empire called *Army Times.*

(It would be reported that they sometimes went to strip clubs together. But while Hoschouer had been content to just watch, Bob had attempted to save at least one of the ladies for the Lord, trying to get her to join what he believed to be the one true church.)

Bob wanted to know what Hoschouer was up to in Germany. You never knew what you could pick up when you asked questions and listened.

A decade ago Bob suggested to the KGB or Komitet Gosudarstvanoy Bezopasnosti—he could both spell and pronounce the difficult Russian phrase—that they try to recruit his friend just before he retired from the army in 1991. The Russians had approached Hoschouer, but the colonel would later say he never knew he was being hustled and was never asked to spy for the KGB.

"If they pitched me, I was too dumb to know it," Hoschouer claimed to Bill Gertz of the *Washington Times*. Others wondered why he hadn't reported the contact as a recruitment attempt.

Hoschouer was dressed and ready for the day. Would he be going to church with them? Bob wanted to know. Why not. So the five of them—Bob and Jack, Bonnie, and the two youngest kids, Greg and Lisa—the ones still living at home—piled into their tan 1993 Volkswagen van. The vehicle had an antibortion sticker on the back bumper that read, *Life Is a Precious Gift / Let Your Baby Live*. They rode the eight miles to Saint Catherine's of Siena in Great Falls, Virginia.

Bob had felt something was wrong. He still did. He knew the steady static in his car radio was not a good sign. What Bob didn't know was that the phone in his home was tapped and that the FBI agents listening in on the line had been in stitches about his daughter Lisa's recounting of a recent date with a school friend. He hadn't seen the agents with their long-lens surveillance cameras and the special night-vision binoculars peeking out from the kitchen window across the street at 9419 Talisman Drive when the family's minivan had pulled out of the driveway. He had missed the unmarked sedan tailing them from a distance and a plane quietly circling above him like a vulture expecting someone to die.

They were back home by noon, and then there was lunch and soon it was time for Hoschouer to go to Dulles Airport to fly on to his parents' retirement home in Phoenix. Bob told Bonnie he had to run a few errands after dropping his friend at the airport, and she bought the story. He changed from his black church suit into a black turtleneck sweater with a black, collared shirt over it. He put on gray slacks.

The two men left before four. Traffic was light on the Dulles Access Road, so it took less than fifteen minutes. Bob had him at the airport by 4:10 P.M., well before departure time. Hoschouer wanted him to come in and hang out with him for a while as he waited for his flight, but his old pal sped off. He seemed to be in a hurry.

"It struck me as slightly odd that Bob didn't come in for a Coke," Hoschouer would say a week later. "In my estimation, I may have been the last friendly face he saw."

Bob was already speeding back down the Dulles Access Road before Hoschouer checked his bags. Eight miles later he was up the ramp at the Route 7 exit and onto the old turnpike. He drove through three lights and pulled into the Pike 7 Plaza Shopping Center. A Kinko's copy shop, Tower Records, and Pier 1 Imports were the largest tenants. The strip mall was just down the street from Tysons Corner, the commercial heart of Northern Virginia. It was 4:21 P.M. The team in the FBI surveillance car watched him getting out of his Taurus and walking to the rear of the car. Bob opened the trunk and pulled out a black plastic trash bag. He put the disc with his farewell letter to his handlers inside it along with seven different FBI documents he had printed. The papers were fresh off the Bureau's Automated Case Support System, the Bureau's intranet database of computerized intelligence files, which had been on-line internally since 1995. All of them had been stamped SECRET, dated between October and December 2000. The papers detailed the Bureau's current surveillance results in several foreign counterintelligence operations against Russian agents. Everything appeared set for his final walk in the woods.

Bob Hanssen was a brilliant computer hacker. In 1992 he had boasted to a pair of FBI officials, Ray Mislock and Roger Watson, that their internal computer system was far from safe. Mislock, chief of the Soviet Intelligence Division, and Watson, the division's deputy assistant director, both said show me, and he had. Bob went back into his office and hacked into Mislock's own computer. He had downloaded the classified document and presented it to him.

Bob had suggested to the Russians that if everyone would just get one of 3Com's Palm VII handheld computers, he would somehow beam them the documents. It would save him a lot of walks in the woods, he said. He had a Palm Pilot III himself and knew what each one could do. Ramon had put in a request for the new gadget in a letter to the successor of the KGB, his new employer, the SVR or Sluzhba Vneshney Razvedki, on June 8, 2000.

Dear Friends:
Administrative issues . . . Enclosed, once again, is my rudimentary cipher. Obviously it is weak in the manner I used it last—reusing key on multiple messages, but I wanted to give you a chance if you had lost the algorythm *[sic]*.

Thank you for your note. It brought me great joy to see the signal at last. As you implied and I have said, we do need a better form of secure communication—faster. In this vein, I propose (without being attached to it) the following:

One of the commercial products currently available is the Palm VII organizer. I have a Palm III, which is actually a fairly capable computer. The VII version comes with wireless Internet capability built in. It can allow the rapid transmission of encrypted messages, which if used on an infrequent basis, could be quite effective in preventing confusions if the existance *[sic]* of the accounts could be appropriately hidden as well as the existance *[sic]* of the devices themselves. Such a device might even serve for rapid transmittal of substantial material in digital form. Your FAPSI *[Federal Agency of Government Communications and Information—the Russian version of the NSA]* could review what would be needed, its advisability, etc., obviously— particularly safe rules of use. While FAPSI may move with the rapidity of the Chinese army, they can be quite effective, in juggernaut fashion, that is to say thorough . . .

New topics: If you are wise, you will reign *[sic]* in the GRU *[Glavnoye Razvedyvatelnoye Upravlenie, which translates to "Russian Military Intelligence"].* They are causing no end of grief. But for the large number of double-agents they run, there would be almost no ability to cite activity warranting current foreign counterintelligence outlays. Of course the Gusev affair didn't help you any. *[Stanislav Gusev, a Russian intelligence officer, had been arrested outside U.S. State Department headquarters on December 8, 1999, and asked to leave the country after it was discovered that he possessed listening equipment and was attempting to overhear conversations in conference rooms that were bugged.]*

If I'd had better communications I could have prevented that. I was aware of the fact that microphones had been detected at the State Department. (Such matters is why I need rapid communications. It can save you much grief.) Many such things are closely held, but that closeness fails when the need for action comes. Then the compartments grow of neccesity [sic]. I had knowledge weeks before of the existence of devices, but not the country placing them. . . . I only found out the gruesome details too late to warn you through available means including the colored stick-pin call. (Which by the way I doubted would work because of your ominous silence.) Very frustrating. This is one reason I say 'you waste me' in the note.

The U.S. can be errantly likened to a powerfully built but retarded child, potentially dangerous, but young, immature and easily manipulated. But don't be fooled by that appearance. It is also one which can turn ingenius *[sic]* quickly, like an idiot savant, once convinced of a goal. The Japanese (to quote General Patten *[sic]* once again) learned this to their dismay. . . .

I will not be able to clear TOM *[an exchange site]* on the first back-up date so don't be surprised if we default to that and you find this then. Just place yours again the following week, same protocol.

I greatly appreciate your highly professional inclusion of old things known to you in messages resulting from the mail interaction to assure me that the channel remains unpirated. This is not lost on me.

On Swiss money laudering *[sic]*, you and I both know it is possible but not simple. And we do both know that money is not really 'put away for you' except in some vague accounting sense. Never patronize at this level.

It offends me, but then you are easily forgiven. But perhaps I shouldn't tease you. It just gets me in trouble.

> Thank you again,
> Ramon

You could buy a Palm VII for less than $500, but Moscow hadn't gone for it. Bob was annoyed. The SVR didn't understand technology. It took them until the last day of July 2000 to answer his letter. The communication was a long one. That was typical of the Russians. They liked to draw things out—maybe it came from those long Moscow winters. This one was chatty enough but still precise in laying out a detailed communications schedule that would take them through the end of the year 2001.

In fractured English they complained about the difficulty in breaking through the security measures he had implanted in the computer. Bob had first used a technique called forty-track mode. He reconfigured the disk to appear to have less capacity, then buried secret documents in the "lost area" at the outer edge of the disk. He used 512-character chunks so it would appear to be a blank disk. Bob had once used the PGP [Pretty Good Privacy] encryption system on the Russians. PGP was newer and the program had worked perfectly. By going to PGP from forty-track mode, Bob thought he was upgrading, but Moscow seemed puzzled at the change. When they didn't get it, he went back to the old system. Their latest letter was direct in telling him of their needs.

Dear Ramon:
We are glad to use this opportunity to thank you for your striving for going on contact with us.

We received your message. The truth is that we expended a lot of efforts to decipher it.

First of all we would like to emphasize that all well known events wich *[sic]* had taken place in this country and in our homeland had not affected our resources and we reaffirm our strong intentions to maintain and ensure safely our long-term cooperation with you.

We perceive your actions as a manifestation of your confidence in our service and from our part we assure you that we take all necessary measures to ensure your personal security as much as possible.

Just because proceeding from our golden rule—to ensure your personal security in the first place—we have proposed to carry out the next exchange operation at the place which had been used in last August. We did not like to give you any occasion to charge us with an inadequate attention to problems of your security. We are happy that, according to the version you have proposed in your last letter, our suggestions about DD *[dead drop]*, known as ELLIS *[Ellis is the code name for Foxstone Park]* coincided completely. However a situation around our collegues *[sic]* at the end of the passed *[sic]* year made us to refuse this operation at set day.

1. We thank you for information, wnich *[sic]* is of a great interest for us and highly evaluated in our service.

2. We hope that during future exchanges we shall receive your materials, which will deal with a work of IC [Intelligence Community], the FBI and CIA in the first place, against our representatives and officers. We do mean its human, electronic and technical penetrations in our residencies here and in other countries. We are very interested in getting of the objective information on the work of a special group which serches *[sic]* "mole" in CIA and FBI. We need this information especially to take necessary additional steps to ensure your personal security.

3. Before stating a communications plan that we propose for a next future, we would like to precise *[sic]* a following problem. Do you have any possibility to meet our collegues *[sic]* or to undertake the exchange ops in other countries? If yes, what are these countries? Until we receive your answer at this questions and set up a new communications plan, we propose to use for the exchange ops DD according to the following schedule:

• DD LEWIS *[the code name for Long Branch Nature Center, in Arlington, Virginia]* on 27th of May 2001 (with a coefficient it will mean on 21 of November 2000) *[Bob had worked out a code that added or subtracted the number six]*. We draw your attention on the fact that we used a former coefficient−6. Sender adds, addressee subtracts. A time will be shown in real sense. We will be ready to withdraw your package beginning by 8 PM on 27 May 2001 after we shall read your signal. After that we put DD our package for you. Remove your signal and place our signal by 9 PM of the same day. After that you will withdraw our package and remove our signal. That will mean an exchange operation is over. We shall check signal site (i.e., its absence) the next day (28th of May) til 9 P.M. If by this time a signal had not been removed we shall withdraw our package and shall put it in for you repeatedly dates with DD EL-LIS—in each seven days after 28 May till 19 of June 2001 (i.e., 13th of December 2000).

Bob *was* brilliant. No one had ever disputed that. But sometimes even he may have had a hard time understanding what Russians meant. That was frustrating. It wasn't as if he could call up their embassy and talk it through with someone. Inside the locked nerve center in the basement of his suburban house, he tried to puzzle them out, but the more he thought about it, the more he felt the exchange doomed to failure.

"We don't go in there," his daughter had told visitors who wondered what was behind the door. Oh, sure, there had been times when he had showed off the technology to neighborhood kids and let them play computer games. But more often than not he was alone. Here in the gloomy room he could again dream he was Emperor Ming. As a child he had read Flash Gordon, but instead of identifying with Flash, he wanted to be Ming, the bad guy, known also by the title Ming the Merciless.

"I have this dream," he had told a classmate, John Sullivan, at Northwestern University in Evanston, Illinois, back in 1967. Sullivan had lived on the same floor as Bob at Abbott Hall. Bob said the dream repeated several times a week. "I'm in the throne room of Emperor Ming and my enemies are brought before me one by one. I have complete power and I can say, 'Guard, take them away!' " he told Sullivan, who never forgot the tale.

Bob's throne room was an obscure basement chamber on a suburban street and he was no Ming—trying to figure out pidgin English for $50,000. Sometimes the thrill, the rush, seemed gone. The Russians wouldn't stop with their dead drops. The SVR's ambitious scheming, the visions of the medals and the promotions and the glory they would receive when they returned to Moscow when all this was over, seemed to have no end. Their letter continued:

- We propose to carry out our next operation on 16 of October 2001 (i.e. 10 of April) at the DD LINDA in Round Tree Park *[the park is between Falls Church and Annandale, Virginia].* If this place suits for your *[sic]* we would like to receive your opinion about that during exchange in May. A time of operation from 8 PM to 9 PM, signals and alternate dates are the same. In the course of exchange ops we shall pass to you descriptions of new DD and SS *[Signal Site: a pre-arranged fixed location in a public place where an agent can alert another to an operational activity, usually with chalk or tape]* that you can check them before. You will find with this letter, descriptions of two new DD—LINDA and TOM. Hope to have your opinion about them.

    In case of break off in our contacts we propose to use DD ELLIS that you indicated in your first message. Your note about a second bridge across the street from the F sign as backup is approved. We propose to use ELLIS once a year on 12 August (i.e., with coeff. it will be 18 February) at the same time as it was in August 1999. On that day we can carry out a full exchange operation—you will enload your package and put out a signal, we shall withdraw it, load our package and put out our signal. You will remove our package and put your signal. Alternate dates—in seven days 'til next month.

- As it appears from your message, you continue to use

post channel as a means of communication with us. You know very well our negative attitude toward this method. (i.e. with coefficient), time and name of DD for urgent exchange are mentioned, you could do it by using address you had used in September (i.e. with coeff.) putting it in a sealed envelope for V. K. *[The initials were those of an SVR officer known to the FBI]*.

In future, it is inexpedient to use the V. K. name as a sender. It will be better to choose any well known name in this country as you did before.

We shall continue to work up new variants of exchanging messages including PC disks. Of course we shall submit them to your approval in advance. If you use a PC disk for next time, please give us key numbers and program you have used.

4. We would like to tell you that an insignificant number of persons know about you, your information, and our relationship.

5. We assess as very risky to transfer money in Zurich because now is impossible to hide its origin.

Others knew about him, the letter had said. That was something to worry about. Not good. Still, Ramon aka Bob could take solace. He had never given them his name, never told them exactly for whom he worked, and never met with them personally. But the money—would he ever see those dollars they said had been deposited in the Swiss and Moscow banks? Perhaps it had all been an illusion.

Ramon/Bob had answered their letter in November of 2000. The package exchanges between the two were not going well. Joined to the teat of Mother Russia since 1985, he had forgotten how to let go, though there had been times when he had tried to wean himself away. After fifteen years the spy and his handler were like an old couple bickering— only now the spy thought he could foresee an end. Not a happy one, though. In his reply he quoted from Shakespeare's *Hamlet* the line that talked about outrageous fortune and impending death. The soliloquy had ended: *For in that sleep of death what dreams may come / When we have shuffled off this mortal coil / Must give us pause.* All that may have been too morbid a thought to include in the letter to his handlers.

In the memo, he desperately begged the Russians to help him one last time.

Dear Friends:
Bear with me. It was I who sent the message trying to use TOM to communicate material to you. On reflection, I can understand why you did not respond to them. I see that I failed to furnish you sufficient information for you to recognize that the message you left for me in ELLIS did not go astray. You do this often (communicate such assurances through the mention of items like the old date offset we used, and believe me, it is not lost on me as a sign of professionalism. I say bear with me on this because you must realize I do not have a staff with who to knock around all the potential difficulties. (For me breaks in communications are most difficult and stressful.) Recent changes in USA law now attach the death penalty to my help to you as you know, so I do take some risk.

On the other hand, I know far better than most what minefields are laid and the risks. Generally speaking, you overestimate the FBI's capacity to interdict you, but on the other hand, cocksure officers, (those with real guts and not as much knowledge as they think) can, as say, step in an occasional cowpie. (Message to the translator: Got a good word for cowpie in Russian? Clue: Don't blindly walk behind cows.)

I have drawn together material for you now over a lengthy period. It is somewhat variable in import. Some were selected as being merely instructive rather than urgently important. I think some instructive insights often can be quite as valuable or even more valuable long-term because they are widely applicable rather than narrow. Others are of definite value immediately.

My position has been most frustrating. I knew Mr. Gusev was in eminent *[sic]* danger and had no effective way of communicating in time. I knew microphones of an unknown origin were detected even earlier and had no regular way of communicating even that. This needs to be rectified if I am to be as effective as I can be. No one answered my signal at Foxhall *[a signal site inside the District of Columbia]*.

Perhaps you occasionally give up on me. Giving up on me is a mistake. I have proved inveterately loyal and willing to take grave risks which even could cause my death, only remaining quiet in times of extreme uncertainty. So far my ship has successfully navigated the slings and arrows of outrageous fortune.

I ask you to help me survive.

On meeting out of the country, it simply is not practical for me. I must answer too many questions from family, friends, and government plus it is a cardinal sign of a spy. You have made it that way because of your policy. Policies are constraints, constraints breed patterns. Patterns are noticed.

Meeting in this country is not really that hard to manage, but I am loath to do so not because it is risky but because it involves revealing my identity. That by someone like me working from whatever motivation, a Bloch or a Philby *[Felix Bloch is a former diplomat and suspected spy whom Bob Hanssen is alleged to have alerted in time to avoid arrest. Kim Philby was a British spy and a hero of Bob's.]*

Bloch was such a schnook *[sic]*. I almost hated protecting him, but then he was your friend, and there was your illegal I wanted to protect. *[An illegal is an agent in a foreign country impersonating a private citizen and who generally has no diplomatic immunity.]*

If our guy sent to Paris had balls or brains both would have been dead meat. Fortunately for you he had neither. He was your good luck of the draw. He was the kind who progressed by always checking with those above and tying them to his mistakes. The French said, "Should we take them down?" He went all wet. He'd never made a decision before, why start then. It was that close. His kindred spirits promoted him. Things are the same the world over, eh?

On funds transfer through Switzerland, I agree that Switzerland itself has no real security, but insulated by laundering on both the in and out sides, mine ultimately through, say a corporation I control loaning mortgage money to me for which repayments are made. It certainly could be done. Cash is hard to handle here because little business is ever really done in cash and repeated cash transactions into the banking system are more dangerous because of the difficulty in explaining them. That doesn't mean it isn't welcome enough to let that problem devolve on me. (We should all have such problems, eh?)

How do you propose I get this money put away for me when I retire? Come on; I can joke with you about it. I know money is not really put into an account at MOST Bank [a Moscow Bank, probably Mosstroyekonombank], and that you are speaking figuratively of an accounting notation at best to be made real at some uncertain future. We do the same. Want me to lecture in your 101 course in my old age? My college level Russian has sunk low through inattention all these years. I would be a novelty attraction, but I don't think a practical one except in extremis.

So good luck. Wish me luck. Okay on all sites detailed to date, but TOM's signal is unstable. See you in "July" as you say constant conditions.

Yours truly,
Ramon

Bob's other employer, the FBI, had suspected he was Ramon for more than two months. Now they knew a lot more about him. Bob was being shadowed by an FBI Special Surveillance Group twenty-four hours a day. The team was known in the Bureau as the SSG, which was sometimes shortened to the G's. It was largely drawn from younger men—the kind Bob would have called "cocksure." Although trained in counterintelligence himself, he didn't see the SSG following him. Ever. They were too good.

The SSG had watched him glide past the Foxstone Park sign on Creek Crossing Road in the Taurus four times on the night of December 12. Bob's eyes squinted, trying to catch a glance of a horizontal piece of white tape or chalk that would indicate that the Russians were ready to receive his payload. The SSG continued to surveil their man from a distance and observed him strolling into a store in a nearby shopping center while a man they identified as an SVR agent stood quietly outside. His movements were captured by a video camera. On the day after Christmas, the SSG photographed their prey again, capturing him on tape as he drove by the yellow-on-brown, etched, wooden Foxstone sign at dusk. That time, according to the G's, Bob stopped in front of it for fifteen seconds, again looking for a chalk marker that would indicate the Russians were ready. He came back to the spot just before nine, this time with a flashlight. Parking the Taurus, Bob got out and turned it on, shining the beam up and down and over the sign and then onto some wooden pylons nearby. Finding nothing, he appeared to beseech the heavens with both arms, lifting them up to the sky in disgust. He shrugged his shoulders and lumbered off, exasperated.

Still, he wouldn't give up. The G-men watched Bob drive to the Pike 7 Plaza and kill time by wandering through Tower Records for ten minutes. He returned to Foxstone Park at nine-thirty. The spy stopped at the sign for several seconds before he sped away.

As the year 2001 began, Bob began driving by the Foxstone sign on weekday evenings almost nightly. On January 9 he drove by at 8:18, stopped, then drove away; on January 23, his Taurus crawled by just after dark at five miles an hour; on January 26, he slowed down near dusk and stared at the sign. The time was just after five. His evening checks stretched into February with the SSG noting that he drove by the Foxstone sign three times between 5:37 and 7:44 on the evening of February 5. What was he looking for? According to the FBI, "Ramon" and the Russians had developed an intricate system for signaling one another whenever there was information to be passed along. In this case, they say, Bob was waiting for his friends to make a drop. He would know they had done so once the sign was appropriately marked.

By now the government had search warrants and was secretly searching Bob's office on the ninth floor at FBI headquarters. They searched his Taurus, parked in the garage, as well. In his E Street side office they found several duplicates of Ramon's letter on a computer memory storage card. The G's copied the data, then replaced it.

When the G-men searched his Ford Taurus, they found white Johnson & Johnson adhesive tape and white Crayola chalk in the glove compartment. In the trunk of the car were seven secret documents Bob had downloaded and was planning to give the Russians. They also found a box of black Hefty-brand trash bags. Everything was photographed. Although they had more than enough for an arrest, they still wanted to catch him in the act. It was only a matter of time now, they reasoned, before the swap took place. The SSG had men assigned to each potential drop site, and Bob was being watched in shifts around the clock. On February 12, they examined the interior of the Ford again. This time there were white and yellow thumbtacks, perfect for placing his own signals on wooden signs. That day they got another break.

Checking the LEWIS or Long Branch Nature Center drop site, the G-men found a concealed package beneath a corner of a community outdoor stage. It was covered by a black plastic trash bag that had been taped up. Inside was another taped-up plastic bag, and inside that was $50,000 in hundred-dollar bills. A brief memo read, *Next 10/31/01 TOM alt 20, 27*. The SSG rushed everything to the FBI laboratory at Quantico, Virginia. Inside the lab all of it was either photographed or copied, then rewrapped and returned to the site. Since it had been deposited on the twelfth, the Bureau was pretty sure their suspect would be making his drop on the eighteenth. All one had to do was to add twelve and six.

Bob slammed down the trunk of his Taurus. The package with the disk and the documents was in place. He drove to Foxstone/ELLIS as the last rays of the cold sun fell below the horizon. It was just after four-thirty and getting colder, below freezing. The G's watched Bob place a piece of white tape on the Foxstone sign. Then he walked into the woods in the direction of the Ayr Hill Avenue entrance. He stopped at the footbridge nearest Creek Crossing Road and put his package under the trestle. He continued strolling down the path, his eyes alert for movement. It was almost dark now and he missed the first signs of spring in the twilight of the mid-February afternoon. That was a shame. He would never have an opportunity to see spring in these woods again.

Bob turned around and began walking back toward the bridge and then suddenly all hell broke loose. There were ten of them, all young men with buzz haircuts. Two pointed automatic weapons his way as they surrounded him. One of them yelled, "Freeze, FBI!" just like in the movies. Another began reading Bob his Miranda rights as his hands were cuffed behind his back, the rough metal digging into his wrists. In the gathering darkness he took on the shapeless form of a manacled black blob. A surprised black blob who was going into shock.

"He knew it was over. You could literally see his shoulders slump," said the FBI's Chris Murray after watching the surveillance video a few days later.

TWO

Dr. Hanssen and the Crazies

How do you start to explain a Bob Hanssen? Enter his mind at the beginning of his life, the psychiatry professionals might say. Then discuss his disassociative identity disorder, they will urge, or show how he has multiple personalities. Detail his troubled, tortured childhood and perhaps people will understand. And while one can make a case for an identity disorder or even argue that he could be a self-made Manchurian Candidate, Bob's childhood appears to be neither troubled nor tortured.

Was he a narcissist? Did he want to have power over other people's lives? Using his alter ego Ramon and not revealing who he was to Moscow, did Bob Hanssen think he had become the master of two worlds? Neither side, he thought, really knew him. But he knew. He was a god, if only for a short time in his life.

Robert Philip Hanssen was born on April 18, 1944, at the Little Company of Mary Hospital in Evergreen Park, in Cook County, just outside the Chicago city limits. His father, Howard Albert Hanssen, had worked for the Campbell Soup Company's Central Division in the 1930s and then became a local cop. When his son was born, he had already been drafted into the navy. During World War II, he rose in rank from seaman to third class petty officer. He was also very lucky. Howard never left U.S. territorial waters.

Bob's mother, Vivian Edith Baer Hanssen, was thirty-one and Howard thirty-two when their son came into the world. It was a late start for the couple considering the times, but at least they were finally blessed with a baby, and a son at that. They named him Robert, simply because they liked it, and Philip because it was a common name used by Edith's side of the family. Howard and Edith called him Bobby when he was a young boy. He would be the only child they could produce, though they wanted more.

"Howard was away on duty at the time. He didn't see our son until weeks later," remembered Vivian Hanssen.

The Hanssens lived on the far North Side of the city then, on Bingham Avenue. Howard's background was mostly German with some Danish—his father was named Theodore Frederich Hanssen—and Howard told Vivian he wasn't sure how much of each nationality he had in him. Vivian was all German, though you didn't brag about how German you were during the war years.

Howard returned to civilian life after the war, rejoining the police department. The Hanssens bought their first and only Chicago house, moving to 6215 North Neva Avenue in the Norwood Park section of the city. The enclave was made up of first- and second-generation Scandinavian and Russian immigrants near O'Hare Airport (Neva is the name of the river that runs through the center of St. Petersburg, Russia). Norwood Park was heavily sprinkled with employees of the Chicago Police and Fire Departments and had the reputation of being "a cop neighborhood." It was a considered a very safe place to live. (That is, until 1978, when Chicago police found twenty-nine bodies under serial killer John Wayne Gacy's house in Norwood Park, though residents claim that was an anomaly.)

The white, modest, two-bedroom, wooden bungalow Howard and Vivian purchased had a single bathroom and a small front porch. It had been built in 1925. The house was fifteen hundred square feet, barely large enough for a family of three. When Howard's widowed mother, Mary Louise Hanssen, came to live with them, he built her a room out of a space in the attic.

"It was a time when you didn't have fences," said one of their neighbors, Warren Peterson. The Hanssens' backyard was only enclosed after Howard Hanssen acquired a second toy poodle, a breed of dog he sometimes appeared to dote on more than his son.

Perhaps because Bobby Hanssen had grown up with three middle-aged adults, he seemed mature, confident for his age. Or maybe it was due to his being an only child. Certainly, by most accounts, he was spoiled and fussed over by the two Hanssen women more than other boys. Whatever it was, he appeared not to need other children around him. Silence was his calling card from the start.

"He would say hello," recalled Pauline Rutledge, who lived across the street, "but he was so quiet. He wouldn't say anything else." Rutledge remembers Bobby Hanssen as being the neighborhood shy child who was more comfortable being alone than hanging out with the other kids.

Bobby Hanssen was a trusted youngster, prized by the neighbors for his politeness. He would be asked to escort the younger children on the block to a kindergarten three blocks away. But at Norwood Park Elementary, he seemed to be taking notes. Years later, in the fall of 1966, he would be introduced to Martin Ziegner at Northwestern University and would begin their conversation, "I know you, but you don't know me."

"I had been a year ahead of him at Norwood Park Elementary," Ziegner recalled. "I was a sixth-grader when he was a fifth-grader, and of course we had little to do with the class behind us. But he remembered me. It was as if he always wanted to have a little something buried away about you that he could reveal at just the right time."

Bobby's passion as a youngster was reading the satirical

magazine *Mad*, as well as action comic books that featured superheroes. His subscription to *Mad*, best known for its regular back-page feature called *Spy vs Spy,* would continue through college, though most teens usually gave it up by the end of high school.

"I was against *Mad* at first," Vivian Hanssen said, "but then I read it myself and thought it was harmless."

In high school, according to friends, Bobby pored over futuristic novels by dystopian British writers. His favorites were George Orwell's *Animal Farm,* an allegory that debunked the idealistic dreams of communism, and *Brave New World* by Aldous Huxley, which warned of a future in which individualism and the family were to be despised.

One snapshot of Bobby and Howard in Vivian Hanssen's photo album was taken when their son was eleven. In it, he could be Opie Taylor, and Howard, Andy, in the opening credits of the *Andy Griffith Show*. The two had stopped to fish on a driving vacation to Florida, and each has caught a small perch. In the photograph they are holding up the fish for the camera. Part of Bob's shirttail is hanging out and he is wearing a white belt. It is a picture of the American dream personified.

His parents pushed Bob, particularly his father. Howard Hanssen had only completed high school and had higher ambitions for his son. Bob gave them little to complain about. Bobby Hanssen was an honor-roll student, a straight-arrow who rarely misbehaved and had no problem getting As in virtually every subject. His list of credits at William Howard Taft High School in Chicago shows that he was active in a Ham Radio Club, the Honors Club, and received something called The Food Industry Award. He was also listed as a teacher's helper. In his senior year, he was allowed to take advanced chemistry classes at nearby Von Steuben High School. Beneath his graduation picture, where he appears as a lanky lad wearing a plaid shirt with a buzz haircut, is the homily *Science is the light of life*. His graduating class was just over two hundred.

"He was sort of a geek," a classmate, Diane Swiderski, recalled. "He wasn't involved in any of the cliques."

Another classmate, Debbie Pienert Hogg, agreed. "He didn't stand out. He was just there. In grade school he had thick, horn-rimmed glasses."

"He was pretty quiet, just not a social guy," said George Hibbeler, who remembered to emphasize that he was an acquaintance and not a close friend.

Was he beaten, abused, in any way? His mother denied it, though Bob would later tell a psychiatrist he had been.

"Oh, no," Vivian Hanssen said. "His father *was* strict. I was the easy one. But aren't most families like that?"

Once, after his mother gave him some advice, Bobby wrote her a formal letter, expressing his appreciation. "He said, 'Thanks for your insight.' I wasn't sure what that meant," Vivian Hanssen remembered.

By now, Howard Hanssen had become part of the Chicago Police Department's intelligence division. His mission was to investigate local political leaders and to report on those who showed any leftist leanings. Called the Red Unit, it was reputed to be on a hunt to unmask communists operating inside the city government. Some neighbors began to view the family as secretive.

"They were a real policeman's family," neighbor Ruth Kremske recalled. "I don't think they wanted anyone nosing around in their business."

In a letter Bob would later write to the Taft High School Alumni Association in May of 1999, he claimed that "my Dad, before he retired, was District commander of the Chicago Police Department's Sixteenth District covering Norwood Park until heading up intelligence operations for the CPD downtown."

However, officers in that district expressed doubt about his claim. And while the Chicago Police Department acknowledged Howard Hanssen was in intelligence, no one would confirm that he headed the division.

Following high school, Bobby, who had begun shortening his name to a more grown-up-sounding Bob, won a scholarship to Knox College, a four-year college 150 miles southwest of Chicago in Galesburg, Illinois. Knox was small, with just eleven hundred students, but had a reputation as selective, with high, no-nonsense conservative standards. Its biggest claim to fame was that Abraham Lincoln had been in the state legislature when its charter was granted and that the historic 1858 debate between Lincoln and Stephen A. Douglas had taken place on its campus. Though Bob didn't plunge into student politics or even evolve as a social butterfly, he did attempt to change his image as awkward and clumsy by playing intramural basketball. His six-foot-two height was a plus, though he was still a string bean in those days, skinny enough to be bent in two by a stiff wind.

He matriculated in chemistry. All Knox science majors were required to study a language for two years, and the choice was narrow: either French, German, or Russian. Bob chose Russian, which, given the German backgrounds of both of his parents, at first seems surprising. However, Russian was popular among college students in the mid '60s. The Cold War had many of them believing that the language could come in handy if a shooting war ever broke out with the Soviet Union.

Bob studied the language with a notable anticommunist Yugoslavian, Momcilo Rosic. When interviewed nearly forty years later, Rosic said he couldn't remember his student but recognized the face. He added that if Bob had attended his classes, he would have gotten a strong dose of anti-Marxist rhetoric.

"I had been a prisoner of war of the Nazis, and then I couldn't go back to my country because of the communists," Rosic recalled. "That he learned Russian from me is

strange. I am anti-Soviet and anticommunist of course and
said so often in my classes."

Bob also studied the country's classic literature. This
included the masters of Russian writing: Dostoyevsky, Che-
khov, Tolstoy, and Turgenév.*

After receiving a bachelor of science degree in chemistry
from Knox College in 1966, Bob applied for a position as
a cryptographer at the National Security Agency in Maryland. He was turned down for the government job, with an
official at the NSA citing a freeze on hiring due to budget
cutbacks.

"He told me he had to make a quick decision and decide
to do something else," said Martin Ziegner. The "something
else" turned out to be Northwestern University's dental
school. By staying in college, Bob got to keep his 1-Y draft
status. The Vietnam War was heating up, and it was not a
place he wanted to be. He breezed through the screening
process and became one of sixty-eight chosen out of more
than three thousand applicants. Bob arrived on Northwestern's 379-acre campus two months after graduation from
Knox, one of the last class members to be admitted.

Northwestern University, bordering Lake Michigan and
twelve miles north of downtown Chicago, was more famous for its drama school (Charlton Heston, Ann-Margret)
than its dental school or its doormat athletic teams.
Although it was fifteen minutes from his parents' house on
North Neva Avenue, Bob chose to live in a dorm. He
shared a room in Abbott Hall with a Hawaiian classmate,
Jerald Takesono, and joined the dental fraternity, Delta
Sigma Delta. Takesono remembered a rigid, introverted
youth who still read *Mad,* appeared to have lots of spending
money, but was caring and kind enough to tutor a classmate

---

* According to Vivian Hanssen, her son never mentioned he was
studying the Russian language. She would learn about it in a newspaper only after he was arrested.

who was failing in chemistry. Takesono sometimes played basketball with him, but since Bob towered over his roommate, it wasn't much of a contest.

"He always wore a suit to class," Takesono said. "Not a jacket and slacks, but a suit, with a white shirt, and tie. Nobody did that in those days. He could never have been called preppy, ever."

His other classmates remembered that Bob was unable to appear in public wearing shorts and a T-shirt, something everyone else did when warm weather hit the Northwestern campus. Being casual, as far as Bob was concerned, was a button-down shirt and slacks. Neither were jeans part of his wardrobe.

Takesono recalled working on cadavers with Bob. His roommate carved up the bodies while still wearing a black suit and tie, the only one dressed that way. He remembers it because Bob Hanssen continued to wear the same outfit for days after the dissection.

"The suit smelled of formaldehyde and he was hanging it up each night in our room. Our place reeked of the cadaver. I finally had to ask him to get it dry-cleaned," Takesono recalled.

Years later, a Knox college friend would ask Bob how it felt to have cut up dead men and women. Bob was unfazed. "You have to pull yourself away and pretend they're not really there," he said.

One curious incident that still sticks out in Takesono's memory is the famous Six Day War in 1967. The conflict took place during May and June between Israel and the Arab nations that bordered it. Though Bob had been raised Lutheran, he took the conflict personally, rooting heavily for the Israeli side and tuning in to the radio for hourly news updates.

"Bob thought he looked Jewish," Takesono recalled. "He followed every minute of it. I remember when it ended. He burst into the dorm room yelling, 'We won! We won!' "

"He was ready to identify with anyone who was strong," explained another classmate, Robert Lauren, who now practices dentistry in Skokie, Illinois. Lauren also remembers Bob's outbursts on the Six Day War:

"He said, 'Those Arabs are weak. Every few years they stand up and then they get their butts kicked.' "

After the war was over, John Sullivan, the classmate to whom Bob had once told his Emperor Ming dreams, asked Martin Ziegner if Bob was Jewish.

"No," said Ziegner, "he just wishes he was."

Ziegner recalled that Bob also had an infatuation for the Kennedy family. He remembers Bob telephoning him before daybreak on a June day in 1968, waking him up to relay the news that presidential candidate and U.S. senator Robert F. Kennedy had been shot and killed by Sirhan Sirhan.

"He was extremely excited and very upset," Ziegner said. "His voice was breaking."

Bob's classmates all marveled at his ability to retain information. Ziegner remembers one episode that he tells to this day:

"I sat across from Bob in a lecture on tooth structure. The professor was someone called Dr. Chasen, who liked to hear himself talk. He was a bit long-winded. I remember that I and everyone else in the class were fervently taking notes. Bob wasn't. I looked across the aisle after forty-five minutes and all Bob had was a single sheet of paper and a pencil. He had used the pencil to doodle a bird and draw a sketch of an anatomically correct nude woman. He had written just one word on the page. The word was *bicuspid*.

"The professor walked around the room as he talked. It was hard for him to miss Bob's naked lady. He came over to Bob's desk and just lost it. He began reaming Bob out. It was something about how Northwestern was a professional school and how he was lucky to get in. Bob sat there and I could see he was pissed off. He began tapping the eraser end of his pencil on the desk as the professor berated him. Finally, Bob couldn't take it anymore and interrupted the tirade.

"He told the professor he had accused him of not listening and didn't appreciate it. He said, 'Why don't you go back up to the front of the class and start over and I'll pick it up from there.' When the professor began, Bob interrupted and began repeating his lecture word for word. It was like he had a tape recorder in his brain.

"Afterward I told him how impressive I found his photographic memory, and Bob said, 'I can remember every conversation I have ever had.' But he didn't say it in a boastful tone. In fact, his voice was wistful and kind of sad. Most people can block out bad memories and keep the good ones, but Bob was condemned to remember everything."

Bob Hanssen quickly tired of dental school. He hated putting his hands in people's mouths, saying, "I don't want to spend my life picking pieces off of someone's teeth." Being a dentist was too static, too proscribed a life. It wasn't a matter of whether he would drop out, but rather when. Perhaps the turning point came when he took impressions of Robert Lauren's teeth and then, when Lauren did the same to him, vomited all over Lauren's clothing, probably because of a gag reflex. In the letter he sent to the Taft Alumni Association in 1999, Bob tried to explain his career choices:

"After college I went to dental school, but didn't like spit all that much—though I was in the 98th percentile on my Dental Board exam—and I decided to get an MBA and a CPA and go into law enforcement."

"He wouldn't have made a good dentist," said classmate John Hargrave, who today practices in Pensacola, Florida. "Bob lacked interpersonal skills. He was competent, but too quiet to succeed at it."

Bob Hanssen began telling his classmates at Northwestern that he had decided to be a psychiatrist instead. His father helped him to get a job at a city-run mental hospital.

Though Bob was a part-time assistant to nurses in a ward of disturbed men, he delighted in pretending he was a doctor on the weekend nights he worked. Bob would call the patients into an office and interview them, taking notes. John Sullivan would often come by to sketch the inmates as Bob talked to them.

"He loved showing people the control he had over the patients," Sullivan recalled. "They were mostly bonkers, but he would perform for his friends, putting the patients through their paces. He wasn't mean; he just quietly interrogated them."

"He seemed to live in a fantasy world," Robert Lauren said. "He pretended to be someone he wasn't. There was always something like that flying around inside his head. He thought the patients were people he could play games with. He would have them address him as Dr. Hanssen, but he was only an orderly."

Why do you think Bob would do something like that?

"He was able to do that because he had amazing confidence. Bob believed that it was only a matter of time before he did it all," Lauren concluded.

Despite these quirks, none of Bob's classmates would categorize him as ever behaving in a malevolent manner. They were unanimous in saying that Bob was simply unable to say bad things about anyone personally. Neither would he gossip or show emotion except when it came to world events, such as the death of a political leader or conflicts between nations.

"Actually, he would have been a good psychiatrist," Sullivan said. "He was always thinking. You could see the gears turning. Back then, we all had this dream to be someone special. More than any of us, Bob wanted to do something big. He wouldn't have cared if others knew about it just as long as he knew about it."

Another classmate, Jeffrey Davee, had the same feeling: "He had a way of carrying himself that I can still see. He would look at you like he knew he was smarter than you, and if you said anything to him, he usually wouldn't answer but just give a smile. But he was plenty smart. His look seemed to say, 'I'm smarter than anyone here.' "

Jerald Takesono agreed, "He was smart enough to be anything he wanted to be."

Robert Lauren remembers going to Bob's house in the late sixties, and in the light of what has happened more than three decades later, the anecdote he tells must be considered remarkable.

"It was a cold, gray house inside. Everything was in its place, but there was no color anywhere. His mother didn't cook—she just opened cans. I was leaving the house—I think it was 1968 or 1969—and Bob handed me a book he wanted me to read. It was *My Silent War* by Kim Philby.* He wanted me to read it because he had just finished the book and thought it was terrific. After a few weeks he became insistent upon getting it back and kept asking me if I had read it. Finally I did return it and he asked me if I had read Philby's book. I had and remember saying something like I found it very interesting. Bob then said—and I've never forgotten it, particularly now—he said, 'You know, someday I'd like to pull off a caper like that.' "

A digression is called for here. In one of the Bob Hanssen/Ramon Garcia letters revealed by the FBI, he wrote this to his Russian handlers on March 14, 2000: *I decided on this course when I was 14 years old. I'd read Philby's book. Now that is insane, eh!* After his arrest, the media noted the line, and in newspapers and on talk shows pundits pointed out that Philby's book was published in 1968 and

---

* The book was written by the British double agent and staunch Catholic Harold Adrian Russell Philby, after he defected to the Soviet Union. Kim was a nickname that honored the boy spy in the Rudyard Kipling novel. Philby's book is considered a classic in Soviet Union communist propaganda.

that—since Bob was twenty-four at the time—he couldn't possibly have read the memoir as a teen. A suggestion was made that perhaps he hadn't read it, but was just trying to flatter the Russians. Another suggestion was that he might be a habitual liar.

There should no longer be any doubt that Bob Hanssen *did* read Kim Philby's book. After viewing the many Bob/Ramon letters to his handlers, a better theory is that he may have intended to hit the *2* key but his finger landed on the key to the left of it, which is the *1* key. There are frequent keystroke errors and misspellings in Bob's letters that strongly suggest he rarely bothered to either proofread or spell-check his communications.

Lauren and others in Bob's Northwestern class recalled him as being somewhat of a stiff when it came to having a good time. Only one incident seemed out of character. While no one can ever remember Bob getting drunk—a college ritual everywhere—he did get high. According to several of his classmates, Bob smoked marijuana on more than one occasion, a practice that was far from unusual in the Vietnam War era. The experiment—remembered as Bob smoking joints until he felt the weed's effect—was accompanied by the music of the Doors and the Rolling Stones. During one pot party, Bob is remembered as getting carried away and putting his hand up the skirt of a female student teacher, who yelped good-naturedly at the pass.

"It doesn't matter," he said. "We'll forget everything in the morning."

Yet, he was mostly a repressed prude. Especially when it came to women.

"There was this restaurant everyone would go to after exams," said Lauren. "It was Greek and we'd celebrate with couscous and baklava. They had a belly dancer and everyone would take a dollar and put it in the belt of the dancer's skirt. We'd ask Bob but he would never go. It was because of the dancer."

Bob certainly seemed able to afford to go. He always appeared to have enough money to eat at the better restaurants while his classmates dined at the drugstore lunch counters of Walgreens.

"It crossed my mind that his father could have been on the take," said Takesono, an assertion echoed both by Robert Lauren and a member of the Chicago Police Department, because of Howard's role with the Red Unit. Takesono recalled that Howard Hanssen seemed to own a racehorse. Vivian Hanssen readily admitted that her late husband had interests in several racehorses. He was trying to earn enough money to build up his social security, so he could get a higher monthly payment when he retired." The horses, she said, raced at Chicago's Arlington Park, and other tracks in the Midwest.

Bob spent two years at dental school, dropping out in May of 1968. He stayed at Northwestern, keeping his draft deferment by enrolling in its school of accountancy, part of its prestigious Kellogg School of Management. It was a surprising choice since many might view the profession as even more mundane than dentistry. This time he finished with an MBA in accounting.

He might have switched majors again or dropped out to try something else. But his life had taken a different turn. The soon-to-be spy had fallen in love, was married to Bonnie Wauck, and their first child was on the way.

THREE

When James Bond Met Natalie Wood

The courtship of Robert Philip Hanssen and his wife, Bernadette "Bonnie" Wauck, is a classic story of opposites attracting one other—a Romeo and Juliet tale set in Illinois instead of Italy. In many ways he was the boy from the wrong side of the tracks who married into not only money, but a higher social stratum. Bonnie Wauck, with her family's adherence to a strict, conservative Roman Catholic culture, couldn't have grown up more differently than Bob Hanssen.

Bernadette Wauck—her mother has an affinity for French names—was born on October 3, 1946, and named for the illiterate peasant girl who Catholics believe experienced apparitions from the Virgin Mary as many as eighteen times in 1858 at Lourdes, France. Bonnie was raised in the affluent village of Park Ridge in Cook County, just west of Chicago's city line, but surprisingly close to Norwood Park. The most famous person to emerge from the suburb has probably been Hillary Rodham Clinton, though that could be argued since screen luminaries Harrison Ford and Karen Black both grew up in the community.

Bonnie's father, Leroy Wauck, is a former university professor who has taught psychology—in particular, political psychology—at prominent Midwestern Catholic universities such as Marquette, DePaul, and Loyola. At each school, he was chairman of its psychology department. After a parochial-school education, Bonnie got her degree in sociology, gratis—as did most of the Wauck children—from Loyola, a Jesuit school, while her father was still teaching on campus.

Roy Wauck also did double time by operating a lucrative private psychiatric practice and serving as a consultant to several hospitals. He has coauthored or translated several religious books, including *The Psychology of Religious Vocations*. Another, *Canons and Commentaries on Marriage*, is still sold at Catholic bookstores. He is also listed in *Who's Wealthy in America*, a two-volume directory of affluent people that is used by charities and stockbrokers. An octogenarian who became semiretired in 1984, the still vibrant Wauck is currently chairman of the board at Northridge Preparatory School, a Catholic institution in Niles, Illinois. Northridge has been attended by several of his grandchildren. He is also a consultant to the Chicago Archdiocesan Matrimonial Tribunal.

Roy Wauck and his wife, Frances or Fran, produced eight children and by the turn of the twenty-first century could boast of twenty-seven grandchildren. Both are members of Opus Dei (the work of God), a conservative—and controversial—Catholic organization that has absorbed much of the Wauck and the Hanssen families' lives.

In February of 1999, when Opus Dei celebrated its fiftieth anniversary in America—it had begun in the United States in Chicago although its worldwide roots are in Spain—the *Chicago Sun-Times* wrote an article stating that some critics considered it "cultlike." The newspaper balanced the piece by saying that its members believed that the rigors of prayer and sacrifice provided a way to holiness for those who chose it.

"In a world of so-called 'cafeteria Catholics' where Catholics tend to pick and choose which church rules they follow, Opus Dei members are fervent followers of the Pope and church law," the story said. The account also claimed that Opus Dei controlled its members by setting limits on contacts with parents, and that members practiced celibacy and bodily self-mortification. This included self-flagellation. A spiked leg bracelet called a *cilice* that digs into the thigh was expected to be worn two hours each day. The device had not been used since the Middle Ages. It was explained that the followers of Opus Dei did this to share the pain of Christ.

"This is not a spiritual movement for everybody," said a member in a bit of an understatement, admitting that the movement had only eighty-four thousand members worldwide and just three thousand in the United States.

The story also said that the bulk of the Opus Dei religious order in America—some two thousand members—was in the Chicago area, where there were eleven Opus Dei priests.

"Opus Dei opponents cite their secrecy as a source of conflict in a democracy," the article said.

An Opus Dei vicar, the Reverend Bill Stetson, responded to the secrecy charge by parsing words: "We're so used to the Knights of Columbus with their capes, plumes, and swords . . . and many pro-life people wear roses in their lapels. Opus Dei doesn't go in for that. But we're not secret, just private."

The article also led to a strong response from Roy Wauck. In a letter to the editor that was published on March 10, 1999, in the *Sun-Times,* he particularly objected to paragraphs about "interventions." One person mentioned in the article, a Tammy DiNicola, claimed that young people in Opus Dei were at first brainwashed into joining the organization by its priests and later had to be spirited away from the group by former members.

Wauck wrote, "I am personally acquainted with the process by which young people meet and join Opus Dei since my youngest son, John, joined when he was a junior in high school. He went on to study at Harvard and is presently a professor of communications at the Opus Dei Pontifical University of the Holy Cross in Rome. He will be ordained a priest for Opus Dei in September. His decision to join Opus Dei in his teens was free, and his continued membership is the result of free choice."

Roy Wauck particularly attacked the intervention groups. To do so, he used his credentials to criticize an organization of former Opus Dei members known as ODAN or The Opus Dei Awareness Network.

"As a practicing psychologist, I can say what is called an intervention is, in fact, a traumatic psychological experience. At the instigation of disgruntled parents, a member of a group is sequestered by deception with the intent of forcibly extracting the person from the group. A team of self-proclaimed 'experts' submits the person to an intense barrage of psychologically intimidating, highly distorted information, without the ability to communicate with the outside world.

"This is followed by several weeks of continued so-called deprogramming," Wauck continued. "The process costs thousands of dollars and leaves the person with permanent psychological scars. One of the psychological techniques used to keep the 'cured' person from going back to the group from which they were forcibly removed is to reprogram them to attack what they formerly found attractive. This is the origin of the Opus Dei Awareness Network."

Bonnie's youngest brother, John Paul, has long been one of the family's more outspoken members. Wauck relatives joke that he applied for Harvard several times before finally being admitted and eventually getting a degree in history at the Cambridge, Massachusetts, university. Why he chose such a liberal bastion of learning to matriculate is puzzling, since his first job after graduating from Harvard in 1985 was to edit the antiabortion magazine *Human Life Review*.

After becoming one of the nation's most vocal pro-life advocates, he went to work as an aide to Robert Casey, the conservative, pro-life, two-time, Catholic, Democratic governor of Pennsylvania. On one occasion John Paul described the Casey family as "the G-rated version of the Kennedys."

John Paul has also written magazine articles debunking so-called New Age thinking and mysticism. One piece in the conservative magazine *National Review,* published in March of 1990, begins: "After the ceremonial dagger, black mass vestments, phallic candles, and human bone earrings, the black cat wasn't strictly necessary, but there it was, basking in the window . . ."

Like his father, John Paul has translated religious texts from ancient Greek scriptures into books that are sold in Catholic bookstores. But then so has another of Bonnie's brothers, Mark. Like Bonnie, Mark has an undergraduate degree in philosophy plus a law degree from Loyola, and his translation of the *Alba House Gospels* is well-known among Catholic scholars. Mark Wauck is also an FBI agent, assigned to the Chicago field office.

In 1999, when John Paul was ordained as an Opus Dei priest at Saint Eugene's Basilica in Rome, both Roy and Fran Wauck were present, as were Bob and Bonnie Hanssen. The trip to Rome by Bob and Bonnie was paid for by Roy Wauck, who thought his son-in-law couldn't afford to make the trip without his help.

In a public statement after his investiture, John Paul said that the United States "is a young nation and its future is fully open. Even though there are places where the Church is still not well-known, people are, however, fully receptive to it." He praised the work of Opus Dei, saying that the secret group "has developed a great deal since 1949" and that "activities of a spiritual nature are now provided in more than twenty cities."

*   *   *

When Bob first saw Bonnie Wauck, in a Chicago court-house where she had taken a job as a clerk, he thought she looked a lot like the film actress Natalie Wood. Indeed, there is a resemblance, though others would later tell her she looked like Pam Dawber, Robin Williams's costar on the 1970s TV sitcom *Mork & Mindy*. Bob may also have seen a mirror image of himself. Though she was nearly a foot shorter, Bonnie had the same deep brown eyes, the same full mouth as Bob. They even dressed alike. Both were formal, with Bonnie shunning slacks and usually only wearing dresses or skirts. When he told her his ancestry was German, she told him she was Polish. When she told him she was from Park Ridge, he said he was from Nor-wood Park, three stops away on the Chicago Transit Au-thority's rail line. When he told her he was Lutheran, she told him she was Catholic. Uh-oh. Nevertheless, soon after that, they went on a skating date.

In the beginning, Bonnie never thought of Bob as mar-riage material. After all, he wasn't even Roman Catholic. "I'll never marry him," she told her sisters. Yet after two dates she changed her story and told everyone she was in love.

"He treated her like a queen," her sister Liz would one day tell *Newsweek*. Indeed, in his own strange way Bob put Bonnie on a pedestal from the beginning.

"There was an understanding that they would be married when he was in dental school," Jerry Takesono remem-bered. "I don't think he dated anyone else."

Bonnie appeared not to be bothered by Bob's long si-lences. After two decades of being around seven brothers and sisters, it may have been a relief.

"I remember going on a double date with Bob and Bon-nie to the movies," said Robert Lauren. "We saw *The Grad-uate* and everyone was blown away by the movie, except Bob. The three of us talked about it for an hour, but Bob didn't react. He never said a word."

"He only had one girlfriend at Northwestern and that

was Bonnie," said John Sullivan. "She cut him a lot of slack."

Bonnie soon found out that Bob was quirky, but she would only cut him so much slack. It is Hanssen family lore that shortly after they were married, Bonnie served Bob a big breakfast of ham, eggs, and coffee while on their honeymoon. Midway through the meal Bob fell totally silent and stared into an emptied cup. Bonnie eventually noticed and asked him why he was staring so intently into the container.

"That's the way my father let my mother know he was ready for his second cup of coffee," he told her.

"Well, I'm sorry, but you're going to have to speak up around here," Bonnie shot back.

"Bob told me he was training Bonnie," Martin Ziegner recalled. "He tried to do things like tip over a glass slowly and she was supposed to catch it before anything spilled. He was big on control, but I don't think Bonnie put up with it for very long."

Another of Bob Hanssen's peculiarities surfaced on their wedding night. He had brought his own freshly laundered pillowcase to the hotel and replaced the one on his side of the bed with his own, informing her he expected her to have a just-washed pillowcase for him each time he slept. Bonnie refused to accommodate his request.

"Bob was wounded. Bonnie may have been so too. With Bob, it was probably because of his father," Martin Ziegner said.

The Catholic question had come up early. Bonnie hoped Bob would convert, and he was not only willing but eager. Incense and Latin combined with pomp and rituals that dated back to the life of Christ appealed to Bob. And when he learned about Opus Dei and the Wauck family's involvement in the mysterious order, it seemed to be a calling.

"I won't marry you unless you're Catholic," Bonnie told him. Bob nearly knocked her down rushing to his first catechism class.

Bob and Bonnie were wed at Mary, Seat of Wisdom Catholic Church in Park Ridge on August 10, 1968, three months after he dropped out of dental school. More than one hundred people attended the large white wedding. The nuptials were performed by a relative of Fran Wauck's, the vice-chancellor of the Archdiocese of Chicago, Monsignor Robert J. Hagarty. The newlyweds began living inside the Hanssens' house, sleeping in his childhood bedroom. Bob rode a bus up to his accounting classes at Northwestern.

After Bob got his MBA, he took a position with a CPA firm in downtown Chicago as a junior accountant. He hated the job. Bob's father had finally been promoted to lieutenant and was able to retire from the Chicago Police Department with a decent pension after thirty years. Howard, his mother, Mary Louise, and Vivian all moved to Venice, Florida, in Sarasota County, where he had purchased them a new home which looked much like their house in Chicago. When they moved in, Howard planted a small seedless-grapefruit tree in the backyard. The tree would grow to be larger than the house by the time he died in 1993. .

Wounded by his father or not, Bob rushed to fill Howard's shoes. He bought the little house on North Neva Avenue with both parents helping out by giving their son a below-the-market deal. Bonnie was already expecting. Their oldest child, Jane, would spend the first five years of her life there.

Howard's official retirement date was July 9, 1972. Bob entered the Chicago Police Academy three months after that, in October. With an MBA from Northwestern, it appeared that he was destined to be more than a beat pounder. Still, he delighted in wearing the uniform, if only briefly.

"I was standing around at O'Hare Airport," a friend from his Northwestern accounting classes, Ron Sanderson, remembered. "Someone tapped me on the shoulder and said, 'Sir, you're under arrest, you'll have to come with me.' I gave a start and turned around and there was Bob Hanssen in a police uniform with a big smile on his face."

The Chicago Police Academy's course took sixteen weeks in 1972 but Bob was pulled out of class by his superiors before graduating and asked if he would like to volunteer for a secret unit called C-5. Secret? Bob leaped at the opportunity and was shipped off to a covert espionage center under contract with the Chicago Police Department without ever having to walk a beat or ride in a black-and-white.

Known in 1972 as the Long-Shutter Spy School, this independent institution had some operatives who once worked for the White House, according to Ernie Rizzo, who attended the school with Bob Hanssen. Rizzo is now a colorful Chicago private detective—he has investigated Michael Jackson for one of the fathers accusing the pop singer of pedophilia. These instructors had done dirty tricks, thefts, and other clandestine deeds for the Nixon White House—the same kind that culminated with a burglary that came to be known as the Watergate scandal. Rizzo said the staff's payroll was flown in each week inside a briefcase. The money was carried by Dorothy Hunt, the wife of E. Howard Hunt, who paid the operatives in cash. A key Watergate figure and a former CIA employee, Hunt was famous for both his disguises and his spy gadgets.*

"Bob Hanssen was in my wiretapping-techniques class," Rizzo said. The school was located on the North Side of the city in the Ravenswood section. It operated secretly by using a television repair shop storefront as cover. The school not only taught counterintelligence but made customized spying devices that it sold to order. Police departments and government agencies sent their more promising men to the institution.

"Hanssen was one of those guys buying equipment and

_____
* When Hunt's wife, Dorothy, died in a Chicago plane crash in the mid-1970s, $10,000 in hundred-dollar bills was found in her purse.

learning the trade, which was counterintelligence," Rizzo recalled. "Being there was an aphrodisiac, and you got higher the deeper you got into it. Hanssen wasn't flashy, but you could tell he was smart. He looked like a plain, churchgoing kind of guy, but that's the kind you get in counterintelligence. He was overqualified to be on the street. The Chicago cops must have spotted him as a sharp guy and sent him there, because you had to know your stuff. We're not talking about doughnut-eating, traffic-watching cops here; this was a real elite group of guys."

The secret unit called C-5 was the brainstorm of Chicago police officer John Clarke, who had sold the program to Chicago mayor Richard J. Daley. Clarke's premise was that Chicago was rife with crooked cops and it was better that the city's police force did something about it before the federal government came in and did it for them.

"I was a consultant to Mayor Daley," Clarke said, "and there were three separate federal grand juries looking into three police districts. It was a major embarrassment, so C-5 asked for volunteer cops to find the bad guys. Hanssen volunteered, and after interviewing him, I felt we had asked for a Ford and got a Mercedes."

"They were the cream of the crop," recalled James Reilley, a former Chicago prosecutor. "You had to be able to do things not everyone in the force was able to do. You couldn't have a problem going after another cop. C-5 seemed to be okay with that."

According to one police source, the thirty-man C-5 unit was so covert that its members would have phony assignments stuffed into their personnel files to help quell suspicion that they were working against their own. In Bob's case, his cover job was as a member of the vice squad.

For the most part, the assignments had the C-5 group posing as drug dealers in sting operations. They tried to catch cops who C-5 believed were being bribed by heroin distributors to look the other way when their deals went down. It was dirty, ugly work, and to this day some members of the police department feel that C-5 abused its authority. Pat Camden, a thirty-year veteran of the force, particularly recalls one raid in front of the now-defunct Chicago Stadium where C-5 members strip-searched two Chicago cops outside the sports arena.

"I thought that was way out of line," Camden said. Other veterans said C-5 had a tense relationship with the rest of their peers, with some police officers going so far as to openly express hatred of C-5 and doing everything they could to bring it down. Taking rookies out of the Police Academy and using them to hunt down their own kind was violently resented, despite evidence of corruption inside the police department.

John Clarke said he eventually grew suspicious of Bob Hanssen. According to Clarke, it got to the point where he began to think his young protégé might be a double agent.

"He was brilliant and he looked like an altar boy. But I always thought he was a spy, a counterspy, when he worked for us. I thought he was working for the police brass who wanted to know what we were doing. I always felt something was wrong, so we held Hanssen on a short leash. I even thought at one point he might be working for the feds because he was so inquisitive about Mayor Daley.

"He seemed to be a good, solid, family-man type, Roman Catholic—the kid next door. He was also wildly ambitious and would volunteer for any wacko assignment we had. He bought a book on wiretapping, as I recall."

Clarke offered his own theory of why Bob may have used the alias of Ramon Garcia in his dealings with the Russians. Speaking to Michael Sneed, the *Chicago Sun-Times* columnist, Clarke said, "I told him the story of an Irish kid from Rhode Island. I had hired him as an undercover agent to infiltrate the Mexican mafia. His code name was Ramon. I used to train people to infiltrate gangs and I trained him."

* * *

Bonnie wasn't as inquisitive. At home, in the little house on North Neva Avenue, her only vice was to sun herself in the fenced-in backyard during the hot Chicago summers. Working on her tan, reading, and caring for Jane took up most of her time. There had already been one miscarriage and there would be others. A second daughter, Susan Elizabeth, would be born in Chicago, in February of 1974. With Bonnie unable to work because of two young toddlers, the family barely scraped by. But they were good years. The constants in their lives were the Catholic Church, Opus Dei, and the large, nearby Wauck family. Their few vacations always involved a car trip to Florida and a visit with Howard and Vivian. On these trips Bob would sometimes open up about his father to Bonnie, describing him as cold and distant. It helped his wife to understand why her husband was that way. Bonnie made the most of the vacations, heading for the beach and a darker tan on the day after they arrived.

Vivian and Howard Hanssen at first applauded Bob's decision to become Catholic, thinking that it was fine that the entire family would be one religion. But after one visit to Florida, Vivian was no longer sure about her son's choice. Howard and Vivian had gone to church every Sunday, but this Opus Dei stuff was over the top.

"I think a child needs a church, especially growing up," she said. "It's good for them. But when they came down here for a visit, they went to church every day. I thought that was too much. You know, they say it's the converts who are the most devout."

Bob took his CPA exam in 1973, passed it, and received his state license. He wound up never using the title. His CPA certificate was requested to be mailed to 11221 State Street—the address of Chicago's police headquarters.

He was a devoted father, concerned about his children's education from the beginning. He told Bonnie he wanted Jane to have a head start in life. When she was three, according to a close family friend, he taught her to read, and when she was four, he helped her through her first novel.

"It was long—more than a thousand pages—there were really hard words in it, and he would read part of it and then she would read part of it. The family still jokes about the one he chose."

Do you recall the title?

"Sure, it was *War and Peace*—the Russian book about the battles against Napoleon. Isn't that weird, knowing what we know now?"

FOUR

Crossing the Rubicon

It did not take long for Bob Hanssen to feel that he was too good for the Chicago Police Department. When he grabbed a defendant in a Chicago courtroom who was trying to escape, his feat wasn't recognized with either a citation or a reward. That upset him. Being part of C-5 had made him controversial. He began looking elsewhere. John Clarke said he advised his discovery as to where his next move should be:

"I told him to get his fanny over to the FBI, and he did. But he didn't get accepted the first time around."

In late 1975, Bob Hanssen took a one-year leave of absence from the Chicago Police Department. On January 12, 1976, employment records show that he was sworn in as an FBI agent assigned to its regional office in Indianapolis. After securing the position he resigned from the Chicago PD.

In his swearing-in ceremony, Bob pledged:

I will support and defend the Constitution of the United States against all enemies, foreign and domestic; I will bear true faith and allegiance to the same; I will take this obligation freely, without any mental reservation or purpose of evasion; and I will

well and faithfully discharge the duties of the office
on which I am about to enter. So help me God.

He also signed a pledge that included:

I accept the obligation in connection with my assignments to consider the information coming into my
knowledge by virtue of my position as a *sacred trust,*
to be used solely for official purposes. In the performance of my duties and assignments, I shall not en-
gage in unlawful and unethical practices. While
occupying the status of a law enforcement officer or
at any other time subsequent thereto, I shall not seek
to benefit personally because of my knowledge of any
confidential matter which has come to my attention.
I am aware of the serious responsibilities of my office
and in the performance of my duties. I shall wage
vigorous warfare against the enemies of my country,
of its laws, and of its principles; I shall always be
loyal to my duty, my organization, and my country.

Finally, Bob Hanssen was also made to sign an employment agreement that, among other restrictions, had him
promising to

prohibit loss, misuse, or unauthorized disclosure or
production of national security information, other
classified information and other nonclassified information in the files of the FBI.
I understand that the unauthorized disclosure of
information in the files of the FBI or information I
may acquire as an employee could result in the im-
pairment of national security, place human life in
jeopardy, or result in the denial of due process to a
person or persons who are subjects of an FBI investigation, or prevent the FBI from effectively discharg-
ing its responsibilities. I understand the need for this

secrecy agreement; therefore, as consideration for
employment I agree that I will never divulge, publish,
or reveal either by word or conduct, or by any other
means disclose to any unauthorized recipient without
official written authorization by the Director of the
FBI or his delegate, any information from the inves-
tigatory files of the FBI or any information relating
to material contained in the files . . . unauthorized disclosure may be a violation of Federal law and pros-
ecuted as a criminal offense.

Following his final signature, Bob Hanssen received a
Top Secret security clearance. It was his third involvement
with organizations (Chicago Police counterintelligence and
Opus Dei being the other two) that were shrouded in secrecy and elitism. Several years later, he would sign additional classified agreements that gave him access to SCI
(Sensitive Compartmented Information) documents. These
were even blacker secrets that had him signing even more
restrictive documents that cited several sections of the U.S.
Intelligence Identities Protection Act of 1982.

Bob Hanssen was given a GS-10 grade and a salary of just
over $30,000 a year. At first he was assigned to the Indi-
anapolis, Indiana, field office, one of fifty-six regional offices in the United States. After a few weeks he was sent
to the Gary, Indiana, resident agency and put on a team
that investigated white-collar crime. It wasn't glamorous.
Gary, a decaying rust belt town of two hundred thousand,
was Indiana's second-largest city, but was first in crime and
boarded-up downtown storefronts. On the other hand, Gary,
in the left-hand corner of the state, was hard on the Illinois
border, and just forty miles from Bob's house on North
Neva Avenue. He could drive there in less than an hour.
The Hanssen family's life was hardly disrupted.

In Chicago, it was getting crowded. Their first son, John,
whom they would call Jack, was born in April of 1977. The

girls sometimes slept in the attic, where Howard's mother had once lived.

Gary became a tryout for New York. The FBI wasn't going to have an MBA from Northwestern, and a former big-city cop with intelligence experience, languish in Indiana. Midway through 1978, Bob Hanssen received orders transferring him to New York City.

In November of that year, Bob and Bonnie purchased a three-bedroom house in Westchester County, on the southern border of Scarsdale, population seventeen thousand. Scarsdale, the Waspy-appearing, quintessential New York suburb, evokes martinis and John Cheever novels, though neither the cocktails nor the author shared any part of Hanssen family values.

The wood-framed, pale yellow, two-story residence at 150 Webster Road was marked by a stucco fireplace chimney in front that ran from the ground to the roof. It had been painted white and stood out from the rest of the home. The five windows on its face were bordered by black, nonfunctional storm shutters. A detached, single-car garage was in the right rear of the yard, with a small, open lawn between the house and the street. In April of 1980, Bob and Bonnie would have a second boy while living there, Mark Edward. Family, Opus Dei, and the FBI were still the three constants for the Hanssens. Bob appeared to be on a fast track in the Bureau. The family were members of Immaculate Heart of Mary Catholic Church, a ten-minute walk away. Jane and Susan Elizabeth attended its parochial school.

"They enjoyed Scarsdale," said Fran Wauck. "And I enjoyed visiting them because I love New York. Their house wasn't in the best part of town, and sometimes we joked and said they were living in the slums of Scarsdale."

Bob and Bonnie purchased the house for $43,500 from an older couple, John and Loretta Donovan. Perhaps because John Donovan was a dentist and Bob became a patient of his, John and Loretta became casual friends of Bob and Bonnie's with the two couples going out to dinner on a couple of occasions. John Donovan knew Bob was in the FBI and in some sort of intelligence work. "He kept very much to himself," Donovan recalled, but remembered Bob telling him, "I wanted to be a spy ever since I was a child."

On another occasion, while discussing taxes, Bonnie let slip to Loretta that she and Bob had a secret Swiss bank account. Bonnie didn't know why, but was about to find out.

During his Scarsdale period, Bob approached several GRU agents in New York and offered them secrets in exchange for money. Exchanges were made, but he made the mistake of counting out $20,000 in the basement of the house. Bonnie caught him and he boasted about the deal to her. Bob told her he had tricked the Soviets by giving them meaningless information for money. The exchange was made in nearby Riverdale, fifteen minutes away. (Many Soviet families lived in a Moscow-owned apartment house there.) His wife was horrified and made her husband promise to discontinue the grown-up *Spy vs Spy* game immediately.

Bonnie also made her husband confess the sin to an Opus Dei priest, Robert P. Bucciarelli.* The priest at first considered turning Bob in, but after realizing it would be a breach of clerical ethics instead told him to give the illegal cash to charity. Bob did so, dispensing it over several years to the charities of the famed Albanian nun Mother Teresa.

In New York City, where the FBI occupied the twenty-third through the twenty-eighth floor of the Jacob Javits Building at 26 Federal Plaza on Broadway, Bob Hanssen could feel he had arrived. The New York City offices had the second-largest number of agents in the country, exceeded only by the Washington headquarters. The daily commutes weren't

---

* Bucciarelli is a published priest. His summary of Edward Leen's *The Holy Ghost,* now modernized as *The Holy Spirit,* on "the principles of supernatural growth," is sold in most Catholic bookstores.

bad. Scarsdale was some twenty-one miles away and only thirty-five minutes from Manhattan by train.

Bob's CPA degree was at first put to work in the criminal division. Tallying up expense accounts and the budget for sting operations wasn't what he had had in mind when he joined the FBI, but outwardly Bob had no complaints. He was confident that someone like himself would be noticed. He soon was—reassigned to counterintelligence, something that others avoided because the cases were slow and required painstaking attention to detail. The CI department was called Sleepy Hollow, and the CI people gibed back by referring to those who worked in domestic criminal cases as "knuckle draggers." CI was considered a bad career choice—CI people rarely got headlines, while everytime an agent busted the mob, the stories made headlines in the New York tabloids. Bob's most important assignment was to install an automated counterintelligence database that tracked the diplomatic base at the United Nations and the city's foreign consulates.

"The counterintelligence agents read the *New York Times,* and the criminal agents read the *Daily News,*" a former agent, who worked with Bob in the late 1970s, later told *Time.* "Espionage cases are the best cases in the world because they're very cerebral. So was Hanssen. He read voraciously, everything from spy novels to Marxist tomes to the richly detailed logs filed by surveillance squads overnight. He really wanted to do counterintelligence work."

In June 1980, Bob got his first clearance that gave him access to "sensitive compartmented information." The definition was for important intelligence data above Top Secret.

"The unit was involved with more than budget matters," explained Bob's predecessor, Richard M. Alu. "It functioned as staff for the assistant director in charge of foreign counterintelligence and terrorism. If you are staff for the boss, you get unique assignments and special knowledge."

What was Bob like?

"He was different. I thought he was an intelligent guy, but he was something of an introvert. Most agents, they're introverts. But the ideal agent is a used-car salesman—you've got to be able to sell yourself. Hanssen simply didn't have any interpersonal skills. He was able to see problems, see solutions, and implement them. His solutions were not always easy for his peers to follow. He would have to explain them and he did not suffer fools gladly."

Alu told the *Los Angeles Times* that Bob was not only "very bright, but knew he was very bright. Arrogance came from that self-assessment."

Bob was soon to find that his advancement within the Bureau was limited. "You can only go so far on brains alone," Alu said. "You still have to have personal skills to rise up in management."

In the next four years Bob would realize that a glass ceiling existed for him, no matter how brilliant his analysis work in counterintelligence. This would eventually work to the advantage of the KGB. By not being a people person, he was instead given more and more access to sensitive materials to study alone.

In Scarsdale, Bob rarely spoke to neighbors. When he came out to rake the leaves in the fall, he never even bothered to wave to the family across the street, who were doing the same chores. Still, he appeared to be a perfect suburban father—a little harried, what with his important law enforcement job in the city and the pressure of getting his kids to their parochial schools and the family to mass each Sunday.

Bonnie matched Bob by becoming Scarsdale's Betty Crocker. Her chocolate-chip oatmeal cookies with walnuts were legendary, and she baked her own bread. Mrs. Hanssen could even make Kung-Pao chicken from scratch. She made the dish better than any Chinese restaurant, her children boasted to their friends. And compared to her husband, she was outgoing, vivacious.

But if Bonnie controlled the kitchen, Bob controlled the

checkbook. He was as sparing with money as he was in his compliments to her. Largely silent at the dinner table, he only opened his mouth to complain or make a request.

"I thought he was a mute at first," said a guest of the Hanssen children who stayed at the house for more than a week and observed his behavior firsthand. "He would sit there and say nothing, going for days without speaking, and then it was a kind of a mumble that you couldn't understand. When Mr. Hanssen got some kind of vegetable he didn't like, he'd carp about it like a little child. He would hang his head, stare at the food, and whine something like, 'But, Bonnie, you know I don't like this.' She would try to hug him in front of us at times, but he would never hug her back. He was very strange."

Exactly five years after joining the Bureau, on January 12, 1981, Bob Hanssen was assigned to the FBI's center of operations in Washington, D.C. The job was part of the track on which the Bureau put favored agents—a few years in the field, a few years in headquarters, and then back out to a field office again.

Rising nine stories where it fronted on Pennsylvania Avenue and eleven stories in the back along E Street, the J. Edgar Hoover Building's reputation as one of the ugliest government buildings in Washington is well deserved. It had been carved from the District of Columbia's tenderloin district at a cost of $126 million, forcing the destruction of the venerable Gayety Burlesque. The death of the theater had saddened many a congressman.*

* Wilbur Mills, the former chairman of the House Ways and Means Committee, had once sat in the front row of the Gayety in the early 1970s besotted with lust for the "Argentine Firecracker," Miss Fanne Fox. He lost his power when Fox jumped out of his limousine at two in the morning and into the Potomac River's Tidal Basin while both were drunk. After that Mills went to a rehab center and Fox changed her description to the "Tidal Basin Bombshell."

The FBI's ludicrous overhang on the E Street and Ninth Street sides gave those walking below the impression that the building was about to fall on them. It was to have been J. Edgar Hoover's living monument, designed while he still headed the Bureau, but was completed two years after his death. Tourists visiting Washington for the first time sometimes asked when it would be completed. The exterior of tan concrete looked as if it had yet to be finished and was awaiting a smoother facing.

For Bob Hanssen, just working in Hoover's 2.5-million-square-foot monstrosity with its worldwide budget of $3.2 billion was humbling. Bob told Bonnie that "Mr. Hoover" had been a great leader. He was happy to have finally arrived at the epicenter of the Bureau and felt that it was now just a matter of time before he would be part of the hierarchy.

The Hanssens nearly doubled their money when selling the Scarsdale house in June of 1981 for $83,000 and were thus able to move up and pay $150,000 for their first Vienna house in Northern Virginia the same month. A closer look, though, would have shown them to be financially skating on thin ice. The sellers had to offer them a $53,000, 12 percent second-mortgage loan to make the deal go through. Bob and Bonnie's first-and second-mortgage payments totaled $1,700 a month.

The four-bedroom, two-bath Dutch colonial on Whitecedar Court was directly in the center at the end of a cul-de-sac. A deck and a gazebo were attached to the back of the house with the lawn in the rear running right out to Courthouse Road, broken only by a thin veneer of woods. Across Courthouse Road were eighty-four acres of greenery—a large outdoor recreation center of soccer and baseball fields called Nottoway Park.

The new house at first seemed comfortable enough for a couple with four children, but then there was a fifth child, Greg, born in 1983, and in 1985, a sixth, Lisa. Bonnie was now thirty-nine, Bob was forty-one, and her life still revolved around diapers and feedings for the younger half of the family while arranging first communions for the older ones. Bob didn't help with the housework or the children. An Opus Dei dictum was that women did housework, so Bonnie never complained. Public displays of affection, always rare, had ended. He appeared too busy, too distracted. Bob had an important job at FBI headquarters.

His title now was supervisory special agent, and at first Bob was assigned to plan and justify the Bureau's multibillion-dollar budget that was presented to Congress each year. In 1983 he was bumped up to the Soviet Analytical Unit, which supported the FBI's foreign counterintelligence operation. Here, Bob Hanssen began to see more compartmentalized classified documents. He was asked to serve on a foreign counterintelligence committee and was responsible for coordinating some highly sensitive technical projects.

Despite these heady assignments and the air of importance Bob was able to project simply by looking over a coworker's or a neighbor's head and saying nothing, the pay didn't match the job. Bob was barely making $40,000 a year, and with six young children, four of whom were already in parochial school, the family was barely scraping by. Summer vacations still meant packing the kids in the car and driving to Florida to see his parents. They would crowd into the little house in Florida with some of the family sleeping on the floor. At home, Bonnie would sew curtains and hem skirts and make duvet covers for the bed out of cheap sheets. She was always busy trying to save money, at times baking her famous cookies and then telling the children they could only have two per day to stretch them out.

In September of 1985, the FBI had the Hanssens on the move once more, to New York City. Bob shuddered at having to uproot the family again. Sometime in the next couple of years he would have to come up with cash for five parochial school kids. Lisa had just been born. He was too old to begin a new career.

FBI employees, some of whom made so little that they were literally applying for food stamps in New York, considered places like Manhattan and San Francisco hardship posts. Agents were quitting—a half dozen each month—in New York City. The Bureau had yet to realize that cost of living allowances were sorely needed if one were reassigned from Nebraska or New Mexico to a place like the Big Apple.

Though Bob and Bonnie made a small profit ($25,000 before real estate commissions) on the sale of the Whitecedar Court house, they now had to move even farther out into Westchester County. Even with a promotion and a boost to $45,000 a year, his salary forced them to buy out in Yorktown Heights. They were so far from the city they were bumping up against Putnam County. It didn't seem fair. Bob was more than forty miles from the Manhattan office, and the drive to work could be an hour and a half, even in light traffic. The new house at 2861 Mead Street was a step down—one less bedroom, one less bathroom, for six kids and two adults—and it was $165,000, nearly the same as the Whitecedar Court house but more than twice as far a commute to Bob's office. Other agents had it even worse in those days, driving into the city from as far away as Pennsylvania.

Supermom Bonnie found time not only to host Bible study groups at the house, but also to join a local Opus Dei chapter that met at Saint Patrick's Catholic Church. Saint Pat's had an adjacent school, and Jane, Susan, John, and Mark were enrolled. The invoices for all of them would give some parents earning the Hanssens' salary pause, but Bonnie and Bob had no choice—they were too devout. Public school was simply out of the question.

Bob's boss, Thomas L. Sheer, had felt the squeeze himself. Just before Bob arrived, he warned FBI headquarters that a beginning agent in his office made less than a New

York City trash collector. He told his superiors that his men were vulnerable, and if the Russians were to make someone a good offer, there might be an agent in the Bureau who couldn't resist the money. Tom Sheer himself, as chief of the office, was making just $72,500 a year, and when the Bureau ignored his warning, he quit. Bob Hanssen didn't. Instead, he changed sides.*

Intelligence agents use the expression *crossing the Rubicon* to describe going over to the other side. The words have their origin with Julius Caesar. In 49 B.C., when Caesar's army crossed the Rubicon River while marching toward Rome, Caesar is said to have exclaimed, "The die is cast!" meaning that upon entering the waters of the Rubicon, he could not turn back. Days later, Caesar's army defeated the republican government's forces and he became dictator for life. In espionage, once an agent begins doing business with the other side, he is said to have "crossed the Rubicon" and to be unable to retreat.

Bob Hanssen, who had already crossed his Rubicon at least once, made it permanent on October 4, 1985, nine days after arriving in New York for his second tour of duty. The question will always be why? The answer is complicated, and no single explanation suffices.

"To someone in espionage, what's the worst thing you can do to sabotage someone who doesn't appreciate you, and who doesn't promote you or support you?" David Charney, a psychiatrist, would explain to the *Washington Post*. "Give away their secrets. But here's the crux. There's no turning back once you've stepped over the line. You're trapped. There are no credible exits. So you have to resign yourself to living this life."

* In 1988, a year following Sheer's departure and three years after Bob Hanssen began working for the Russians, the FBI raised salaries for New York–based agents by 25 percent. The Bureau had little choice—the New York office had more than two hundred vacancies and they couldn't fill the positions.

According to espionage experts, an acronym explains the motivation for double espionage agents. The term is *MICE*, which stands for Money, Ideology, Compromise, and Ego. In Bob Hanssen's world, all of these reasons came into play, but none of these can be explained by a single word.

While *money* was a reason, in Bob Hanssen's case it was *need* rather than *greed* that made him cross the line. Unlike with Rick Ames and others, none of the funds were used to foster a lavish lifestyle. Bob didn't even buy a new suit. The first dollars went to pay the children's parochial schools.

According to Cambridge history professor Christopher Andrew, the days of ideological agents who betray their country are largely over. This is because the dream of creating a worker state where class differences are eliminated has been shown to be unworkable. Robert Hanssen *was* indeed fascinated by Kim Philby's *My Silent War,* but it was likely more for "a caper," as Bob told his friend Robert Lauren, than *ideology.* He may also have been influenced by the forward to *My Silent War,* which was written by Graham Greene, the distinguished twentieth-century British novelist and, at one time, a spy himself. Greene's books are heavily laced with Catholic guilt and thought. In the foreword to *My Silent War,* Greene implied it was better to betray one's country than one's friends. It would have been easy for Bob Hanssen to substitute the word *family* for *friends.* Greene wrote: "He betrayed his country—yes, perhaps he did, but who among us has not committed treason to something or someone more important than a country? In Philby's own eyes he was working for a shape of things to come from which his country would benefit."

Bob Hanssen despised communism, but he nurtured a love affair with the best aspects of Russian culture. The books and music he had read or listened to while learning the language in college had made a big impression upon him. By the late 1980s, according to a family friend, Bob would not allow his children to speak inside his car while he was driving them to and from their expensive parochial schools. Instead, he would serenade them with tapes of Russian symphonies and then only by Kremlin-approved composers such as Tchaikovsky and Prokofiev.

"Occasionally, he would play Beethoven," a former schoolmate of his two oldest girls, Jane and Susan, said, "but that was once in a blue moon." In that decade, Oakcrest, a Catholic girls' school affiliated with Opus Dei, was located in Chevy Chase, Maryland. Bob Hanssen would drive his daughters to Metro Center near FBI headquarters and drop them off there, with the girls transferring onto the subway to finish their journey. The route would be reversed in the evening.

Compromise usually involves blackmail. The agent succumbs to traps that usually revolve around sex or money. Bob Hanssen compromised himself. He thought he was immune from extortion and exposure from the Russians as long as he didn't meet with them or reveal his name. How naive. Did he think that they would not record his license plate number from a distance and then have his name and address within twenty-four hours? Bob was willing to fool himself into believing all was fine. If he had ever attempted to twist the Russian bear's tail, his "friends" could just as easily have played rough and used coercion.

Ego comes last in the MICE equation, but was likely the second-greatest factor in Bob Hanssen's mind. He wanted to be famous and may have been contented to be so only in the closeted world that occupied one part of his reasoning. Bob's Russian handlers may have understood that too, for as their letters reveal, they massaged his ego at every opportunity, flattering him by paying compliments and suggesting he had a "sharp-as-a-razor mind," or he possessed "a superb sense of humor," at times even enclosing a personal thank-you note from the head of the KGB. Everyone is vulnerable to flattery, and Bob Hanssen, disappointed that he had not advanced as far as he felt he should have at the Bureau, welcomed these compliments.

In his warped world, the praise may have been one of the few recognitions of his abilities.

On the day after Bonnie Hanssen's thirty-ninth birthday, October 4, 1985, Viktor M. Degtyar, a KGB colonel living in Alexandria, Virginia, received an unsigned letter from Bob Hanssen. At the time, the Justice Department had a program that flagged mail to "known foreign agents." The post office was supposed to photograph the front and back of each envelope. But the program was spotty at best, and many letters went through without any examination at all. Bob Hanssen, an FBI agent working in counterintelligence, had access to a list of targeted spies, Justice Department officials now conclude. The communication, written entirely in capital letters, bore a postmark of October 1 from a Washington suburb, Prince George's County in Maryland. The letter had an inner envelope, which gave an order to Colonel Degtyar in capital letters: *DO NOT OPEN. TAKE THIS LETTER TO VICTOR* [sic] *I. CHERKASHIN.* Inside the second envelope was a letter that would confirm information the KGB had recently received from the CIA's Aldrich Ames. It may have meant a death sentence for two Soviet double agents who had been spying for America, and years of hard labor for another.

DEAR MR. CHERKASHIN:
SOON, I WILL SEND A BOX OF DOCUMENTS TO MR. DEGTYAR. THEY ARE FROM CERTAIN OF THE MOST SENSITIVE AND HIGHLY COMPART-MENTED PROJECTS OF THE U.S. INTELLIGENCE COMMUNITY. ALL ARE ORIGINALS TO AID IN VERIFYING THEIR AUTHENTICITY. PLEASE RECOGNIZE FOR OUR LONG-TERM INTERESTS THAT THERE ARE A LIMITED NUMBER OF PER-SONS WITH THIS ARRAY OF CLEARANCES. AS A COLLECTION THEY POINT TO ME. I TRUST THAT AN OFFICER OF YOUR EXPERIENCE WILL

HANDLE THEM APPROPRIATELY. I BELIEVE
THEY ARE SUFFICIENT TO JUSTIFY A $100,000
PAYMENT TO ME.

I MUST WARN OF CERTAIN RISKS TO MY SE-
CURITY OF WHICH YOU MAY NOT BE AWARE.
YOUR SERVICE HAS RECENTLY SUFFERED
SOME SETBACKS. I WARN THAT BORIS YUZHIN
(LINE PR, S.F.), MR. SERGEY MOTORIN (LINE PR,
WASH.) AND MR. VALERIY MARTYNOV (LINE X,
WASH.) HAVE BEEN RECRUITED BY OUR "SPE-
CIAL SERVICES."
[*PR* is the Soviet abbreviation for "political," *X* was for
"science and technology."]

Bob described some highly sensitive classified material
for Cherkashin, then head of American KGB counterintelligence, to give his chosen handler a taste of what he could
expect next. Bob also gave personal observations on what
he knew of the three Russian agents' activities on behalf
of the United States against the Soviet Union. Bob may
have wanted Cherkashin to know he would be getting his
$100,000 worth, labeling the information TO FURTHER
SUPPORT MY BONAFIDES, and finished:

DETAILS REGARDING PAYMENT AND FUTURE
CONTACT WILL BE SENT TO YOU PERSONALLY.
MY IDENTITY AND ACTUAL POSITION IN THE
COMMUNITY MUST BE LEFT UNSTATED. I AM
OPEN TO COMMO SUGGESTIONS BUT WANT NO
SPECIALIZED TRADECRAFT. I WILL ADD 6 AND
YOU WILL SUBTRACT 6 FROM STATED
MONTHS, DAYS AND TIMES IN BOTH DIREC-
TIONS OF OUR FUTURE COMMUNICATIONS.

The die had been cast. Best of all, the new double agent
believed he was going to be calling the shots. Like Ming
the Merciless, Ramon Garcia thought he was about to be a
master of two worlds.

PART TWO

SLAVE: The slaves obey, O Ming the Merciless.
FLASH: Get your hands off me. I will meet your emperor as a free man and an equal.
MING: So, Earthman, you are a free man and my equal?
FLASH: All men of Earth are equal, and one day they will all be free.

—FLASH GORDON,
"Episode One: The New Planet"

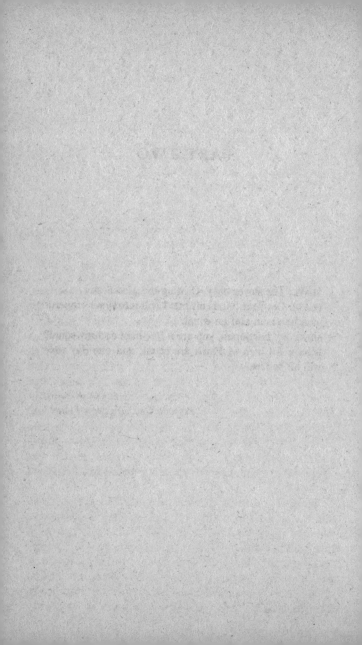

FIVE

The Secret World of "B"

A year after receiving the first letter from Bob Hanssen, Viktor I. Cherkashin would receive the Order of Lenin, the second-highest award the Soviet Union offered, akin to a knighthood from the queen of England. Cherkashin has claimed that he received the honor for his handling of Rick Ames and, to a lesser degree, the Yurchenko affair. In that scandal, a top Soviet KGB official, Vitaly Yurchenko, had publicly defected to the U.S. embassy in Rome during August of 1985. After being debriefed in Washington and sampling a U.S. lifestyle, he redefected to Moscow three months later. The Soviets made the episode into a propaganda coup, staging a lively press conference where it was suggested that Yurchenko had been drugged and kidnapped by the CIA.

The real reason for the defection could have been made into a spy novel as written by bodice-ripper novelist Nora Roberts. Yurchenko had left the Soviets because he was in love with the wife of a Soviet diplomat assigned to Canada. He demanded the CIA reunite him with her in Montreal, and the pliant Agency did just that. But when he showed up at her doorstep, she spurned him. Yurchenko decided to take his chances and return home. Because of his newly minted value as a Soviet show horse, he was not harmed and, instead, was given a hero's welcome.

Ames, after fortifying his nerve with vodka, had marched into the Soviet embassy at 1125 Sixteenth Street in Washington on April 16, 1985. During the next two months he gave them the names of the same three Soviet double agents that Bob Hanssen would later divulge in exchange for five hundred new hundred-dollar bills. But the name on the letter Ames initially dropped off at the embassy was that of the KGB *rezident* in Washington, Stanislav Andreevich Androsov, not Cherkashin, the counterintelligence chief. Though Cherkashin would eventually supervise much of the dealings with Ames, the Androsov letter was not one he could have flashed around in Moscow. But the letter from Bob Hanssen did have his name on it, though he might have been affronted at first by Bob's slight misspelling of his name. Thus one can make a strong case that Viktor Cherkashin's coveted Lenin medal came at least partly as a result of Bob's entry into what was already a crowded field.

A crowded field? The year Bob began spying, 1985, has long been designated as "the year of the spy." Tripped-up espionage agents on both sides were either being tried or arrested for all kinds of reasons. John Walker, his brother, a son, and an accomplice were arrested in June. The four were charged with selling U.S. navy nuclear-submarine secrets and other classified material to the Soviets. All would be convicted and receive a variety of sentences, from twenty-five years to life. In California, there was the fall trial of FBI agent Richard W. Miller, who would be convicted of selling classified materials to the Soviets, the first FBI agent ever to be convicted of spying for the Russians. A portly, slovenly agent who had been sexually entrapped by beautiful Russian émigré Svetlana Ogorodnikov, Miller had a need for money that ultimately led to his arrest. He had sold FBI materials to a private investigator and, pathetically, had stolen a $113 social security check from his wife's grandmother. At his first trial, which took place at the same time Bob Hanssen delivered his first shipment of classified documents to the Soviets, the hapless Miller got two life sentences plus fifty years.*

Jonathan Pollard, a civilian intelligence analyst for the navy, was arrested in November of 1985 and accused of spying for Israel. He eventually received a life sentence. His wife, Ann, got a five-year term. Unlike the others, who spied for either sex, money, or both, Pollard was an ideological spy. There was also the case of Edward Lee Howard, a CIA employee who failed a polygraph exam in Moscow in 1983 and was fired. Suspected of selling secrets to the Soviets, he was watched twenty-four hours a day by the FBI after returning to his New Mexico home. After Yurchenko defected, Howard was certain he would be one of the double agents revealed by the Russians. While returning home from a restaurant near Santa Fe with his wife, Mary, driving, he rounded a turn on an isolated road, quickly placed a dummy in the seat next to his wife, and dove out of the car without being noticed. He made his way to Finland and on to the Soviet Union, becoming the first CIA agent to defect to Moscow. There was further embarrassment for the FBI when it was learned that the surveillance agent had missed the Howard departure and that his daring car escape hadn't even been necessary. The CIA blamed the FBI for Howard's escape, and in turn the FBI blamed the CIA for not telling everything it knew about Howard.

Which brings us somewhat full circle and to an important question. Bob Hanssen gave up the names of the three double agents in his first letter to Cherkashin. Did he? Bob undoubtedly knew they were already compromised and were therefore doomed. When Edward Howard arrived in the Soviet Union on September 21, he immediately re-

* After eight years and three more trials, his sentence was reduced to nine years.

vealed both Martynov and Yuzhin's duplicities, though sources are unsure if Howard knew about Motorin. So the KGB had probably already been told twice—first by Ames and then by Howard—about the double-agent activities of at least two of the names. Ames had definitely revealed Motorin's name, and Howard might have done the same. Bob Hanssen, working in Soviet counterintelligence, likely knew or assumed that Yuzhin, Martynov, and Motorin were marked men because of Howard's defection or because of an unexplained silence by the trio. All had been under suspicion for years. Motorin and Yuzhin were already in Moscow. Martynov, however, did not leave the United States until November, as part of Yurchenko's honor guard, escorting him home.

There is an important issue here: Was Bob Hanssen's information about the activities of double agents Martynov and Motorin the catalyst that led to their execution by firing squads? (Yuzhin served six years of a fifteen-year sentence inside a hard-labor prison camp in the Ural Mountains.) As the third person to drop their names, he might have known that they were already as good as dead.

Bob Hanssen's actions against his country can never be defended. On the other hand, evidence suggests that, for the most part, he spent most of his adult life as a caring, religious man, despite his disturbed personality. The FBI says he never offered the Russians any documentation on Martynov, Motorin, and Yuzhin, only his personal knowledge. Further, though the FBI has charged that Bob exposed as many as six more double agents, they have yet to name them or tell of their fates. So while Bob may have used his position at the FBI's Soviet counterintelligence unit to give his handlers at least nine names of Russian moles over fifteen years, there is not yet any evidence, except for one, that they were harmed. Bob Hanssen may have deluded himself, because his religious beliefs would never have permitted him to feel responsible for someone's death.

*   *   *

Valeriy Fedorovich Martynov was burly, six feet tall, and like Bob, very much a family man. He and his wife, Natalya, had a boy and a girl, and their apartment was a twenty-minute drive from Bob Hanssen's home in Vienna. According to David Wise, author of *Nightmover,* one of five books on the Aldrich Ames case, the FBI's Soviet intelligence unit met with Martynov several times between 1983 and 1985. Martynov was recruited by the CIA in 1982. Bob Hanssen had joined the FBI's Soviet Analytical Unit, which supported the Bureau's counterintelligence operations and investigated Soviet intelligence services, in 1983. Bob Hanssen met face-to-face with both Martynov *and* Motorin. As Wise reported:

> The FBI and the CIA had different priorities in the meeting with Martynov. The Bureau was interested in detailed information about the KGB residency in Washington . . . the FBI, for example, wanted PI-MENTA'S (Martynov's code name) assessment of which KGB officers might be vulnerable to recruitment.
>
> Martynov also turned over documents to the FBI and the CIA. He provided Xerox copies; he did not use a camera. From the CIA's point of view, Martynov's real importance was not so much what he could provide, although that was valuable, but his potential as a sleeper agent. "Here was a bright young guy who would move ahead," one SE division officer said, "and someday might become a very important agent."

Motorin had come to Washington in 1980 to gather political intelligence for the KGB. He was the same height as Bob Hanssen, six foot two, but he was Bob's opposite when it came to family life. Though he was married and his wife, Olga, and their two daughters were with him in the United States, the blond, wispy-mustached Motorin seemed to need extramarital sex. The FBI found him with a prostitute in his car in 1982 and later used that as part of a package they put together for his conversion to double agent. The other part came when an FBI surveillance team photographed him trading two cases of vodka and some boxes of Cuban cigars for a stereo system at a downtown Washington discount electronics store. Motorin was supposed to be using the cigars and vodka as bait to entice Americans to work for his side. Using the goods to buy the latest excesses of capitalist materialism could earn him a few years in a labor camp somewhere in the Gulag archipelago.

FBI agents confronted Motorin with photographs. Motorin didn't cave in immediately. Mike Morton, the FBI agent assigned to him, would appear out of nowhere every few weeks brandishing the photos. It took nearly a year of threats. Was Motorin blackmailed into his job as a double agent?

"We try never to do that," an agent said. "Moles that get forced into working for us more often than not can be disasters. But sometimes you do what you have to in order to make someone cooperate."

Soviet spies offer a different version of FBI benevolence. According to former KGB agent Yuri B. Shvets in his memoir, *Washington Station,* Konstantin Koryavin, a handler for an American mole, was caught by the FBI at midnight gathering up documents that had been left for him in a park. The FBI blindfolded him, threw him in a car, drove to a cemetery, and had him stand at the edge of a freshly dug grave, where they removed his blindfold.

"Tell us the name of your contact and we'll let you go. If you don't we're going to shoot you and bury you," an FBI agent said. "Nobody will know what happened to you. You'll just have vanished into thin air. You have exactly a minute to make up your mind."

According to Shvets, Koryavin looked into the grave as an FBI agent counted off the seconds. When he reached sixty, several pistols were loudly clicked, but he was in such shock he couldn't speak. A few minutes later the agents jumped in their cars, slammed the doors, and drove off. Spared, Koryavin wound up walking home.

There were to be no empty threats from the KGB for Motorin and Martynov. Instead, both were tortured while being debriefed over a two-year period. When Motorin was finally brought to trial, his blond hair had turned gray and he was forced by the prison guards to dye it back to its original shade before going into court. Martynov, who had received only $100 or $200 each time he delivered documents to the FBI—the total amount was less than $10,000—was allowed just four visits by his wife and children in the two years he was held captive. Both men were executed by firing squads separately in 1987.

Yuzhin was a different matter. He had been under suspicion for years. The CIA had given him a camera disguised as a cigarette lighter, and he had stupidly left it behind at the San Francisco offices of the Soviet consulate. Was he really luckier than Martynov and Motorin? The camp in the Ural Mountains, called Perm-35, was surrounded by ten rows of barbed wire and was noted for its numbing cold. Wooden planks were fastened to walls and doubled as beds. There were no blankets or bedding. Prisoners sat in concrete chairs. Solitary confinement was a frequent punishment, and Yuzhin was never told where he was being held, was denied all visits, and was never given news of the outside world. On the other hand, he stayed alive.

Yuzhin got lucky. He was released in February of 1992 as part of an amnesty decree by Boris Yeltsin when Yeltsin rose to the Russian presidency. He was allowed to move to the United States and today lives quietly in northern California.

On October 15, 1985, Viktor Degtyar received a package at his Alexandria home from Bob, signed "B." The package contained classified documents, many of them originals. Degtyar rushed them to the Soviet Union's embassy on Sixteenth Street. To get into the embassy—Degtyar was photographed by the FBI as he walked in the front door because of the unusually large package he was carrying— one would at first have to dial in a code at the front door. After that, he, like all employees or visitors to the embassy, was forced to remove his coat and hang it up near the front door. The Soviet philosophy was that the fewer pockets one had, the less chance one had of entering with spy gadgets or miniature electronic devices that could transmit to the outside. Degtyar took the package to the top floor, a dim, windowless space of under a thousand square feet that housed forty KGB operatives. The floor was partitioned into four divisions—Political Intelligence, External Counterintelligence, Scientific and Technological Intelligence, and Technical Operations.

The KGB's offices were far from glamorous. In 1985, they could even be described as crude. The lighting was so bad, one had to place a newspaper under a lamp to read it. When KGB agents left the building, they were expected to put a primitive pin into a map of Washington that let everyone know where they were headed. By law, all Soviet embassy employees were allowed to travel only twenty-five miles in any direction from the agency.

The KGB operatives in those years felt defeated. They had never been able to directly recruit an American agent in Washington—all had been walk-ins. The FBI was far more sophisticated, they thought. The KGB believed—with some justification—that not only were its members followed by the FBI everywhere in the Washington area, but that the FBI had installed silicone optical sensors in the headrest of every car they owned. When they drove through a major intersection, they were certain that an actuator was triggered by the sensors as the weight of the car rolled over it, and a tiny light, affixed to a giant electric grid, would blink on and off somewhere inside an FBI war room at its headquarters. Thus even if they lost their pursuers, they could be located by the Bureau's tag team. No pins were stuck in maps at the FBI.

The KGB had its own methods to counter the high-tech capabilities of the Bureau. They seemed primitive, but were effective. One was to put a group of four embassy employees into a bugged car and head for a shopping mall. Arriving there, the Russians would hurry into the mall and scatter while an FBI team tried to keep them in sight. After ten or fifteen minutes, when it seemed certain all parties were inside a department store, a KGB agent would roll out of the trunk of the Russian car and either hail a cab or walk to a bus stop to reach his clandestine destination.

On the top floor of the embassy, the KGB eagerly examined the contents of Bob Hanssen's first package containing classified documents. Besides Degtyar and Cherkashin, their boss, Stanislav Androsov, was present. The documents were a treasure trove. One of the revelations from Bob was that the United States had built a tunnel under the new Soviet embassy on Wisconsin Avenue to eavesdrop on them, though other reports would say it was disclosed four years later, on September 25, 1989.

Cherkashin, the counterintelligence chief, couldn't believe his good fortune. Just six months before, Rick Ames had walked through the door of the embassy and offered to spy for cash. The amount had been $50,000. For that kind of money he had not only given up the names of the double agents but unloaded seven pounds of secret cable communications from CIA stations around the world. Between Bob Hanssen and Rick Ames, so many documents were stacked up for examination on the top floor of the Soviet embassy one could easily have joked the Russians needed to place a help-wanted ad in a Washington newspaper.

The documents in this new package, except for revealing the same double-agent names, were nonduplicative. They appeared to be from the FBI. And unlike Ames, who liked to go out for long, boozy lunches, this mole only wanted money. Who needed to recruit spies for Moscow when operatives were literally falling through the front door or mailing information in gift boxes?

More than a decade later, in 1997, well before Bob was suspected, but after Aldrich Ames began serving his life sentence, Cherkashin would play down the damage Ames had done to America. In retrospect he may have been hinting that there might have been someone else. In an interview with the *Los Angeles Times*, he said, "I think Ames's damage has been exaggerated a bit in the West. Maybe because of Ames himself. I think he exaggerated in his confessions to the FBI, maybe he told them he did everything—even things he *never* did."

As one might expect, Rick Ames was a hero to Cherkashin. "Ames was a man of great self-control and courage," his former handler said. "I think the Russian government should help his family."

Nine days later Degtyar got a third piece of mail that Bob signed—rather damningly—"B." The address was handwritten, postmarked from New York City, with an October 24, 1985, date stamp. The no-nonsense note was typed and read in part:

DROP LOCATION
Please leave your package for me under the corner (nearest the street) of the wooden foot bridge located just west of the entrance to Nottoway Park. (ADC Northern Virginia Street Map, #14, D3)
PACKAGE PREPARATION
Use a green or brown plastic trash bag and trash to cover a waterproofed package.
SIGNAL LOCATION
Signal site will be the pictorial "pedestrian crossing" signpost, just west of the main Nottoway Park entrance

on Old Courthouse Road. (The sign is the one nearest the bridge just mentioned.)
SIGNALS
My signal to you: One vertical mark of white adhesive tape meaning I am ready to receive your package.

Your signal to me: One horizontal mark of white adhesive tape meaning drop filled.

My signal to you: One vertical mark of white adhesive tape meaning I have received your package.

(Remove old tape before leaving signal.) I will acknowledge amount with my next package.

Bob put the date and the times for the signals for the drop. Nottoway Park, which the KGB would assign the code name of PARK, was, as mentioned, just across the street from the backyard of Bob's former Whitecedar Court home and a half mile off the I-66 interstate highway. Assuming the Russians shook their FBI "tag team," which in this particular case would be imperative, the drop would be easy to find. He had given them time to do several dry runs.

On November 2, the KGB placed a package containing $50,000 in hundred-dollar bills under the footbridge. (In his letter, Bob had asked for $100,000, but the KGB chose to give him half that amount. It was the same amount they had paid to Rick Ames, six months earlier.) They also proposed procedures when future contacts were to be made. Bob replied six days later. For Cherkashin, it was like receiving a love letter.

Thank you for the 50,000.
I also appreciate your courage and perseverance in the face of generically reported bureaucratic obstacles. I would not have contacted you if it were not reported that you were held in esteem within your organization, an organization I have studied for years. I did expect some communication plan in your response. I viewed

the postal delivery as a necessary risk and do not wish to trust again that channel with valuable material. I did this only because I had to so you would take my offer seriously, that there be no misunderstanding as to my long-term value, and to obtain appropriate security for our relationship from the start.

Bob Hanssen became known by the code letter *B* to the Soviets in late 1985. B rejected the KGB's contact plans and suggested an alternative. His was a bit too technical for his handlers. He suggested using a personal computer bulletin board, a device used by computer enthusiasts in the mid-1980s before the Internet came into widespead use. He told the Soviets there would be "appropriate encryption." Bob, or B, continued, "Let us use the same site again. Same timing. Same signals." B said the next date would be September 9, which, using the 6 coefficient, meant March 3, 1986. He played down receiving only $50,000 rather than the $100,000 he had asked for:

As far as the funds are concerned, I have little need or utility for more than the 100,000. It merely provides a difficulty since I cannot spend it, store it or invest it without triping *[sic]* "drug money" warning bells. Perhaps some diamonds as security for my children and some good will so that when the times comes, you will accept by *[sic]* senior services as a guest lecturer. Eventually, I would appreciate an escape plan. (Nothing lasts forever.)

Bob reiterated the names of Yuzhin, Motorin, and Martynov as double agents and told them that Martynov was wired with a transmitter that relayed conversations to the FBI. The names were a redundancy since all were either under suspicion, arrest, or in prison, a fact Bob undoubtedly knew.

I can not provide documentary substantiating evidence without arousing suspicion at this time. Never-the-less, it is from my own knowledge as a member of the community effort to capitalize on the information from which I speak. I have seen video tapes of debriefings and physically saw the last, (Martynov) though we were not introduced. The names were provided to me as part of my duties as one of the few who needed to know. You have some avenues of inquiry. Substantial funds were provided in excess of what could have been skimmed from their agents. The active one has always (in the past) used a concealment device—a bag with bank notes sewn in the base during homes [sic] leaves.

Besides repeating the names of the already compromised three double agents, Bob revealed a secret technique used by the NSA, explaining it in full. He also gave them the details on Pocketwatch, which was the FBI's surveillance of Soviet commercial businesses in New York they believed were fronts for spying activities. The Pocketwatch operation included Amtorg, a Soviet trade organization into which Bob himself had headed the investigation. Finally, he told them of Spiderweb, an FBI system that monitored potential dead drop sites, signal sites, and embassies.

If Bob Hanssen believed he was only B to the KGB by this time, he would have been extremely naive. He had already mentioned "my children" in one communication, and by describing a meeting where Martynov was present, the Soviets had undoubtedly connected enough dots through his letters and the documents. They undoubtedly knew he was with the FBI. Surely, they would have had a sleuth in the woods of Nottoway Park to note his appearance, photograph his car, and record its license plate number. If Bob wanted to be anonymous, let him. However, it was important for them to know who their contact was so they could protect his identity if it got to that point. On the other hand, if he went cold on them, blackmailing him by threatening to expose his activities was an option. And finally, from time to time they wanted to guide him into giving them information that only he would know about. The KGB had no intention of being a passive lover.

On March 3, 1986, the KGB again loaded the dead drop site—the first pedestrian footbridge in Nottoway Park—with a package of cash. But Bob was a no-show and the money was removed the next day.

SIX

A Work of God

In 1985, Bob Hanssen's quandary may have been a chicken-or-an-egg type of question. Is it better to betray one's country or one's family? Perhaps the answer might have been neither, if not for the warped standards of piety Bob created for himself and the members of his family. A convert to Catholicism, he chose not only to abide by the strictest standards of the Roman Catholic Church, but to become a member of a small, elitist sect within the Church. Opus Dei set even higher standards for its members than the Church. In hindsight, it may have been a recipe for disaster.

Religion and politics are always a dangerous blend. Several conservative Christian movements in the United States would gladly move the country into a theocracy if they could garner enough votes. Islamic militants want to do the same in the Middle East and are succeeding. The Opus Dei organization is less than one hundred years old and still in its infancy. Opus Dei also seeks to align a nation's political policies with those of the Catholic Church, blurring or erasing the line between church and state.

Opus Dei seems small at first glance. There are some eighty thousand to ninety thousand members around the globe and just over two thousand priests. Despite the minuscule numbers and its short life, Opus Dei is potent, partly because it is a favorite organization of Pope John Paul II's. The organization is said to be a powerful personal prelature within the Roman Curia, a body of twenty-five hundred prelates and laymen who govern the Church.

At the beginning of the twenty-first century, Opus Dei can already claim at least two near misses in electing an Opus Dei slate and peacefully gaining control of a country by reaching its top political office. The first example is Chile, where an Opus Dei member in 1999, financially backed with large contributions from organization members outside the country, came within two percentage points of winning its presidency. The candidate, Joaquin Lavin, had been an economist in the regime of Chile's former dictator, Augusto Pinochet, and had served as a mayor of Las Condes, the richest suburb in the capital city of Santiago.

In the December primary, Lavin finished in a statistical dead heat with Ricardo Lagos, the centrist candidate. Both received about 47.5 percent of the vote, though Lagos had a slim thirty thousand margin out of more than 7 million votes cast. Lavin's numbers were far more than Pinochet himself had received when he became president in the 1980s, and more than any other right-wing candidate had received in fifty years. At least part of his strong showing can be credited to financial backing from Opus Dei members and sympathizers. Lavin was able to outspend his opponent by seven to one, promising to pick a government from the "most able," regardless of political allegiance. His campaign also offered absolutes. He was for a strong death penalty and would have banned both abortion and divorce if elected.

After the primary and facing a runoff election, Lavin went into the desert of northern Chile to pray at the shrine of La Tirana, whose Virgin is an object of pilgrimages by devout South American Catholics. But in the second vote a month later, Lagos beat Lavin 51 to 49 percent, partly due to a Communist Party candidate who had received 3 percent of the vote in the primary and who chose to back Lagos, believing him to be the lesser of two evils.

"We had a spectacular number of votes," Lavin said on election night. "I am confident in the future the message of change that we brought into Chilean politics will prevail."

In Peru, an even more spectacular Opus Dei candidate ran in early 2001. The Peruvians, seeking an antidote to the scandal-ridden administration of Alberto Fujimori, nearly voted in their first female president, Lourdes Flores. The forty-one-year-old Flores was single, lived next door to her father, and was rumored to be an Opus Dei numerary, or a member who chooses to live a life of celibacy. Flores, in fact, at first encouraged comparisons with the Virgin Mary.

"For a large segment of Peru's population, women are saints or sinners, with little room between," the *Washington Post* reported, adding that "Flores, a religious woman who has never married and who has close links to the conservative Opus Dei Catholic organization, is going for the saint. In fact, many Peruvians openly wonder whether she remains a virgin, a question Flores has never felt obliged to answer when asked by reporters.

"Flores seems to work that image deliberately. On her campaign tour in Jauja, she allowed news crews to follow her into the magnificent colonial-era church. There, in front of a gilded shrine of the Virgin Mary cloaked in glorious powder-blue robes, she knelt with a serene face to offer a prayer as delighted photographers snapped pictures and TV crews rolled their tapes."

Lourdes Flores was careful to define herself as an anti-feminist. "I am not a feminist. I do not think of myself as a feminist, and I will never be a feminist. I don't like the sound of the word," she said in an interview during the campaign.

Maria Esther Mogollon, a Peruvian women's rights leader, responded, "She is against a woman's right to choose and she is against the idea of feminism as an equalizer in society. She is someone whose view of the role of women is overly defined by her religious beliefs."

Flores said that if elected, she planned to channel social spending by the state through religious charities and "the Church." Opponents said that because of her Opus Dei membership and ties to the upper classes—who were descended from wealthy Europeans—she had a right-wing secret agenda.

In the end, she may have been mistrusted simply because she was too good to be true. Her main competition, Alejandro Toledo, a former-shoeshine-boy-cum-Stanford-University-graduate was accused of testing positive for cocaine and fathering a child he refused to recognize and seemed always to be surrounded by sleaze.

"Lourdes would have been a better candidate if she had done a few naughty things in her life," a Peruvian television news commentator, Jaime Bayley, said. "She is a kind of immaculate virgin who has tried to be flirtatious but in reality is a nice girl. While Toledo has twenty skeletons in his closet, Flores just has religious prints."

Like Lavin in Chile, the Flores campaign was fueled by large contributions, and in an eight-candidate field, she rocketed from 8 percent to 26 percent and second place in the polls. Flores attempted to broaden her appeal by naming the head of a communist trade union as her running mate. In a desperate last-minute bid for votes, she tried to shuck her virginal image by appearing in front of several half-clad male strippers on Peruvian television. The moment was viewed by voters as calculated, an end-justifies-the-means move.

But it was Toledo's broad Amerindian features that resonated with the poor, and since half of Peru's population lived in abject poverty, he defeated his opponents with a plurality of the votes, Lourdes Flores finishing a close third.

Toledo then won the run-off. Flores promised to return in the next election.*

Opus Dei heavily supported Polish leader Lech Walesa in his efforts to bring down Poland's communist government in 1980. In 1994, it worked hand in hand with Islamic fundamentalists to defeat an attempt by the United Nations to declare abortion a global women's right. Any protestations of not being involved in politics, then, cannot be considered. As one of Bob Hanssen's non–Opus Dei priests at Saint Catherine's of Siena, Franklyn McAfee, has put it, "They're trying to get people in the upper echelons of government and business to change the world. They believe that if you convert the king, you convert the country."

Opus Dei was founded in 1928 by Josemaria Escriva de Balaguer. The comfortable, twenty-six-year-old son of a textile maker in Aragon, Spain, Escriva objected to the liberal atmosphere he found at the University of Madrid. Escriva's and Opus Dei's goals were noble—to elevate laypeople in a church that had seemed to emphasize the clergy. He highlighted three passages from the Bible as requirements for anyone who wanted to be a Christian. They were daunting. The initial phrase, from the book of

* In 1996, Tupac Amaru rebels seized the Japanese embassy in Peru and held its residents hostage for 126 days. Opus Dei had backed then President Alberto Fujimori in his election, although Fujimori was not a member. Fujimori paid back Opus Dei by leapfrogging over Lima's Jesuit cardinal, Augusto Vargas Zamora, and choosing an Opus Dei archbishop, Juan Luis Cipriani Thorne, to mediate the crisis. Cipriani was from the faraway mountain diocese of Ayacucho, and his handling of the situation was lauded. His actions put him first in line to become the next cardinal of Lima, and indeed, he was named cardinal of the Peruvian capital in January of 2001, becoming the first Opus Dei cleric to gain that title and thus eligible to be voted into the papacy.

Matthew, read, *Be ye therefore perfect, even as your Father in heaven is perfect.* The second, from the first book of Thessalonians, as voiced by Paul, said, *For this is the will of God, even your sanctification, that ye should abstain from fornication.* The third was from the book of John: *But to all who received Him, who believed in His name, he gave power to become the children of God.*

Escriva believed that *everyone* is called by God to become a saint and that each person should aspire to that apex. After death, he said, Opus Dei members who had lived that way would not only ascend to heaven but would be in its hierarchy, second only to Jesus Christ and his mother, the Virgin Mary. Sainthood could not be accomplished through charity or love, he said, but through prayer. These thoughts were viewed as radical within the Catholic Church. It had been taught that priests and nuns were the ones who could become holy. Now everyone could, according to Escriva, though the price was high.

Before Escriva, Catholic priests in the twentieth century were telling their parishioners that God was understanding; he had put man on earth to struggle. Even if one led a sinful life, one could still be in heaven, the clergy said. A pure life was impossible, beyond most people and therefore not expected. To lead a holy life, the modern priests said, one had to live a life of isolation in a monastery or a convent. Escriva and Opus Dei were not only saying the opposite, but claiming that Jesus Christ demanded it.

At first blush then, Opus Dei seems simple. Pray a lot, tell everything to a spiritual leader, wear the *cilice* or otherwise flagellate yourself two hours a day, donate money, and you too can be a saint. But be sure to keep what you are doing a secret.

Escriva's teachings have been accused of having all the elements of fascism. This made him a darling of Francisco Franco. Everything must be under the control of a leader, he taught. He had little tolerance for other religions. Priests are more valuable than other people, he wrote. He called Queen Elizabeth II a "demon." He railed against Voltaire and his teachings of respect for the individual and his deist philosophy. Escriva's book, *The Way*, a manifesto of 999 thoughts or maxims, some as short as a sentence, is a text-book of elitism and control. For instance, No. 339 reads:

> You shall not buy books without the advice of an experienced Christian. It is so easy to buy something useless or mischievous. Often people believe that they are carrying a book under their arm . . . but they are carrying a load of mud.

From its beginning, Opus Dei has been mired in contro-versy. At first it was largely identified with post–Spanish Civil War Spain and the politics of its dictator, Franco. Today it operates in forty-two countries. The organization claims to be poor, but it has a lavish, opulent headquarters in Rome's Parioli District with twenty-four chapels. In America it has completed its own $55 million, seventeen-story office building at Thirty-fourth Street and Lexington Avenue in midtown Manhattan, complete with separate en-trances for men and women. There are six chapels, twenty-six guestrooms, a gym, and a cafeteria inside. Despite this wealth, Opus Dei publishes no financial statements or mem-bership lists and is required to report on itself every five years and then only to the pope. Opus Dei has its own doctrine, which it claims to be divinely inspired. Thus it is the only organization within the Roman Catholic Church—other than the Church itself—that believes it was created by God.

In the 1950s, two leading Opus Dei strategists, Rafael Calvo Serer and Florentino Perez-Embid, wrote a lengthy paper proposing that Opus Dei serve as an instrument to regenerate the Catholic Church in countries around the world. They argued that the coming emergence of a revi-talized Spain presented the best opportunity to return to a type of conservative Catholicism since the reign of the Holy Roman Emperor Charles V, in the sixteenth century. (Charles V's most famous quote was "I speak German to my horse, French to my ministers, and Spanish to my God," which speaks for itself.) While Charles V did bring Spain to its height as a nation, he also created a schism between Catholics and Protestants that ended the Roman Catholic Church's dominance in Europe.

The Opus Dei scholars argued in their manifesto that secularism was persuasive in the West, and the only way to revitalize Christianity was through a powerful international Catholic movement led by Opus Dei. Their first opportunities, they wrote, would be in Latin America. United States Catholics who disapproved of Opus Dei's political goals began calling the group Octopus Dei, and sometimes the Holy Mafia.

To become a member of Opus Dei takes six months of study, and one has to write to the Opus Dei vicar in the United States—currently the Very Reverend Arne Panula—and declare that God has asked one to become a saint and to live in the real world. One then chooses to be either celibate or noncelibate, though it is permissible to change one's mind on that count. (Both the Hanssen and the Wauck families have celibate Opus Dei members.) A celibate member does not make a vow but rather signs a contract. Breaking that contract requires the approval of an Opus Dei bishop. There is also a secret initiation rite and a special salutation that Opus Dei members use with one another. Celibate members who live in group houses must agree to have their mail opened by a superior and to have their reading materials restricted.

After being inducted into Opus Dei, one swears obedience to a prelate-general and other "authorized persons of the prelature." Members then submit to the "formative norms," which critics charge is a form of mind conditioning. They are required to report weekly to a director, who has a right to question their activities, both personal and professional. They may not publicize their membership. A weekly confession to an Opus Dei or Opus Dei–approved priest is mandatory. Daily attendance of mass is also required. Members are asked to send their children to Opus Dei schools or affiliated ones, which are usually separated by gender.

Opus Dei members have alternate forms of self-mortification in addition to the spiked thigh band, the aforementioned *cilice*. These range from walking with sharp pebbles in one's shoes to sleeping on a hard wooden floor once a week and taking ice-cold showers. Celibate numeraries are expected to rise each morning and utter the Latin word *serviam,* or "I will serve," then pray while flagellating their buttocks with a special macramé-like woven whip.

When Escriva died in 1975, Opus Dei members immediately attempted to elevate him to sainthood. Other prominent Catholics objected, with Spain's leading theologian, Juan Martin Velasco, analyzing the life of Escriva with these words: "We cannot portray as a model of Christian living someone who has served the power of the state [Franco's Spain] and who used that power to launch his opus, which he ran with obscure criteria—like a Mafia shrouded in white—not accepting the papal magisterium when it failed to coincide with his way of thinking."

In papal politics, John Paul II is said to have favored quick sainthood for the Opus Dei founder, partly because elements of the sect had done everything possible to raise him to the papal throne. John Paul II had publicly prayed at Escriva's tomb just before being voted in as pope in 1978. In 1994 he attended the funeral of Escriva's successor, Bishop Juan Alvaro del Portillo, and knelt before his funeral bier. This raised eyebrows within the Church as protocol dictates the pope must only bow to the remains of a cardinal.

On May 17, 1992, John Paul II, in front of more than three hundred thousand people gathered in Rome at Saint Peter's Square, beatified Escriva, which is considered a first step toward sainthood. The beatification process was, like nearly everything that surrounds Opus Dei, awash in controversy. Critics charged that no one had ever before been so sanctified within twenty years following death. Others in the Vatican who were speaking out against Opus Dei said they weren't allowed to testify before the tribunal investigating Josemaria's life. One, Maria Del Carmen Tapia, a celibate Opus Dei member and Escriva's personal secretary for eighteen years, claimed she was not only denied the right to speak and held against her will, but was accused of being depraved and having no conscience by pro-beatification lobbyists. (This is understandable, since in a published memoir Tapia quoted Escriva as railing against a woman who had witheld information, "She has to be spanked throughout! Draw up her skirts, tear down her panties, and give it to her in the ass! In the ass! Until she talks!")

As one might expect, Opus Dei has been the target of even wilder allegations. Perhaps the most serious one came in 1978, when Italian newspapers accused Opus Dei of complicity in the death of Pope John Paul I, John Paul II's predecessor. The first John Paul died suddenly thirty-three days after being voted to the papacy. After his death, several allegations were made that he was murdered because he favored birth control and was about to make a speech favoring contraception.

Some Vatican observers have charged that John Paul II has been so heavily influenced by Opus Dei that he is under the group's control. His press secretary, Joaquin Navarro-Vales, is an Opus Dei member. The papal secretary, Monsignor Stanislaw Dziwisz, is an Opus Dei associate. An

Opus Dei archbishop, Juliarl Herranz, is cochair of the Papal Council of Advisers. Dziwisz makes a habit of exchanging the Opus Dei salute when meeting organization members. Opus Dei members are said to have a heightened chance of a private audience with the pope, an apogee all Catholics seek.

Despite its influence in the Vatican, Opus Dei has suffered some setbacks in recent years even as its worldwide political power has risen. In 1997, a parliamentary commission in Belgium put Opus Dei on a list of dangerous religious sects. The Socialist Party in France has been able to overcome the efforts of President Jacques Chirac's wife, Bernadette, an Opus Dei enthusiast who has attempted to install Opus Dei members throughout her husband's cabinet. Opus Dei in France has lobbied for wide-ranging legislation that ranges from criminalizing homosexuality to privatizing a television network.

Most of Opus Dei's worldwide works outside the political arena are done through schools, study centers, and youth clubs. Opus Dei often seeks financial alliances with the United Nations—Unesco's director general, Frederico Mayor, is an Opus Dei member—or with national and sometimes local governments. The schools and youth groups are fertile grounds for the organization's recruitment efforts.

"Sometimes in life we are called to do great things." George W. Bush said in his presidential inauguration speech in January 2001. "But as a saint of our times has said, every day we are called to do small things with great love." It is not known if George W. Bush knew that the "saint" he was quoting was Josemaria Escriva, but certainly the speech—written by evangelical Christian Michael Gerson—and the quoting of Escriva's words, caused hearts to leap inside Opus Dei chapters everywhere. The president had quoted Opus Dei's founder and called him a saint. What could be more exhilarating?*

Opus Dei members in Washington begin at the very top. Bob Hanssen's own boss during many of his years at the Bureau, former FBI director Louis Freeh, is reputedly an Opus Dei member whose son attended an Opus Dei–affiliated institution, the Heights School in Maryland, with Bob Hanssen's son. At one time, Bonnie Hanssen, working as a part-time teacher, taught one of Freeh's sons. In September of 2000, the FBI director gave a speech at the Heights with Bob listening attentively in the front row. Following his employee's arrest, Freeh was forced to admit to knowing Bob and Bonnie through church activities, but said they were never "social friends."

When asked to confirm Freeh's affiliation with Opus Dei, the FBI's public affairs spokesman, John Collingwood, responded only, "While I cannot answer your specific questions, I do note that you have been informed incorrectly." Still, Freeh is deeply religious, whether or not he belongs to the organization. A framed photo of the late Cardinal John O'Connor was on his desk in his seventh-floor FBI office when he headed the Bureau, and he nearly always found time to steal away to daily mass at nearby Saint Patrick's Church. Freeh's brother, John, has been the celibate director of an Opus Dei center in Pittsburgh, Pennsylvania.

In the U.S. Supreme Court, both Antonin Scalia (who also attended the same church as Bob Hanssen) and Clarence Thomas are rumored to be Opus Dei members, though neither will confirm nor deny it. Scalia's son, Father Paul Scalia, converted Thomas to Catholicism in 1997. (The Court's third Catholic member, Anthony M. Kennedy, is con-

---

* Reportedly, Bush political operatives now meet regularly with conservative Catholic leaders in an attempt to gain their votes for the Republican ticket in the year 2004. Underlining this policy, Bush chose to give a 2001 college commencement speech at Notre Dame University in Indiana and received an honorary doctor of laws degree in return.

sidered a centrist who often votes against Scalia and Thomas.)

Although American Opus Dei priests deny it, there is little doubt that their clerics target the elite and the wealthy. Opus Dei centers border many major universities, including Harvard, Princeton, Dartmouth, and of course Notre Dame and Georgetown Universities. In Washington, an Opus Dei center in the wealthy upper-northwest section of the city grooms high schoolers for the Ivy League. The center's biggest draw is a program that elevates SAT scores. Washington's other Opus Dei–affiliated Catholic school, Oakcrest—the female equivalent of the Heights—was attended by Bob Hanssen's three girls. Its headmistress, Barbara Faulk, knows exactly where she wants her students to go. "We're out to change the world," she has said.

Washington's most visible Opus Dei priest, C. John McCloskey, who heads an Opus Dei–run information center two blocks from the White House, has admitted to *Newsweek* that "we are interested in people who can have an influence." Father McCloskey, a graduate of Columbia University who often appears as a talking head on MSNBC, practices what he preaches by counting conservative newspaper columnist Robert Novak (he converted to Catholicism in 1998) as a pal.* Father McCloskey is also credited with helping the Wall Street economic wizard Lawrence Kudlow find his way to Christ. Someone like Kudlow would be welcomed at Opus Dei. Though Protestants cannot join, the conservative Christians often work or pray with the organization in an unofficial capacity. Father McCloskey also writes articles for *Crisis* magazine, some with authoritarian overtones. An excerpt from one written in 1993 suggests how to choose a college: "Be sure to read the colleges' mission statements. If you encounter words like *standard*, *belief maturity*, *conviction*, *marriage*, *family*, *evangelization*, *culture*, *character*, *truth*, and *knowledge*,

* Bob Hanssen was a confidential source for Novak in a November 24, 1997 column he wrote on the subject of U.S. intelligence assets in the People's Republic of China.

take a closer look. On the other hand, if you encounter words like *values, openness, just society, search, diversity,* and *professional preparation,* move on."

McCloskey stresses recruiting members at elite universities. "These people are going to be leaders in the world and in the Church," he once wrote, and posted on his Web site.

James Bamford, the investigative author of two bestselling books on the NSA, would meet Bob Hanssen in the early 1990s. The two men became pals and sometimes flew to gun shows together in a CIA friend's small private plane. Bamford married a few years after they met; both Bob and Bonnie attended his wedding. The men were also pallbearers at the funeral of the same mutual CIA friend after he died of cancer in 1996. When Bamford was sent to Moscow to interview Bob's handler, Viktor Cherkashin, for ABC News, Bob expressed a keen interest in seeing the extra film footage, perhaps worried that Cherkashin might have said something that could compromise him. Bamford also later recalled Bob's fascination with Felix Bloch, the State Department official whom the FBI suspected of spying and who the Bureau believes was tipped off by Bob Hanssen.

Bamford said Bob spent a lot of time writing papers for the FBI about the evils of communism and gave him duplicates of the essays. "They were like something out of the 1950s," he remembered. What was really surprising to Bamford, though, was that Bob had written these long treatises against Marxism in the mid-1990s, years after the Soviet Union and the international communist movement had essentially collapsed. But Bamford, a lapsed Catholic, believed his friend's membership in Opus Dei was genuine.

"He was a little obsessed about it," he said. "Bob would rant about the evil in organizations like Planned Parenthood and how abortion was immoral." Bamford would later write about the preoccupation with Opus Dei in the *New York Times*:

Hanssen squeezed religion into most conversations and hung a silver crucifix above his desk. Occasionally he would leave work to take part in antiabortion rallies. He was forever trying to get me to go with him to meetings of Opus Dei, a secretive, conservative arm of the Catholic Church. After weeks of urging, I finally agreed. At the meeting, Hanssen was in his element. He reveled in that closed society of true believers like a fraternity brother exchanging a secret handshake. Even today, despite all the allegations against him, his faith seemed too sincere to be a ruse.

David Major, one of Bob's bosses at the FBI, noticed the same zeal: "He was a religious person who put the Soviets into a religious context. He would say that the Soviet Union is bound to fail because it is run by communists and communists don't have God in their life. He said to me, 'Without religion, man is lost.'"

After the Opus Dei meeting, Bamford dropped Bob Hanssen as a friend. Bamford found Bob's fixation with Opus Dei, Catholicism, and fighting godless communists a bit too much to handle.

SEVEN

All for the Greater Good

If he could find someone willing to listen, Bob Hanssen loved to lecture on religion. He would say that because the teachings of Lenin were the opposite of Jesus Christ's, communism was doomed and would eventually fail. Marxists weren't moral, he claimed.

In the 1980s, much as he had at Northwestern two decades earlier when he had refused to visit a belly-dancing restaurant after exams, Bob refused to attend strip clubs. In New York and Washington, farewell parties for departing agents commonly included naked dancers. A former FBI China analyst and a longtime friend, Paul D. Moore, recalled that Bob would lecture him against going to the raucous celebrations.

"He said, 'You shouldn't do that, because it's an occasion of sin,'" Moore told the *New York Times*.

In Washington, the Bureau would often stage going-away dinners at the Old Europe, a German restaurant on Wisconsin Avenue famed for its sauerbraten and Dortmunder beer on draft. Directly across the street from the staid dining establishment was a strip club called the Good Guys. Both places had been in the same location for several decades, and after the heavy dinners, many of the agents would wander over to the Good Guys, which was shaped like a long boxcar. The club had three stages, each occupied by a young woman who danced totally nude except for a pair of spiked heels or leather boots and a thin, jeweled belt on which men were invited to affix five-dollar bills. Referring to it as a strip club was misleading, since the women never slowly stripped or even teased but rather leapt to the stage, shucked a kimono, and began nakedly gyrating to whatever was blaring on the jukebox.

The club was just two blocks from the new Russian embassy and attracted young men from that quarter as well. It was a joke among the dancers that they wouldn't accept rubles. Whether the FBI men knew they were rubbing shoulders with their Moscow counterparts is not known, but Bob wouldn't go near such a place of sin—then. That would soon change.

According to Jack Drescher, MD, a psychiatrist, someone can separate his religious beliefs from business practices. Devout people sometimes have secret sex lives that are forbidden by their church. "As long as these contradictions are kept out of conscious awareness and remain a secret from others, living as if one has two separate lives can go on indefinitely," Drescher says.

Jerrold M. Post, a former CIA employee who once psychoanalyzed and profiled world leaders for the government based on their actions and backgrounds, largely agrees. "Spies have a pattern of split loyalties. [They] can sham loyalty on the surface while being disloyal under the surface."

Post, who founded the CIA's Center for the Analysis of Personality and Political Behavior, believes that all spies are narcissistic and self-absorbed, full of egocentricity. Speaking generally of Bob Hanssen, he said, "For a mid-level individual, what a profound satisfaction to look into the mirror each morning and say, chuckling to oneself, 'If they only knew what I am putting over on them.' For Hanssen, it may well be that there was joy in putting one over on people who hadn't treated him very well at the Bureau."

Using the MICE theory, Post focused on the last letter of the acronym: "The greatest of these is assuredly ego. Again and again, I'm struck by the narcissistic wounds that have often been inflicted on an individual, so the act of treason can be seen as narcissistic rage, which leads to this revenge."

Still, Bob's piety appeared to be real, his convictions carved in stone. Paul Moore recalled riding in a car with his friend and listening to a radio talk show host discuss morality and whether morality should be based on social contracts. Bob "leaned over and turned off the radio. He said, 'That's enough of that.' Bob said that the foundation for morality is not an implied social contract. It's God's law."

There is a greater-good theory that partly explains Bob Hanssen. His definition of the greater good may have been that even though he was betraying his country, he was using the money from the Russians to put his six children through approved—though expensive—Opus Dei–affiliated schools. His children were good students, and he could have believed they might in the future be part of a holy war that would remerge God and country, whose leaders would then ban abortion, divorce, and all the other evils of the world that he and Opus Dei opposed.

A 1998 research paper from Brigham Young University studied 139 spies and concluded that half of them did it for the money. "People usually spy for some combination of emotional gratification and remuneration," John Pike, a specialist in intelligence issues, said, "but in all cases, money is how they keep score."

Bob Hanssen, always the loner, always unable to fit in, was Walter Mitty squared. His hero, Kim Philby, may have explained Bob's mind. Just before his death in 1988, Philby said, "To betray, you must first belong. I never belonged."

*   *   *

Not everyone in the FBI's New York office in the mid-1980s believed Bob Hanssen to be a patriotic American. Vladimir Azbel, an early-1970s Russian immigrant who worked part-time in the New York office's counterintelligence unit translating documents for $16.50 an hour thought Bob was dirty. Years later, he told *Newsday* that when he had passed sensitive information about the Soviets to Bob, he would ignore the papers and not process them through proper channels.

"I handed them to him and he just discarded them. I was kind of surprised by his attitude," Azbel said. "I pointed out someone doing something very wrong, and nobody did anything about it." When Azbel reported Bob's actions and charged him with mishandling and misinterpreting information, Azbel believes that Bob sought revenge. Azbel said he was subjected to several polygraph exams, each lasting a full day. He now believes Bob was behind the testing, harassing him because he was Russian.

"Hanssen believed the Russians at the FBI were not to be trusted," Azbel said. "But we were actually the guys to trust because we hated communism and we would have never sold secrets to the Soviets for money."

According to Azbel, the FBI's office was a leaking sieve in those years. Russian journalists were easily able to sneak into the offices, he said.

If Bob felt he never belonged, he had many opportunities along the way to change his profile, but he appeared not to have a clue how to go about it. The FBI was in the middle of several New York cases that resulted in Soviet spies being expelled from the country. Bob volunteered to work on these cases, even when it was above and beyond his unit's responsibilities. But his lack of humor, his arrogance, and his aloofness earned him no friends. "If you had entered him in a trivia contest or tested his IQ, he would have won," said a former colleague, "but he couldn't deal with people."

Bob couldn't get people to listen to him either. When called upon to make an oral presentation, his lack of animation or maybe just a basic inability to show enthusiasm for a subject usually had his audience nodding off in minutes. His appearance was also a handicap. Bob's habit of wearing frayed and sometimes less than clean black suits five days a week was monotonous and off-putting. Behind his back his coworkers were referring to him as either Dr. Death or the Mortician.

On June 30, 1986, Viktor Degtyar received a new letter from B. It was his first communication from their agent since November of 1985. After the missed drop in March, they had reason to suspect that B had been arrested. Their American double agent was clearly concerned about Viktor Gundarev, a KGB colonel who defected on February 14, 1986, after Vitaly Yurchenko. Gundarev was questioned by the FBI a few days later and at that time was shown a photo of Viktor Cherkashin and asked if he knew him. B may have gone to ground temporarily because he believed that somehow he had been betrayed or was about to be compromised by Cherkashin.*

> I apologize for the delay since our break in communications. I wanted to determine if there was cause for concern over security. I have seen only one item which has given me pause. When the FBI was first given access to Victor [sic] Petrovich Gundarev, they asked if Gun-

---

* Gundarev would later complain about his treatment and the endless interrogations by the CIA, writing that "those people who would like to defect with the help of the CIA should think twice." Because of his mistreatment at the hands of the CIA, he considered redefecting in 1989. At that time, defectors were thrown into the unfamiliar surroundings of a capitalist culture with no preparation for what lay ahead. Scientists and elite military men wound up as waiters or janitors and quickly became disgruntled with their decision.

Robert Hanssen spent most of his early years in this two-bedroom
bungalow in Chicago, at 6215 North Neva Avenue.
AP PHOTO/WIDE WORLD PHOTOS

William Howard Taft High School in Chicago, which Robert Hanssen
attended in the early 1960s. AP PHOTO/WIDE WORLD PHOTOS

Above and right:
Robert Hanssen in
Chicago, 1968
PHOTOS BY DR. JOHN
L. SULLIVAN

The Hanssens' former home in Scarsdale, New York, where Bonnie Hanssen discovered that her husband had been paid by the Russians for information.
GEORGIANA HAVILL

The J. Edgar Hoover Building in Washington D.C. Robert Hanssen worked in the FBI headquarters from 1981 to 1985, and from 1987 until his arrest.
FBI PHOTOGRAPH

Right: Valeriy
Fedorovich Martynov
Below: Sergei M.
Motorin

Robert Hanssen
reported the double
agents to his KGB
handlers and both
were subsequently
executed.
FBI PHOTOGRAPHS

In July of 1986 the KGB placed this ad in the *Washington Times* in order to contact Robert Hanssen.

Above: Felix Bloch, seen here leaving his lawyer's office on August 4, 1989
AP PHOTO/WIDE WORLD PHOTOS

Left: One method Robert Hanssen used to inform his handlers that he was holding information for them was to drive tacks into this telephone pole. If and when a Russian agent spotted the signal, he would know Hanssen was ready to make a drop.
FBI PHOTOGRAPH

Left: Code-named PARK, and later referred to as PRIME by the Russians, Robert Hanssen made more dead drops inside Nottoway Park than any other location.
GEORGIANA HAVILL

Above: The Hanssens' current home in Vienna, Virginia. Located at 9414 Talisman Drive, the house is within easy walking distance of Foxstone Park.
GEORGIANA HAVILL

The bridge over Wolf Trap Creek in Foxstone Park, the ELLIS drop site, where federal agents apprehended Robert Hanssen in the early evening of February 18, 2001
GEORGIANA HAVILL

The $50,000 that was left for Robert Hanssen at drop site LEWIS
FBI PHOTOGRAPH

Agents discovered the money hidden at the corner of this community outdoor stage six days before they took Hanssen into custody.
FBI PHOTOGRAPH

This group photo of the Office of Foreign Missions appeared in the State Department's annual report of 1999. Hanssen can be seen in the middle foreground. STATE DEPARTMENT PHOTOGRAPH

Plato Cacheris talks to reporters outside the U.S. District Court in Alexandria, Virginia, on July 6, 2001, soon after Robert Hanssen entered a guilty plea.
AP PHOTO/WIDE WORLD PHOTOS

Former FBI director Louis J. Freeh
FBI PHOTOGRAPH

darev knew Viktor Cherkashin. I thought this unusual.
I had seen no report indicating that Viktor Cherkashin
was handling an important agent, and here-to-fore he
was looked at with the usual lethargy awarded Line
Chiefs. The question came to mind, are they somehow
able to monitor funds, ie., to know that Viktor Cherkashin received a large amount of money for an agent?
I am unaware of any such ability, but I might not know
that type of source reporting.

After showing his concern about the possibility of being
betrayed by Cherkashin, Bob told his handlers about a
highly classified surveillance technique the intelligence
community was using against the Soviet Union. He then
continued:

> If you wish to continue our discussions, please have
> someone run an advertisement in the Washington Times
> during the week of 1/12/87 or 1/19/87, for sale; "Dodge
> Diplomat, 1971, needs engine work, $1000."
>   Give a phone number and time-of-day in the adver-
> tisement where I can call. I will call and leave a phone
> number where a recorded message can be left for me in
> one hour. I will say, "Hello, my name is Ramon. I am
> calling about the car you offered for sale in the Times."
> You will respond, "I'm sorry, but the man with the car
> is not here, can I get your number." The number will
> be in Area Code 212. I will not specify that Area Code
> on the line.
>
>   Ramon

Using B's 6 coefficient, the actual week that the ad was
to run would be July 6, 1986 or July 13, 1986. Between
July 14 and July 18 an ad did appear in the *Washington
Times*:

DODGE-'71, DIPLOMAT, NEEDS ENGINE WORK,
$1000. Phone (703) 451-9780
(CALL NEXT Mon., Wed., Fri. 1 P.M.)

The phone number put in the ad was for a public telephone booth at the edge of a strip shopping center that was anchored by a supermarket and a drugstore. The center was on the corner of Rolling Road and Old Keene Mill Road in West Springfield, Virginia, located about halfway between Bob's old house on Whitecedar Court—which had been separated only by a street from Nottoway Park—and I-95 where the interstate highway marked the halfway point between the Pentagon and the FBI Training Center in Quantico, Virginia. On Monday, July 21, and on a day the *Washington Post*'s lead story detailed the delicate negotiations on nuclear weapons between Ronald Reagan and Mikhail Gorbachev, Bob called the number at the phone booth. The phone was answered by a KGB agent with the Soviet embassy, Aleksandr Kirillovich Fefelov. Fefelov had been waiting for the call, sweltering in the humid, ninety-degree sun for nearly an hour. Bob said the seven digits slowly, skipping the area code. Then he hung up.

An hour later, Fefelov dialed the number in New York and began by apologizing to Bob, or B, as they were referring to him at the KGB offices inside the Soviet embassy. Fefelov admitted that the KGB had probably loaded the dead drop at Nottoway Park incorrectly, saying someone had placed B's money under the wrong corner of the footbridge. They would try again. A few weeks later, on August 7, 1986, Viktor Degtyar, the KGB colonel, received a letter in the mail from B complaining he still hadn't found the package of money in Nottoway Park and would be calling the phone booth next to the shopping center again, this time on Monday, August 18. The situation would have been comical if not for the amount of money and the secrets involved. This time, perhaps to prove to his KGB superiors that it wasn't his fault, Fefelov recorded the conversation.

The two spoke using veiled metaphors about the botched drop and the missed money.

B: Tomorrow morning?

FEFELOV: Uh, yeah, and the car is still available for you and as we have agreed last time, I prepared all the papers and I left them on the same table. You didn't find them because I put them in another corner of the table.

B: I see.

FEFELOV: You shouldn't worry, everything is okay. The papers are with me now.

B: Good.

FEFELOV: I believe under these circumstances, ummm, it's not necessary to make any changes concerning the place and the time. Our company is reliable, and we are ready to give you a substantial discount which will be enclosed in the papers. Now, about the date of our meeting. I suggest that our meeting will be—will take place without delay on February thirteenth, one three, one P.M. Okay? February thirteenth.

B: February second?

B appeared to find the date inconvenient and tried for an earlier one. But Fefelov was adamant.

FEFELOV: Thirteenth. One three.

B: One three.

FEFELOV: Yes. Thirteenth. One P.M.

B: Let me see if I can do that. Hold on.

FEFELOV: Okay. Yeah.

There was a pause while B checked his calendar. When he came back on the phone, he was whispering so low that Fefelov couldn't understand him.

FEFELOV: Hello? Okay?

B: Six . . . Six . . . That should be fine.

By saying the word *six* twice, Bob Hanssen was telling Fefelov that they should deposit the money six days after the thirteenth of August or the nineteenth. The second *six* meant they should move the drop from 1 P.M. to 7 P.M.

> **FEFELOV:** Okay. We will confirm you, that the papers are waiting for you with the same horizontal tape in the same place as we did it at the first time.
> **B:** Very good.
> **FEFELOV:** You see. After you receive the papers, you will send the letter confirming it and signing it, as usual. Okay?
> **B:** Excellent.
> **FEFELOV:** I hope you remember the address. Is . . . if everything is okay.
> **B:** I believe it will be fine and thank you very much.
> **FEFELOV:** Heh heh. Not at all. Not at all. Nice job. For both of us. Uh, have a nice evening, sir.

B attempted a word from his college Russian to end their conversation. The good-bye word in the language, in Bob's Midwestern voice, came out flat and unaccented.

> **B:** Do sivdaniya.
> **FEFELOV:** Bye-bye.

On August 19, 1986, the KGB loaded the Nottoway Park "PARK" dead drop site with $10,000 in cash, plus several new instructions and proposals. Degtyar was being reassigned to Moscow, and the KGB wanted their agent to send his letters to a KGB political officer, Boris M. Malakhov, who also lived in Alexandria, Virginia. Malakhov's cover at the embassy was as a Soviet press secretary, the same title that Degtyar held. B was instructed to write Malakhov's last name as Malkow so that the Soviets would be able to separate their spy's communications from others. They also gave B an emergency address to use, ironically in Vienna, Austria. They also gave B an alternative safe address to use—or in spy terms, an "accommodation"—that they codenamed NANCY. The Russians also named two dead drop sites they wanted to use.

Bob picked up the $10,000 and the new list of proposals by the KGB. He immediately fired off a memo to Degtyar, which tersely said: RECEIVED $10,000. RAMON. The handwritten return address read: *Ramon Garcia, 125 Main St., Falls Church, VA*. (There is no Main Street in Falls Church.) His letter was postmarked from Northern Virginia's main post office in Merrifield and dated August 19, 1986. A few weeks later, on September 8, Bob fired off a longer letter. This one was to B. N. Malkow at the new NANCY address. The letter found him in his full Emperor Ming mode, setting the terms and calling the shots, even though he ended with a salutation that softened the blow.

Dear Friends:
No, I have decided. It must be on my original terms or not at all. I will not meet abroad or here. I will not maintain lists of sites or modified equipment. I will help you when I can, and in time we will develop methods of efficient communication. Unless a *[sic]* see an abort signal on our post from you by 3/16, I will mail my contact a valuable package time to arrive on 3/18. I will await your signal and package to be in place before 1.00 pm on 3'22 or alternately the following three weeks, same day and time. If my terms are unacceptable then place no signals and withdraw my contact. Excellent work by him has ensured this channel is secure for now. My regards to him and to the professional way you have handled this matter.

                                        Sincerely,
                                        Ramon

The letter was, in a way, perfect timing. In late July of 1986, Bob, Bonnie, and their six children had returned to

Northern Virginia. Bob was back at headquarters, this time as supervisory special agent in the FBI's Intelligence Unit, again assigned to the Soviet Analytical Unit. This time his supervisory duties—astoundingly—included searching for potentially disloyal Americans, particularly those with a liberal bent. The fox, in the guise of Bob Hanssen, was now in charge of the hen house.

EIGHT

Mondays Are for Dead Drops

Two of Bonnie Hanssen's sisters—Peggy and Jeanne—had moved to Northern Virginia. When Bonnie let them know the family was coming back to Washington, Jeanne—who had married a Greek architect by the name of George Beglis—said there was a home in their price range just down the street from her. So Bonnie and Bob wound up in the split-level house at 9414 Talisman Drive, almost across the street from her sister and about two miles away from their first, much larger, house on Whitecedar Court in Vienna.

Bob put $80,000 down on the $205,000 nine-room house. He had both cash from the Soviets and a $47,000 profit from the sale of the Yorktown Heights house. Bonnie may not have known about the substantial payment Bob made at the time of the settlement. She had signed a power-of-attorney permission for her husband in order to stay behind in Yorktown Heights and pack up and supervise the movers. Bob signed the documents with Gary Peterson, a prominent Northern Virginia lawyer who specialized in real estate matters and the same attorney who had handled the Whitecedar Court transaction.

The house was far from perfect. It had been built in 1978 and, after ten years, was already showing its age. There was a one-car garage, three bedrooms, two full bathrooms, and an unfinished basement—about twenty-one hundred square feet of living space. The back of the house led into woods and a path that ended on the next street, Delancey. In fact, that was another good thing. Talisman Drive was located inside a honeycomb maze of streets. You could drive down Talisman and take a left and then another left and a right and go out to the main thoroughfare of Beulah Road that way or by choosing a half dozen other routes. If an organization wanted to stake out his house, it would either have to expose itself by parking on Talisman or have six different cars parked at the various exit points. The neighborhood was an espionage agent's dream come true.

Still, the new dwelling wasn't really large enough for a couple with six children—two of them now girls in their teens. But Bob seemed to have plenty of money and immediately set about making the house more livable. He had a home-improvement crew come in and divide the basement into three rooms. The first, to the left at the bottom of the stairs, became a bedroom for Jane and Susan Elizabeth (she had begun calling herself Sue). The middle room was made into the recreation room, complete with a fireplace, TV set—viewing was strictly regulated to harmless fare such as *Agatha Christie Mysteries* on PBS—and a computer for the family. The room to the right was kept locked. It was understood by family and visitors alike that this was Bob's private kingdom, and one was never to go inside unless invited. The improvements—including a deck off the kitchen—cost more than $80,000 and were paid for with cash.

The family always ate in the kitchen even though there was a separate dining room. The kitchen table had benches on both sides, and Bob would sit on one end of the table with Bonnie at the other. The living room was rarely used. Bob sometimes sat in a wing chair near the front door to read the mail or his newspaper, and unless there was special company, that was about it for the living room. Upstairs was Bob and Bonnie's bedroom, with the three boys sharing another bedroom, and Lisa, who was still a toddler when they moved in during 1987, sleeping in her parents' bedroom. The extra bedroom was a combination study and guestroom.

The affluent county in which they were living—Fairfax—had some of the best public schools in the country. There were good, nearby parochial schools as well, and some of the children did go to Our Lady of Good Counsel when they were younger, but by the seventh grade, they were attending the two Opus Dei–affiliated schools—Oakcrest and the Heights. At that time, both were between thirty and forty miles away. They were expensive and seemed hardly worth the daily struggle, but Bob and Bonnie both agreed the effort was necessary.

On September 14, 1987, shortly after the Hanssen family had moved into the Talisman Drive house, Bob Hanssen mailed some secret documents, many of them from the National Security Council marked Top Secret. A day later the KGB loaded the PARK drop site under the Nottoway Park bridge with another $10,000. With the money was a letter proposing two new sites. The KGB wanted to give the first one the code name AN. The site was in the Ellanor C. Lawrence Park on Route 28, nearly fourteen miles from Bob's new house. The park had been named after the wife of David Lawrence, the conservative, rabidly anticommunist founder of *U.S. News & World Report*. Lawrence had donated the 660 acres for the park, though it was doubtful the KGB knew or cared about the political beliefs of the park's donor.

The second place, which the KGB wanted to code DEN, was even farther away. The Soviets suggested that B load either PARK or AN with new documents on September 26, and that they would respond by loading DEN with cash.

Bob cleared the sign at Nottoway Park the next night

and ten days later put a package under the bridge. This time the letter was in B's handwriting and read:

> My Friends:
> I am not a young man, and the commitments on my time prevent using distant drops as you suggest. I know in this I am moving you out of your set modes of doing business, but my experience tells me the [*sic*] we can be actually more secure in easier modes.

Bob tried out some new ideas on the KGB, including leaving a document package inside a parked car instead of the park sites they had been using. Writing as Ramon, B gave them some other ideas as well but wound up compromising:

> If you cannot do this I will clear this once AN on your schedule date, rather than the other site. Find me a comfortable Vienna, Va. signal site to call me to an exchange any following Monday. Good luck with your work.
>
> Ramon

Besides his letter, Bob enclosed a document with the title *National Intelligence Program for 1987*. The KGB suggested that the signal site be on the post below a stop sign at the junction of Courthouse Road and Locust Street, in Vienna. The Soviets gave the stop sign the code name of V. The signal site was five blocks from Bob and Bonnie's new home on Talisman Drive, again suggesting that the KGB knew the identity of "Ramon" and took seriously his assertion of not being "a young man."

The KGB told Bob that $100,000 had been deposited in his name at a Moscow bank, most likely Mosstroyekonombank, on September 29, 1987. The financial institution was a favorite of the government's.

The machinations of spy tradecraft continued. Bob sent

off another letter to Malakhov/Malkow in Alexandria, which was postmarked November 7, 1987. This time, B used a return address of "J. Baker, Chicago." He told the KGB that Saturday, November 14, was impossible and suggested Monday the sixteenth instead. In his letter he teased his handlers by saying he had an urgent package for the KGB and told them to place the appropriate piece of white tape at the PARK signal site. The Soviets did so immediately. Bob also let them know that whenever the word *Chicago* was used in a return address, he wanted a dead drop exchange to occur on the following Monday. On Sunday night, November 15, the Soviets deposited a package of money for B at the site inside Ellanor C. Lawrence Park, but he didn't show and they removed it on Tuesday evening. There had been a mix-up, and he dashed off a letter, which this time had the return address of "G. Robertson, Houston" and was postmarked November 17, the same day the Soviets had removed the money from AN or Ellanor C. Lawrence Park. B appeared to be a bit miffed, writing as Ramon:

Unable to locate AN based on your description at night. Recognize that I am dressed in business suit and can not slog around in inch deep mud. I suggest we use once again original site. I will place my urgent material there at next AN times. Replace it with your package. I will select some few sites good for me and pass them to you. Please give new constant conditions of recontact as address to write. Will not put substantive material through it. Only instructions as usual format.

Ramon

On Monday, November 23, B and the KGB exchanged gift packages at Nottoway Park. The package contained a cable report of a secret meeting that had taken place only a month ago with a mysterious source the KGB called M, some information that Vitaly Yurchenko had provided the

FBI, and a technical document describing COINS-II, the acronym for Community On-Line Intelligence System, a classified computer intranet system that linked the CIA and NSA with the U.S. Defense Department and three other smaller intelligence agencies.*

Bob's package contained $20,000 in cash—which may have come in handy when he was faced with the invoices from the home-improvement contractors who were redoing the basement—and a letter from the KGB expressing their "regards" and telling him that the $100,000 that had been deposited in the Moscow bank would compound at interest rates of between 6 and 7 percent.

The KGB, perhaps feeling emboldened by its claim of $100,000 in B's name in a Moscow bank, demanded in the letter several specific types of information it needed. The spy was also given two new accommodation addresses, and in turn, he was asked to name two new dead drop sites.

When they moved into the Talisman Drive house in 1987, Bob, Bonnie, and the children at first attended the parish church, Our Lady of Good Counsel in Vienna, a mile away, where they were sending the youngest children to its parochial school. After a year they began to feel that OLGC was too liberal for them and began attending another church out of their parish, Saint Catherine's of Siena in Great Falls. Saint Cat's had it all—a Latin mass, monthly Gregorian chants, Opus Dei meetings, Dominican meetings, all on fifteen beautifully landscaped acres. Best of all in those days, it had an outstanding, charismatic priest, Jerome Fasano, whom Bob and Bonnie would come to know and love.

Father Fasano, who was invited to dinner more than once at the Hanssen house—one of the few times each year the formal dining room was used—was not an Opus Dei

---

* Today, a newer version of COINS is available to authorized users. The system has a front end that can be used with a Web browser and features both XML and Java support.

priest but a Dominican tertiary who had a special ability to affect people's lives. The conservative Republican U.S. Senator Rick Santorum, who also attended Saint Cat's, once said that Fasano had convinced him to speak out in the Congress for the pro-life position and for the partial-birth-abortion amendment.*

Fasano spoke fervently to Bob about the Soviet Union. Fasano was considered an expert on the relationship between Russia and Fátima, a Portuguese town where many Catholics believe the Virgin Mary had spoken several times to three peasant children in 1917 about war and the eventual fate of Russia. One of the Virgin Mary's alleged messages to the children at Fátima was that armed conflicts between nations were punishments for sin, and thus because of so much sin being committed, the earth would soon be overwhelmed by war, hunger, and the persecution of Catholics. Russia was to be God's "instrument of chastisement," and atheism would be spread by Russia around the world. The Virgin Mary told the children that this could be prevented through special prayers and also said that the pope and every bishop in the world should publicly consecrate Russia, making it a sacred place as a condition for world peace. Among Catholics, the message of Fátima is often called the Peace Plan from Heaven. The message of Fátima would also become the basis of one of Bob's research papers at the FBI.

Fasano wasn't a follower of Opus Dei's Josemaria Escriva, but rather Padre Pio de Pietrelcina, a Capuchin priest in Italy who was said to have lifelong stigmata—five wounds that duplicated Christ's on the cross—and bled a cup of blood each day. Fasano had lobbied heavily for the beatification of Padre Pio because he believed that Friar Pio had cured a family friend of lymphatic cancer in 1949. Fa-

---

* This was after his wife, Karen, had refused an abortion when doctors told her that their daughter would be born with a heart-valve problem. The baby lived two hours.

sano had written to Pio seeking his intercession with God on behalf of his mother, who also had cancer. In 1975, Fasano had gone to Italy to pray at Pio's tomb, and in 1998, shortly after Pio's beatification, Father Fasano helped dedicate a shrine to him in Northern Virginia.

Father Fasano and Senator Santorum were just a few of the star-studded members who helped to make up Saint Catherine of Siena's staff and congregation. Supreme Court justice Antonin Scalia, his wife, and their nine children also attended ("five–four in favor of boys," he would joke). Scalia had once shown up out of the blue and asked to join Saint Cat's eighteen-member choir, who wore bright red robes and sang Bach and Mozart. He explained to the choir director that he traveled a lot and wouldn't be able to make every practice but was accepted just the same. "So, what should we call you?" a choir member had asked.

"Just call me Niño," Justice Scalia replied.

Niño Scalia and his family were not the most glittering celebrities who found time to attend Saint Catherine's of Siena. Two quarterbacks from the Washington Redskins, Gus Frerotte and Mark Rypien, had been regulars when they led the NFL team and drew far more attention, with small children standing near the priest outside the church to get their autographs. House Minority Leader Richard A. Gephardt, the Democratic congressman from Missouri, and his wife, Jane, were there many Sundays. So was Kate O'Beirne, the Washington editor of the conservative magazine *National Review*. CIA and FBI employees were sprinkled everywhere. When Franklyn McAfee, a priest at the church, was once asked by the *Washington Post* if any of the congregants were in intelligence, he answered, "Maybe. If I ask somebody what they do and they don't tell me, I don't ask again."

The most important congregant after Scalia was Louis J. Freeh, Bob's boss. Freeh, his wife, Marilyn, and their brood often sat across the aisle from Bob, Bonnie, and their children. But the egos of everyone, famous or not, were expected to be checked at the door. "There's no VIP section," a parishioner explained.

Bob Hanssen's youngest son, Greg, became an altar boy at Saint Catherine's. (The church is located in one of only two dioceses in the United States that does not allow girls to serve at the altar.) Modern without being stark, there were Byzantine-styled icons of Jesus and Mary flanking a large crucifix at the front of the church, and outside, nearly two hundred rosebushes made the manicured grounds fragrant for much of the summer. Saint Cat's could afford it. Members tithed more than a million dollars each year.

Bob, though, was never a big giver to either Saint Catherine's of Siena or Opus Dei. Records show that between 1988 and 1992, for example, he gave a total of $2,690 to the Woodlawn Foundation, the group that funds American Opus Dei activities. At Saint Cat's, he gave the bare minimum.

"He didn't support our parish," Father McAfee said after Bob's arrest. "I can safely say he didn't donate to us."

On February 4, 1988, Bob sent a letter to the KGB at one of the new accommodation addresses. The chit said simply "OK" and had a new return address, "Jim Baker, Langley." It had been mailed from Washington, D.C., the day before.*

Four days later both B and the KGB hit Nottoway Park at nearly the same time. B's package had a letter that acknowledged receipt of $20,000 on November 23. He also suggested two new drop sites, reported on a new Soviet defector, and promised more information on him as soon as he found time to read the defector's file, writing, "A full

---

* Jim Bakker, the televangelist, confessed in 1987 to adultery, was indicted in 1988 for defrauding his followers of $158 million by selling them nonexistent time-shares, and was sentenced in 1989 to forty-five years in prison. Stories about his legal woes and about his colorful wife, Tammy Faye, were in the papers and on the television evening news during that period nearly daily.

report will follow as soon as possible." According to the FBI, he revealed the identity of a KGB double agent who was working for the United States without diplomatic immunity. He also enclosed a memo that detailed the U.S. intelligence community's capabilities, an encrypted computer disk, and other classified documents.

In return, the Soviets gave their double agent $25,000 in hundred-dollar bills and a personal thank-you letter from the chairman of the KGB, Vladimir Aleksandrovich Kryuchkov. The new KGB spy chief had been appointed to that position only one month earlier by Mikhail Gorbachev. (Ironically, Kryuchkov's first speech as the head of the KGB would be an impassioned harangue against the CIA, accusing the Agency of conducting a "wide-ranging campaign of spy mania and brutal provocation employed against Soviet institutions." In 1991, Kryuchkov would be one of the leaders in a coup against Gorbachev. It failed and he was imprisoned.)

Kryuchkov wrote that he wanted more information about M and the FBI's agent network in New York City. He also wanted to know what the FBI knew about a certain KGB agent. B cleared the drop the next day.

According to Jack Platt, a former CIA agent who once recruited Russians to spy for the United States in the 1980s, M was Gennadiy Vasilenko, his counterpart with the KGB. In the spy-vs.-spy game of the Cold War era, the two had tried to recruit each other, failed, and then become friends, going to ball games together and socializing with each other's family. Platt says Bob Hanssen told his handlers that M was Vasilenko and that M was meeting regularly with a CIA case handler.

Vasilenko was sent to Havana for what he thought was a KGB conference in the sun. Instead, he was nearly beaten to death by his fellow agents, who broke his arm and cracked his skull. He was transported back to a Moscow prison for execution and underwent several months of questioning under duress. During the interrogation Vasilenko managed to convince his KGB captors that it was all innocent fun with Platt, and he was released after six months.

"Hanssen turned Gennadiy in," Platt said after Bob's arrest. "I know that now. He nearly lost his life."

A grateful Bob mailed the KGB a second computer disk at one of the new accommodation addresses a month later, on March 16. This time he used a "Jim Baker, Chicago" return address, although the envelope was mailed from Washington the day before.

The next day the KGB got yet another letter from Bob at the accommodation address with the same "Jim Baker, Chicago" as the return address in the upper left-hand corner. It had been mailed from Northern Virginia. Bob ordered the KGB to use nearby Nottoway Park for dead drops until a suitable location was found on which both could agree. The Soviets had taken to calling Nottoway by the code name of PRIME now instead of PARK. On Monday, March 21, 1988, the KGB saw that B had placed a signal with tape for them at Nottoway but couldn't get to the dead drop location as a group of teens were hanging out on top of the bridge, smoking cigarettes.

On March 24, B sent yet another computer disk to the accommodation address from Washington. Again he used the "Jim Baker, Chicago" return. His computer knowledge was apparently too sophisticated for the Russians—the KGB was unable to find any text on the disk. They assigned it a file and put it on a shelf, labeling it D-3.

A few days later, on Monday, March 28, Bob and the KGB carried out a successful gift exchange at Nottoway Park. B handed over his fourth computer disk. This time they were able to decipher it and found two valuable documents on it marked TOP SECRET. The first was entitled *The FBI's Double Agent Program,* and the second was marked for the director of the U.S. Central Intelligence

Agency and seemed to be a training program called *Stealth Orientation*.

The exchange package from the KGB contained another $25,000 for B and a letter of apology explaining why its agents had been unable to check the dead drop site the previous Monday. They also complained about not being able to read the third disk. Finally they requested information on various intelligence codes and cryptograms, documents about intelligence support for the Strategic Defense Initiative, nuclear submarines, and a plethora of other materials. Bob removed the pickup tape signal the next day.

Annoyed that the Soviets didn't yet know how to decrypt a computer disk, Bob dashed off a letter on March 31 using a "Jim Baker, Alexandria" return address with a terse message inside: "Use 40 TRACK MODE, this letter is not a signal." (Forty-track mode, described in chapter One, is simply a technical process that uses the outer edge of a computer disk so that it conceals information. The data is put onto specific tracks on the disk and can be read only when one uses the correct code. If one doesn't know the code, the disk appears to be blank.)

Bob sent the KGB a fifth computer disk on April 5, 1988. The disk provided information that told them almost everything the FBI knew about an unidentified KGB officer, and two specific Soviet recruitments. Bob asked that part of his compensation be diamonds. Finally, there was intelligence about a KGB major, Victor Sheymov, who had defected to the United States with his wife and their five-year-old daughter in 1980. At one time Bob had been his FBI case officer.

Sheymov was a threat to the Soviets. He had once been the fair-haired boy of Moscow and at thirty-two was the youngest major in the KGB. After he settled in the United States he said he was convinced that the KGB had been involved in the attempted assassination of Pope John Paul II in 1981. Sheymov based his claim on a 1979 cable he had seen authored by then KGB chief Yuri Andropov, who later succeeded Soviet leader Leonid Brezhnev. The wire said in part, "Find out how to get physically close to the pope."

The former KGB agent was also an inventor and an expert on communications intelligence who may have escaped with documents that detailed the Soviets' work on information warfare, or IW. The Soviets were on the verge of perfecting a new technology that used quick, concentrated bursts of radio frequencies (RF) to shut down all computers and telephones in an area the size of a city, including the tiny computer chips that controlled gasoline distribution in modern cars and trucks.

The Soviets had been using RF with varying degrees of success since the 1960s. In 1968, using RF, they had jammed nearly every telephone in Czechoslovakia when they invaded the country to quell an uprising. In 1977 they had aimed an RF device at a piece of computer hardware in the U.S. embassy in Moscow for so long the equipment caught on fire. Because it was in a sensitive area, the embassy had no choice but to rely on the Moscow fire department. The firemen arrived to put out the fire, and among them were KGB operatives who planted electronic bugs throughout the embassy. The KGB had tested RF against the embassy again in 1985, this time aiming it at the alarm system and harassing the employees by setting it off over and over again. Sheymov was going to tell the CIA everything about the technology. So Sheymov was a worry. He knew a lot.*

---

* Although Bob Hanssen gave the KGB classified information about Victor Sheymov, the double agent apparently harbored no animosity towards him. The Hanssens later became social friends with the Sheymov family, according to former CIA chief R. James Woolsey. And as we shall see, Bob Hanssen would ask Sheymov for a job with an American company the defector ran just three weeks before being arrested.

* * *

Bob continued to send computer disks in rapid succession. The sixth was mailed on May 17, 1988, from "Jim Baker, Chicago" and contained information about a recent FBI Soviet recruitment operation.

Just after 9 P.M. on Monday, May 30, Bob Hanssen and Viktor Degtyar nearly bumped into each other—literally— at Nottoway Park. The KGB pulled up just as Bob was removing a piece of adhesive tape from the signal site. They watched Bob drive away, but made no attempt to follow or otherwise spook him. After that they didn't hear from him for a month. When he did reply in mid-July, the envelope with just a "Chicago" in the upper left-hand corner and posted from Washington, Bob seemed unaffected by his brush with his handlers.

I found the site empty. Possibly I had the time wrong. I work from memory. My recollection was for you to fill before 1:AM. I believe Viktor Degtyar was in the church driveway off Rt. 123, but I did not know how he would react to an approach. My schedule was tight to make this at all. Because of my work, I had to synchronize explanations and flights while not leaving a pattern of absence or travel that could later be correlated with communications times. This is difficult and expensive.

I will call the number you gave me on 2/24, 2/26 or 2/28 at 1.00 A.M., EDST. Please plan filled signals. Empty sites bother me. I like to know before I commit myself as I'm sure you do also. Let's not use the original site so early at least until the seasons change. Some type of call-out signal to you when I have a package or when I can receive one would be useful. Also, please be specific about dates, eg., 2/24. Scheduling is not simple for me because of frequent travel and wife. Any ambiguity multiplies the problems.

My security concerns may seem excessive. I believe

experience has shown them to be necessary. I am much safer if you know little about me. Neither of us are children about these things. Over time, I can cut your losses rather than become one.

Ramon

P.S. Your "thank you" was deeply appreciated.

NINE

Diamonds Are Not Forever

It is hard to decide which are the most damaging materials that Bob Hanssen was charged with handing over to the KGB. Certainly, his activities during the last half of 1988 were devastating to the security of the United States and, because nuclear secrets were turned over, would make him eligible for the death penalty many times over.

On Monday, July 18, 1988, Bob handed over 530 pages of documents to the KGB including a CIA paper dated November 1987 that contained details of the current U.S. nuclear program that was stamped TOP SECRET and marked NOFORN NOCONTRACT ORCON. (In government speak, NOFORN is an acronym for "not releasable to foreign nationals"; NOCONTRACT stands for "not releasable to contractors or contractor consultants"; and ORCON means "dissemination and extraction of information controlled by originator.") Another document was titled *Compendium of Future Intelligence Requirements: Volume II* and dated September 1987. It had been prepared by the staff of the Intelligence Producers Council and classified TOP SECRET/SCI (Sensitive Compartmented Information) with a NOFORN stamp on it.

Also in the package was a CIA counterintelligence staff

study labeled *The Soviet Counterintelligence Offensive: KGB Recruitment Operations Against CIA* which had been produced in March of 1988. It was classified SECRET and also contained the NOFORN NOCONTRACT ORCON caveat. It was also marked WNINTEL (Warning Notice: Intelligence Sources and Methods Involved) and said, "Unauthorized Disclosure Subject to Criminal Sanctions." Finally, there was a paper labeled TOP SECRET that was a historical FBI review of allegations from spies and counterspies that spanned several decades and documented all the times that the Soviets had penetrated various U.S. intelligence services. It described a number of Soviet defectors and the information they had provided. The following warning was printed in all capital letters on the front page:

IN VIEW OF THE EXTREME SENSITIVITY OF THIS DOCUMENT, THE UTMOST CAUTION MUST BE EXERCISED IN ITS HANDLING. THE CONTENT INCLUDES A COMPREHENSIVE REVIEW OF SENSITIVE SOURCE ALLEGATIONS AND INVESTIGATIONS OF PENETRATION OF THE FBI BY THE SOVIET INTELLIGENCE SERVICES, THE DISCLOSURE OF WHICH WOULD COMPROMISE HIGHLY SENSITIVE COUNTERINTELLIGENCE OPERATIONS AND METHODS. ACCESS SHOULD BE LIMITED TO A STRICT NEED-TO-KNOW BASIS.

In return, the package from the KGB contained $25,000 in hundred-dollar bills and a list of demands. They obviously considered B a treasure trove who somehow had virtually unlimited access to intelligence secrets. As if ordering from a menu, they requested information about the FBI's surveillance system, more on the FBI's agent network in New York City, some documents on illegal intelligence, and news on several ongoing FBI recruitment operations. They also proposed two new dead drop and signal locations. Both were under five miles from Bob's home, again strong clues that they knew their informant's identity and home address, even though his defense attorney would later claim that the KGB never knew his name.

The first drop, in Idylwood Park, halfway between Vienna and Falls Church, was rather brazenly named BOB. The other, named CHARLIE, was in Eakin Park, just south of Vienna. In both cases, the dead drop sites were under footbridges. They told their double agent to load the bridges with his package by 9 P.M. on the designated day and it would be cleared by 10 P.M. and then the location would be loaded with cash and a memo. He could clear it anytime after ten that night. On the last day of July, the Soviets got the seventh computer disk in the mail. The disk had new information on technical surveillance systems, news of a recruitment in New York City, and the names of several Soviet KGB agents whom the FBI wanted to recruit. Three weeks later the Soviets would claim in a letter that they had deposited another $50,000 in his Moscow bank account.

Computers and the havoc they can wreak have long been of interest to the intelligence community. The technology is used well. The NSA, for example, employs hackers whose sole mission is to break into the computer networks of foreign governments, drug cartels, and international terrorist organizations. Computer viruses have been invented in the various intelligence agencies and never used, in preparation for a war or crisis of such magnitude that it will be necessary to shut down the rest of the world's networks.

Bob Hanssen was a self-taught computer hacker of the first order, a member of a minority that foresaw the impact the technology would have on the world well before words like *spamming* and *cyberspace* became commonplace. He taught himself to program in C and Pascal and created a system that automated the teletypewriting operation at FBI headquarters. In one Internet posting he made on a computer chatline, he made the believable assertion that he had been a regular computer user since September of 1986.

Bob proselytized members of his family to become wired early on and attempted to bring both them and his more Luddite supervisors at the FBI into the electronic age. No one in Bonnie's family was safe from Bob's efforts. Records show Bob lent his brother-in-law George Beglis several thousand dollars to buy an Apple Macintosh II computer system for his architectural firm in early 1990. The desktop model came with all the bells and whistles for the time—laser printer, color monitor, and special software. Bob insisted that the loan to Beglis be secured with a court-recorded memorandum of understanding.

At the same time he was getting his family, friends, and employer into the technology picture, he was also imploring his KGB handlers to get cyber-connected. In a 1991 letter to the Soviets, Bob suggested they communicate "directly using a computer that will be specially-equipped with certain advanced technology." The explanation was his awkward way of explaining E-mail to them long before most people had ever heard of the term.

The Emperor Ming kingdom he built for himself in the basement of his house always had two or three computers, a server, and several E-mail addresses that included hanssen@nova.org and hanssen@orion.clark.net. One of the computers, the IBM ThinkPad 365E, had twenty-four megabytes of RAM with Linux-distributed Slackware 3.0 with a 2.0 kernel. Computer enthusiasts rolled their eyes at these configurations, considering them primitive.

Bob often joined computer chatlines to discuss the latest advances in the field. One of his entries, made at 8:52 P.M. on Valentine's Day of 2001, four days before he was arrested, underlines that Bob may have been more interested in his Palm III than a romantic candlelight dinner with Bonnie. That the word *I* is used twelve times in two short paragraphs speaks volumes about his ego:

From: Robert P. Hanssen (hanssen@orion.clark.net)
Subject: 3.5 Question

Newsgroups: alt.comp.sys.palmtops.pilot
Date: 2001-02-14 11.52.46 PST
I have a Palm IIIx which I upgraded the OS on to 3.5.2.
When I did, I still got the old style menu with no list
option. In order to see the programs in the newer style
I needed to click on the Applications icon. I now have
a Palm Vx. It showed up of course with the new style
of applications selector on first booting. After I synched
over my information and applications from the Palm
IIIx, however I now have reverted to the old style se-
lection icon menu as the default. When I synched I saw
a bunch of files get transfered *[sic]* of course and some
I didn't recognize which seemed administrative.

Obviously, one of these 'updated' my new Vx to the
look and feel of the original 3.0 Palm IIIx. Does anyone
know how I can fix this easily?

In a way, Bob was hoisted by his own petard. When he
was arrested four days later, his Palm IIIx contained the
code name ELLIS and the date of February 18 recorded in
his calendar. When asked to comment on Bob's use of the
handheld computer, Julia Rodriguez, the spokesperson for
the Santa Clara, California–based Palm would only say
primly, "Palm does not condone the use of our products for
espionage or any other unsavory practices."

Bob sent his eighth computer disk to the KGB on September 21, 1988, this time by mail to an accommodation address in Alexandria. It contained information about Soviet
recruitment targets of the FBI. Again the left-hand corner
read "Chicago" but was postmarked from Washington.
There was a two-word message—"at BOB"—which meant
that the next exchange would be in Idylwood Park. The
BOB exchange was made on Monday, September 26. B
enclosed three hundred pages of materials that included an
FBI analysis of a KGB KR (foreign counterintelligence)
officer in New York City, information on what the FBI

knew about the technology Soviet intelligence used in their work, a transcript of an FBI Counterintelligence Group meeting, and other documents. In return, the KGB enclosed a large, cut diamond that had been appraised at $24,720, and a message saying that an additional $50,000 had been deposited in B's Moscow bank account. The KGB also enclosed another thank-you note from KGB chief Vladimir Kryuchkov and enclosed its usual wish list, which seemed to be getting longer and more specific with each contact. This time they wanted information on missile technologies, agent networks, and what the FBI knew about classified technical operations within the Soviet Union.

Some six weeks later, on December 1, 1988, B mailed the KGB his ninth computer disk. The Soviets would label it D-9. This time, he put a new wrinkle on the return address, writing "G. Robertson, Baker's Photo" in the left-hand corner. The information on the disk was a potpourri of classified material.

On the night after Christmas of 1988, B and the KGB made an exchange at the new CHARLIE site in Eakin Park, near Bob Hanssen's house. This time Bob gave his handlers 356 pages of material and his tenth computer disk. Six documents were from the most recent National HUMINT (spy speak for human intelligence) Collection Plan or NHCP. One, which the KGB must have particularly relished reading, was rather sweepingly titled *Soviet Armed Forces and Capabilities for Conducting Strategic Nuclear War Until the End of the 1990s*. Moscow, in its gratitude, gave the spy $10,000 cash, a second cut diamond, which had been appraised at $17,748, and the usual laundry list of demands.

If anything, B appeared to be willing to work like a beaver for the KGB. The combination of money and thrills, after living such a repressed life for so long, was exhilarating. Bob was like a tube of toothpaste being squeezed with the cap on. He was oozing out in several directions.

On the last day of January of 1989 the Soviets noticed that their spy had activated a signal at an emergency site in Washington. The location was just above Dupont Circle at the junction of Connecticut Avenue and Q Street NW. This meant B had unloaded a package at the BOB dead drop in Idylwood Park. Rushing to the park, they found a package containing an overseas cable and a breathless memo that read, "Send to the Center right away. This might be useful." In addition to the encrypted cable there was a computer disk with their agent's own helpful analysis of the message as well as several profiles of intelligence people in whom the KGB had expressed interest.

Another such signal was placed by Bob Hanssen six weeks later. This time a signal was put at the Taft Memorial Bridge, a graceful overpass in upper northwest Washington noted for its stone sculptures of lions abutting each end. The dead drops were made at CHARLIE or Eakin Park. This time Bob passed the Soviets a TOP SECRET SCI NOFORN NOCONTRACT document that was prefaced with this caveat:

Warning Notice
Intelligence Sources or Methods Involved
(WNINTEL)
NATIONAL SECURITY INFORMATION
Unauthorized Disclosure Subject to Criminal Sanctions

The document was titled *DCI Guidance for the National MASINT Intelligence Program (FY1991–FY 2000)*. It had been written by the Measurement and Signature Intelligence (MASINT) Committee and was fresh, dated November 1988. The document was highly technical and Bob asked for it back when the KGB had finished reading and copying it. Bob also gave the KGB a twelfth computer disk that contained another 539 pages of classified material.

Bob's gift from the Soviets contained $18,000 cash, a third cut diamond worth $11,700, a letter requesting a personal meeting, new proposed dead drop sites, and concern about the security of the diamonds. (Bob later told the KGB that if he was ever asked about the diamonds, he would say they were a gift from the grandmother who had lived with the family on North Neva Avenue in Chicago and was now deceased.) They also presented their usual list of needs, including a final line that asked "for everything else that's possible."

The depth and the sensitivity of the documents Bob was giving the Soviets were doing wonders for his handlers' careers. In the spring of 1989, several of them were lauded by Moscow. Among the medals that they received were the coveted Order of the Red Banner, Order of the Red Star, and the Medal for Excellent Service. B, on the other hand, was getting cold feet about the diamonds. In May, at the BOB site, he sent two of them back to the KGB (the first and third stones) and asked that they be exchanged for cash. He also passed along the thirteenth computer disk, in which he asked the Soviets to set him up a Swiss bank account. There were eighty pages of material this time, with one document titled *National Intelligence Program '90–'91.**

Though Bob Hanssen got no awards or medals, he may have been due one for what he did to save the skin of alleged double agent Felix Bloch. In 1989, Bloch was a U.S. diplomat and the number two man at the U.S. embassy in Vienna, Austria. The fifty-three-year-old, $81,000-a-year envoy, whom B would later call "a schnook"—thirty documents on Bloch would be found inside Bob Hanssen's

---

* By now, the Soviets had to be ecstatic with both the quality and quantity of intelligence they were receiving. In 1982, their only double agent in Washington had been a janitor who filched classified papers off a government contractor's desktops and out of trash cans. According to former KGB agent Yuri Shvets, Leonid Brezhnev's successor, Yuri Andropov, made the intial decision to pursue perestroika entirely based on this "garbology," which showed that the United States had a much larger nuclear capability than the Soviets had previously thought.)

office safe a few days prior to his arrest—had found his way into an FBI telephone surveillance net. He was caught talking on April 27 to a known KGB illegal, Reino Gikman, whom he claimed to know only as "Pierre." Leaping at the discovery, the FBI had French intelligence twice photograph Bloch that May handing over briefcases to Gikman during a trip to Paris. With Bloch's every phone call monitored, the FBI then overheard him receiving a call at his home in Washington from a person using the name of Ferdinand Paul.

"I am calling on behalf of Pierre. He cannot see you in the future," the voice said, adding, "He is sick. A contagious disease is suspected." The voice concluded cryptically, "I am worried about you. You have to take care of yourself."

Bloch immediately went to ground. Gikman returned to Moscow.

Bob's boss at the time, David Major, later recalled that Bob would come into Major's office to agonize with him on who had alerted Bloch. According to the FBI and the documents they received from the KGB, it was Bob. FBI records show that they opened a surveillance file on Bloch the day after he was caught talking to Gikman and that Bob Hanssen had access to that file from the beginning. Originally, Bloch was believed to have been tipped off by the French, but according to the Bureau, it was Bob, passing over a duplicate of the FBI file on Bloch to the KGB.

Yet the greatest impediment to Bloch's arrest may have been the rivalry between the CIA and the FBI. The CIA had assembled a team that, working with French intelligence, planned to grab both Gikman and Bloch in Paris while they were making their exchange or, failing that, later on at a meeting the two had arranged in Brussels. The FBI vetoed the plan, saying they were worried about extraditing Bloch from France. Instead they ordered him back to Washington, where they thought he would not only continue his activities but would be easier to arrest. The Bureau cited an executive order signed by President Jimmy Carter that prevented the CIA from spying on U.S. citizens abroad. But the phone call from the mysterious Ferdinand Paul canceled the FBI's plans.

The FBI never gave up trying to prosecute Bloch, even trotting out an Austrian prostitute before a grand jury to testify he had given her $10,000 over the years because he was addicted to sadomasochistic sex. The theory espoused by the FBI was that Bloch had sold U.S. secrets to the KGB to finance his fetish. Others theorized that if he had done what he was accused of, it was more than likely because he—an Austrian-born U.S. citizen whose parents had fled the country and the Nazis in 1939—had twice been passed over for the post of ambassador to the country of his birth. When the FBI questioned Bloch about the exchanges with Gikman, he had a ready explanation. He explained he thought "Pierre" was a philatelist and there had only been his stamp collection inside the briefcase, and thus they were just two hobbyists making an innocent exchange.

In 1989, while Bob Hanssen was making his unobserved dead drops every few weeks with the KGB, Bloch's every move was recorded by the press, who made the suspected spy the story of the summer. It soon became a circus with TV cameras capturing the FBI stealthily following Bloch around and videotaping him while he sat on a bench eating a bag lunch. On one weekend, Bloch and his then wife, Lucille, went to visit a daughter in the New York suburbs. With the network camera crews staking out the house, neighbors brought lawn chairs out on their front lawns to watch the spectacle while their children sold lemonade to the reporters. At one bizarre restaurant lunch with a *Time* magazine correspondent, the FBI sat at the next table. After eating, Bloch told the reporter that he hoped to do it again, "providing I don't defect to East Berlin first." He then turned to the FBI surveillance team across the room and smiled, saying, "Just kidding."

The FBI had let Bloch off, and the Bureau rightly got

the blame instead of the CIA. Desperate, one of Bob's bosses, Tom DuHadway, then the chief of FBI counterintelligence, suggested that the Soviet Union swap files with the United States on Bloch and Edward Lee Howard in exchange for economic aid. "If they want massive aid—and I'm not saying we shouldn't give it to them—there are reasonable quid pro quos that people should ask for, and I don't think handing over those two cases are unreasonable at all," he said.*

Still, the next decade would not be good to Felix Bloch. In November of 1990, he was fired from the State Department and denied his pension for "making false statements and misrepresentations to the FBI." He quietly moved to the university town of Chapel Hill, North Carolina, and may have been forgotten, except in 1992 a reporter discovered him bagging groceries at the local Harris-Teeter supermarket for five dollars an hour and wearing a name tag that said "Felix B." When asked for an explanation, the once suave envoy who had hosted George H. Bush and CIA director William Webster in Austria told the newspaper scribe, "I won't talk to you now or ever."

The story became even stranger. Bloch was actually working two jobs. The other was driving a mass transit bus. Despite the menial employment, he appeared to be living well. He had a custom-built $220,000 house on one acre in a gated golf-course community called the Governor's Club and drove a silver Mercedes to his bag-boy position. An old friend, Henry Mattox, who was a postdoctoral fellow at the University of North Carolina, downplayed the house, telling the local *News and Observer* that the house was "nothing luxurious, bottom of the line for the Governor's Club, much like the Tempo model is the bottom of the line for the Ford Motor Company."

In late 1992, Bloch was promoted to cashier at the su-

---

* DuHadway escaped being chastised for his political statement; he died of a massive heart attack the day after giving the interview.

permarket, which in hindsight may have been past his Peter Principle optimum. He was arrested on January 12, 1993, and charged with stealing $100.59 worth of groceries while in the midst of loading the bags into the trunk of his silver Mercedes. The stolen food was so mundane and so removed from the caviar-and-champagne life he had once enjoyed as a European diplomat that the press had a field day itemizing the stolen food. Included were such items as Gorton's frozen catfish, Campbell's chicken soup, Taster's Choice instant coffee, and various brands of ready-to-eat cereal.

Bloch spent the night in jail and pled guilty a week later, receiving a $60 fine. He was also made to perform forty-eight hours of community service. In a mea culpa to the judge, he wrote, "I sincerely regret the pass to which things came that day and wish to assure you they will not recur. My brief sojourn in the Orange County jail is an indelible and instructive memory."

Were that so. In 1994, Bloch was again arrested for shoplifting. This time he stole $21.74 worth of food and over-the-counter drugs from a discount store called Sav-A-Center. Again the press delighted in listing his haul, which included two nine-ounce pepperoni sausages, McCrustino pita bread, Crystal Light lemonade, and two fifty-tablet bottles of aspirin. When apprehended, Bloch at first attempted to resist being taken to local police headquarters, but when told by the security guard, "We can do this the easy way or the hard way," he crumbled.

By now, his life had completely come apart. He was separated from his wife and, because of the two theft charges, was fired from his job bagging groceries. There, his only interaction with people had come from asking customers if they preferred plastic or paper. At the new trial, where he spoke a lot, he promised to get some counseling. His narcissistic speech had almost as many *I*'s as Bob Hanssen's Palm III Internet posting.

"I'm seeking professional advice about whether therapy

or treatment is appropriate," Bloch told the court, saying in part: "I view this as a onetime, singular occurrence. I feel this asocial behavior of mine is atypical of my behavior. I believe that I will soon begin a new phase of my life."

To mitigate the charges, Bloch produced a Red Cross executive who testified Bloch had put in fifteen hundred hours of volunteer time at the local chapter. After receiving a $100 fine and a thirty-day suspended sentence, the former diplomat was followed by several TV crews to an ATM machine down the block where he withdrew the cash to pay the court. The farcical scene was a near duplicate of the carnival-like atmosphere that had been created in Washington four years before.

Bloch moved to a rented room with shared-refrigerator privileges. When Bob Hanssen was arrested, Bloch had upgraded to a small apartment but was still driving and taking fares on the transit bus. In recent years, Felix Bloch appeared to have developed a fatalistic attitude toward life and, in one of his rare statements, gave this piece of philosophy, which offered an advance look at his tombstone:

"As they say, life is a bitch and then you die. So you live and you die. Then oblivion. I think that's what I'll get when I die. Oblivion."

On Monday, August 7, 1989, Bob and the KGB exchanged packages at the CHARLIE dead drop site. B gave the KGB five rolls of film, which contained a TOP SECRET SCI analysis that was dated May 1987. There was also his fourteenth computer disk, which had the latest information from the FBI on the Bloch-Gikman affair. The Soviets proposed a new dead drop site they dubbed DORIS, in a park near the Canterbury Woods subdivision in Northern Virginia. They also gave B $30,000 in cash and a due bill that promised they would pay him for the diamonds at a later date. The KGB rejected his idea for a Swiss bank account but a week later claimed to have deposited $50,000 more in his Moscow bank account. Moscow also suggested a new dead drop site they code-named ELLIS in Foxstone Park. The signal site they said would be the Foxstone Park sign on Creek Crossing Road.

Some six weeks later, on Monday, September 25, B and the Soviets carried out their first operation at DORIS. B gave them his fifteenth computer disk and a highly sensitive document labeled TOP SECRET/SCI and in turn received $30,000 in cash, a thank-you letter, and for the first time a computer disk from the KGB, marking its first entry into the era of computer technology. B wasn't pleased with their first effort. On October 2 he wrote to his handlers, "The disk is clean. I tried all methods—completely demagnetized."

TEN

Computer Geek Seeks Repentant Stripper

In 1868, Great Britain elected as its leader William Ewart Gladstone. He was to become one of its more important and enduring prime ministers, serving four different terms between 1868 and 1894. Gladstone, and his political rival Benjamin Disraeli, dominated British government for decades during the Victorian age.

Gladstone was a study in contrasts. He was born in Liverpool to a religious, wealthy family who emphasized a moral life. On the one hand, he owned slaves overseas and worked against the abolition of slavery. On the other, he fought for lower-class voting rights in England—the poor had none in that era—and passed a law that said a workingman would never have to pay more than a penny a mile when traveling by train.

For most of his life Gladstone was considered an example of Victorian virtue. He was married to his wife, Catherine, for sixty years, and the couple had several sons. Despite this semblance of normalcy, Gladstone walked the streets of London before and during his terms as prime minister seeking out street prostitutes. His quest was not to hire them for sex, but rather to save them for the Lord. Gladstone believed Christianity required him to do this type of evangelical charitable work. Reclaiming prostitutes for Christ was his passion, and the great political leader co-founded an organization called The Church Penitentiary Society Association for the Reclamation of Fallen Women.

The good works caused him to become racked with guilt. In his diary he worried that he may have committed "adultery of the heart" or *delectatio morosa*—the act of "enjoying thinking of evil without the intention of action." He also—like members of Opus Dei—may have practiced self-flagellation. Some accounts of his life suggest he often turned a whip on himself after merely meeting with a lady of the evening.

An essay by literary critic Trevor Fisher in the magazine *History Today* in February of 1997 analyzed one of the many biographies on Gladstone. The book, by Travis L. Crosby, was titled *The Two Mr. Gladstones: A Study on Psychology and History*. In the article, Fisher attempted to sum up the dual nature of Gladstone's personality:

Individuals handle stress via a "two-stage process." First is cognitive appraisal, by which an individual reflects on the nature of the stress. Second is coping, a process by which individuals manage the perceived stress and thereby restore a sense of coherence and balance to their lives. Gladstone had a profound need for order, coherence and control. When experiencing severe pressure that threatened to deprive him of the control he required, he would respond in one of two ways. His preferred strategy was aggression, whereby he would strive to master his situation by lashing out against those deemed responsible for his discomfort. If this failed, he would adopt a strategy of withdrawal with a view to removing himself from the hostile forces he could not command. Taking in the entire span of his subject's long life, Crosby tries to show how Gladstone's private and public behavior exemplified this pattern. What seemed erratic and wayward to his contemporaries was in fact the product of an internal logic inseparable from his struggle to contend with the difficulties besetting him.

While Bob Hanssen has never tried to bring hookers to the Lord, he has attempted to convert several strippers and other types of exotic dancers. These good works were not performed at the aforementioned Good Guys. Rather he chose clubs around Washington that were similar, but not frequented by G-men. Being seen by an FBI associate at the Bureau's chosen hangout of the flesh would have opened him up to a charge of hypocrisy.

That many of the KGB payments went directly to these women has seemed amazing to many, particularly with Bonnie Hanssen at home doling out cookies at two per day per child to pinch pennies. But the human psyche is often a tangle of contradictions. Certainly that was the case with our modern Gladstone as embodied by Robert Philip Hanssen. How else can one explain this example—the attempted conversion of Priscilla Sue Galey, a young woman from the wrong side of the tracks in Columbus, Ohio?

In 1980, Priscilla Sue Galey was a twenty-three-year-old high school dropout who told anyone who would listen that she had been molested by a stepfather at fourteen, married at sixteen, and then divorced at nineteen. She was looking for a fresh start that year. To her, that meant a one-way ticket out of the Buckeye State.

Priscilla had been taking off her clothes for money since she was seventeen. So when a contest was announced that would decide the Ohio "Stripper of the Year" at the Garden Burlesque Theater on North High Street in Columbus, she was among the first to enter. The odds seemed stacked against her. Priscilla was one of ninety-five women competing for the crown, and the competition appeared fierce. Still, she surprised everyone by winning the crown, the sash, and the honor of calling herself Ohio's 1980 Stripper of the Year. Using the title as a calling card, Priscilla headed off to Boston, thinking she was about to begin a glamorous career onstage.

On the East Coast she danced under the names Traci Starr and Misty Dawn at clubs like the Golden Banana in Peabody, Massachusetts. After experiencing several raw New England winters, she drifted southward, winding up in Washington in 1984. Priscilla began dancing at a strip club at 1520 K Street NW called Archibald's, whose two levels and four stages was a step up from the Good Guys. The place advertised itself in the yellow pages as being just "two blocks from the White House" and claimed to be "DC's Premier Gentleman's Club Since 1969." Priscilla took a small suburban apartment in Silver Spring, Maryland, had a series of boyfriends, and tried to enjoy life. After three years at Archibald's she brought a revised act over to a smaller, one-level bar called Joanna's 1819 Club, right off Connecticut Avenue at 1819 M Street NW, then just down the block from the Federal Communications Commission.

At the new place she was a sensation, a businessman's dream. Joanna's opened at 11 A.M. and closed at two in the morning, with Priscilla Sue Galey's shift beginning at four. The mostly married men would drop in after work for an overpriced beer and a look at a nude woman before heading home to their wives in rush-hour traffic. Priscilla's trick was to wear unflattering glasses, a starched blouse, and a pin-striped skirt as if she were a legal assistant who sang in a church choir on Sundays. Then she would boldly stride to the stage and take off every stitch of clothing, fulfilling many an office executive's fantasy.

"I loved stripping. I just loved it," she said. "I'd go up to that stage, take off my glasses, set down my briefcase, and go to work. The guys all saw me as the secretary they worked with or a woman they saw walking down the street."

In the summer of 1990, she met Bob Hanssen at

Joanna's. According to FBI sources, Bob usually attended strip clubs whenever his friend Jack Hoschouer was in Washington. But while Hoschouer was there for a good time, Bob would sometimes preach to the strippers and tell them to quit their job. When he met Priscilla Sue Galey she became one of his special missions.

Bob began the relationship by sending over a ten-dollar bill and an admiring note to Galey after she finished dancing, writing that he didn't think it was possible to ever find that kind of grace and beauty in a place like Joanna's. Priscilla, more used to getting leers than handwritten letters, ran from the back of the club and caught him just as he headed out the door. Bob gave her his FBI business card and asked if she would like to have lunch. Priscilla said yes, gave him her phone number, and their unusual two-year friendship began.

"He said he already had my phone number and address," Priscilla told the *Washington Post*. "He told me he knew I had a clean record but wanted to see if his instincts were right."

Bob claimed he had only been in the club to meet someone who was supposed to give him information. Priscilla recalled their first meeting: "He was dressed in a dark suit, not a hair out of place, not a piece of lint, not a wrinkle. To be honest, I was a little afraid of him at first."

Within days Bob gave Priscilla several thousand dollars in hundred-dollar bills to get her teeth fixed. Just before Christmas that year, he handed her an expensive diamond and sapphire gold necklace.

Priscilla Galey said that although she fell in love with Bob, they were never lovers. Even when she attempted to hug him, he would resist. It was all about bringing her closer to God, she said, though her mother, Linda Harris, would have a different opinion.

"She told me they never got physical or anything," Harris said after seeing Bob's picture and arrest chronicled on a television news program. "It was a fatherly thing. But he

wouldn't have bought her a car if he wasn't getting something out of it. It could be he was trying to recruit her to
help him out later in the spy thing."

If one can fall in love by being showered with material
gifts and cash, Priscilla had to have been head over heels.
Bob was handing over hundred-dollar bills as if shaking
M&M candies out of a just-ripped-open bag. Fine jewelry
and flowers followed, and in 1991 he gave her the car of
her dreams, a used 1985 silver-gray Mercedes-Benz 190E
sedan that he purchased for cash from a car dealer in Alexandria, Virginia, that specialized in imported cars. "When
you drive up in a Mercedes, they won't ask you if you've
been to college" was his reasoning. "They're not going to
ask you anything. They're going to treat you right."

Bob made the gift an event by taking her to lunch at
Jaimalito's, a Mexican restaurant on the Potomac River.
There, over taco salads, he gave her an envelope with several hundred-dollar bills inside, the keys to the Mercedes,
and her own American Express card made out to P. S.
Galey, saying the monthly charges would be sent to his
house and paid by him. Priscilla was ecstatic.

"I went fifty miles out of my way on the way home just
to drive it," she recalled. "I would look out of the apartment
window each day just to make sure it was there. He was
the nicest person on earth. I thought he was my personal
angel."

One time Priscilla asked her angel if he had ever done
anything wrong in his life. Bob thought for a moment and
then revealed to her that he had altered some test scores in
college.

Bob never hid that he was happily married or that he
had several children. He told her he was only there to try
to convince her to leave stripping, find God, and better
herself. At one point, Priscilla said, she tried to please him
by showing up at Saint Catherine's of Siena and attending
a Sunday service. But she pulled into the church parking

lot at the same time as Bonnie and the Hanssen children, and their presence made her lose her nerve.

"He thought I could do much better with my life," she said. "He never criticized me—he just pulled at my heart-strings."

Besides trying to convert her to God, it appears that Bob also tried to play Professor Henry Higgins to her Eliza Doo-little. He would take her to the National Gallery of Art on Constitution Avenue and explain the paintings to her. They would take long walks together, with Bob pitching God as they strolled along, and repeatedly telling her it was the way to a better life. Once, while walking near the White House, he made her trade her stripper-style, white, spiked heels for more presentable blue pumps, which he purchased for her on the spot. "He didn't want me to stand out like a sore thumb," she recalled.

He also tried to impress her with his position at the FBI, taking her to private dining clubs that were reserved for law enforcement officers. She would watch, fascinated, as Bob and others checked their service revolvers at the door. They went to expensive restaurants where she was given a menu printed on parchment that had no prices next to the entrees. He drove the two of them fifty miles out of town to the FBI Training Center at Quantico Marine Base just to give her a personal tour of the facilities. On the way back he drove by his house and pointed out how ideal life was on Talisman Drive.

Thinking the FBI could find anyone, Priscilla once asked Bob to help find her real father, who had deserted the family when she was six. Bob couldn't.

Bob next gave her a $5,000, top-of-the-line laptop computer, which he said had a secret code. When she couldn't crack it or learn to operate the device, he became disappointed.

Was there anything that made you think he might be a spy?

"Sometimes he would mutter German or Russian

phrases, but I never thought he had anything to do with espionage," she said.

There seemed to be no limits as to what Bob was willing to do or how far he would go for her. If she needed money for the rent or a bill that the American Express card wouldn't cover, then out would come Bob's wad of hundred-dollar bills and he would peel off a few and hand them over. Still, Bob was keeping tabs on the amounts he was spending. At one point he asked Priscilla to guess how much he had given her so far, and when she guessed $50,000, he corrected her and said it was more like $80,000.

"She would ask him what he was doing with all that money," her mother, Linda Harris, chortled. "He would always laugh and say, 'I could tell you but then I would have to kill you.' Priscilla kept trying to advance the relationship, but when she tried to reach out to him, he would push her back and tell her he was a family man."

Priscilla's younger sister, Vanessa, flew to Washington and the two of them went to an Aerosmith concert—a rock group definitely not on the list of approved Soviet composers—that August. "My sister didn't have a care in the world," Vanessa remembered of the time. "If she came into a problem, all she had to do was to pick up the phone and he would take care of it."

In April of 1991, Bob asked Priscilla to go to Hong Kong with him, ostensibly so she could develop an appreciation for Asian art. He had told her he was going and she had asked him to bring her back a gift. Instead, he showed up at Joanna's and walked her over to a travel agency, where she was handed a reserved plane ticket. When he learned she didn't have a passport, he pulled some strings and she had the document within hours, even though she couldn't find her birth certificate. According to Priscilla, they flew to Hong Kong on separate planes, stayed in separate rooms, and met for breakfast and again at dinner.

They would talk about their disparate lives and how they had turned out so differently.

In the Asian metropolis she tried again to make a pass at him, but he refused her advances. One night after dinner she finally got Bob up to dance. It was at a piano bar, and according to Priscilla, the tune was his favorite song, the pop standard "As Time Goes By." The tune was from *Casablanca,* the classic movie of intrigue and espionage that starred Humphrey Bogart and Ingrid Bergman.

"I explored all day and partied all night," she recalled, reveling in the memory of the good times. But after the two-week trip to Asia their relationship went sour. Bob found out she had a photo of him taken at night in Hong Kong. He grabbed it and ripped the snapshot in half.

After returning, Bob promised to take her to France. "We were going to see something called the incorrupt saint and there was possibly a position," Priscilla told Larry King on his CNN show. (An incorrupt saint in the Catholic faith is one whose body does not decay after death, despite not being embalmed.)

Of course, the best-known incorrupt saint in France is Bonnie's namesake, Bernadette. The corresponding miracle with which she is associated are the many apparitions of the Virgin Mary she saw at Lourdes. Was Bob planning to have Priscilla healed of her loose behavior through prayer and holy water at this legendary destination? Or was he going to get her a job serving the thousands of Catholics who annually made pilgrimages to the Lourdes shrine? Perhaps he was simply going to recall the Virgin Mary's message to the long-suffering Bernadette and repeat it to Priscilla there: "I do not promise to make you happy in this world, but in the next."

When a former lover from Columbus telephoned her in Washington and implored her to come home to be with him, Priscilla did so, but neglected to tell Bob she was leaving town. Back home, she began using crack cocaine and using the KGB's money to pay for the drug. She returned to Washington a final time, but when she drove back to Columbus for the Christmas holidays in 1991, she began smoking crack again and became addicted. It was the beginning of the end. Bob said he was planning for her to accompany him to Paris in 1992 and kept promising to help her get a proper job. Instead their relationship became ugly.

During the Easter holidays of 1992, it ended. Priscilla had used the American Express card to buy cigarettes for herself and dresses for her nieces. Bob, who had told her the card was only to be used for gas and car repairs, suddenly took umbrage at the extra spending. A week later he drove out to Columbus just to retrieve the card. Priscilla's mom remembers meeting him.

"He had an air about him," she told *USA Today*. "He acted like he was too good for people like us."

A year later when Priscilla was arrested on drug charges, her mother called Bob on his direct line at the FBI. By now he wanted nothing to do with them.

"He said that Priscilla had made her bed, and now she had to lay in it," said her mother. "He completely turned away from her, like she never existed."

The following years were not good to Priscilla. She began working as a streetwalker on West Broad Street in Columbus to pay for her crack habit and eventually wound up in a group house with eight others. She wrecked the Mercedes by running a light and driving it into a truck, pawned the laptop, sold the jewelry, was convicted several times for prostitution, and in 1999 did a year of hard time in an Ohio state prison for "complicity to aggravated trafficking," or in plain English, being an assistant to a drug dealer. By the year 2000, she was often disappearing for various lengths of time to live in abandoned houses where men paid her for sexual favors with drugs. The bottom came just before Bob was apprehended. A dog chewed up her upper plate of false teeth while she was passed out from an all-nighter.

"Then we saw him on the news being arrested," her mother recalled. "Me and Priscilla about fell off our chairs. We knew it would only be a matter of time before the FBI came looking for us."

The Bureau did, interrogating Priscilla in Columbus at first, then flying her to Washington to appear before a federal grand jury. Since then Priscilla has asked herself many times what Bob may really have been seeking.

"He had to have wanted me for something," she wonders. "He wanted to see how I handled myself. He wanted to see if he could trust me. I trusted him completely, and if he had asked me to do anything, I would have." She now claims that Bob was probably grooming her to help him in his espionage work and says she would have refused. She talked about that subject in somewhat hysterical terms to *The Columbus Dispatch.*

"I could have been killed," she said. "If I ever knew any secrets, they could have got rid of me."

Her friends who live with her in a vinyl-sided group house riddled with bullet marks from drive-by shootings agree with her summation. They say that she should never have gone public with her story. "If he did what they say he did, he's got friends everywhere," said Francis Gannon, one of the residents. "Priscilla should have kept her mouth shut."

Priscilla Sue Galey's only joy in life by the summer of 2001 was a three-year-old son, Joshua, born to her and a boyfriend, a former marine named Sam Bryant. Legally, her mother has custody, gaining the guardianship when her daughter went off to prison, though Priscilla sees the toddler as often as she can. When she was asked if she knew that Joshua was the name of the first spy mentioned in the Bible, she said she didn't.

Bob Hanssen's friend Paul Moore thinks that his behavior with Priscilla Sue Galey is consistent with his personality. In an interview with ABC News Moore said, "Bob believed that you should do good. He believed that you should try to give people a nudge to go in the right direction if you possibly could. Those of us who saw him saw a very good person."

If Priscilla Sue winds up writing a book about her experience—and she says she will—Moore believes it won't be about sex. That's not what Bob was about, Moore claimed, saying, "It's much more believable to think of the young lady eventually writing a memoir about, say, the spy who didn't love me than the opposite. Bob just believed—he had a good talent for cutting to the bone of an issue. He could, with a few words, make you see that what you were doing was not the best thing for you to be doing and that you should be doing something else.

"I don't know specifically, but knowing Bob—and we go back twenty years—he probably went in [the strip club] with the purpose of seeing whether anybody would talk to him and calling their attention that this was probably not the kind of thing that God intended for her to be doing.

"He was as sincere a spy as he was a Christian. He did more damage than he needed to, gave the Russians more than he had to, and earned the money. He was overperforming, and he also overperformed in his day job. He had the same work ethic for both."

B's work ethic for his KGB handlers had yet to falter. On October 17, 1989, he sent his sixteenth computer disk to the KGB, this time with a new return address that read "G. Robertson, 1101 Kingston Ct., Houston, TX," but mailed with a postmark from close to his home. On Monday, October 23, an exchange was carried out, the first ever from ELLIS or Foxstone Park, just blocks from Talisman Drive. B enclosed the same disk with an update and additional classified information. The package from the KGB contained $55,000 in cash and a letter advising him that another $50,000 had been deposited into his Moscow bank account. But the double agent never signaled that he received the money, and the KGB retrieved the package only to redeposit the cash and the letter on Halloween night. There was another thank-you letter from KGB chairman Vladimir Kryuchkov, who put in a pitch for what items he personally needed on U.S. intelligence activities against the Soviet Union.

Nobody ever told Kryuchkov that so many of the KGB's hundred-dollar bills might soon be going to maintain a stripper's lavish lifestyle; or that some of the money would be spent for crack cocaine on some of the meanest streets in Columbus, Ohio. If told, he might have shipped the informant off to the Gulag for lying against the state.

ELEVEN

An Unusual Unraveling

It might seem a bit perverse that Bob Hanssen scheduled a dead drop exchange on a holiday like Christmas Day, especially when the temperature was in the teens, with snow and ice covering the roads. But B was a creature of habit and it *was* a Monday. As for the Soviets, well, they were godless communists, so why should they care? Besides, who would be hanging out in the sea of white that was Idylwood Park and named BOB, perhaps just for him, on December 25, 1989?

Their agent had a heck of a holiday present for the KGB that day. On the seventeenth computer disk were several documents, including an important piece of intelligence that had just been published the month before. The paper was titled *The Soviet System in Crisis: Prospects for the Next Two Years*. The research was so new that some of the Joint Chiefs of Staff at the Pentagon had yet to read it. The paper had a long list of warnings: SECRET NOFORN NOCONTRACT and WNINTEL, including the phrase "Unauthorized Disclosure Subject to Criminal Sanctions." B wrote a holiday bread-and-butter note that complimented the KGB on its efficiency and told about recent FBI efforts to recruit several KGB intelligence officers. He also gave information on three FBI sources within the KGB, and four recent defectors. Finally, he offered an update on the latest moves by the FBI in the Bloch-Gikman affair.

B's own package included a timely Christmas greeting from the KGB and $38,000 in cash. The Soviets said the money was for the two diamonds he had returned and compensation for the work period between October 16 and 23. The Soviets had by now jumped into the computer age with zeal as their new parcel contained two disks, trumping Bob's single offering.

The next exchange was on Monday, March 5, 1990, this time at Eakin Park/CHARLIE. Considering this was B's eighteenth computer disk, one might think he had given his handlers virtually every secret available to him. Again, he did not disappoint. There was classified information on four Soviet nationals—one a Soviet-embassy employee, one Soviet illegal, and two KGB defectors—all from either FBI or CIA sources. B also supplied a profile of an NSA employee and the sensitive department where he worked. Perhaps the best document—which again was so fresh the ink may still have been wet—dated February 1990, was titled *Soviet Armed Forces and Strategic Nuclear Capabilities for the 1990s.*

B received $40,000 in cash, and a KGB computer disk. On the disk he was asked to analyze and report on some of the most recent materials they had received from him.

It would be nice to report that life in the Hanssen household had become relatively stress-free because of Bob Hanssen's ill-gotten prosperity during the early 1990s. He spent little of the money on his family—particularly on creature comforts—instead using a large chunk of the KGB's cash to save wayward strippers. Both parents seemed to be frazzled much of the time. Picture Bonnie Hanssen, deservedly called a saint by her friends, driving her large brood from school to school in an old minivan. Some of them were Opus Dei–affiliated institutions that were more than thirty miles away. Others, like Our Lady of Good Counsel, where four of the Hanssen children attended elementary school, were much closer. Then there was the housework and the cooking. She got no help from Bob or the children. How frazzled? County court records show she received five traffic tickets between 1992 and 1996, all minor, and only two for speeding. Bob received a couple, even though he was a law enforcement officer, and the Hanssen children got their share, though one expects that from teens.

Still, their children were turning out well. Grounded with a life that revolved around family, church, and Opus Dei, they were exceptional by most people's standards. Jane, the Hanssens' eldest, went off to nearby George Mason University and, at a Young Republican mixer, met and eventually married a young man named Richard Trimber. By the end of the century they would have several children.

Bob and Bonnie's second daughter, Susan Elizabeth, decided to become an Opus Dei numerary and stay celibate. She became the Hanssen family scholar. In 1991 she made her way to the national high school debate finals of the Catholic Forensic League. Sue then won a scholarship to Boston University, attending the school while living off campus at an Opus Dei center. In 1996, she was named the most outstanding student among the school's history majors. Sue then pursued her master's degree at Rice University while teaching part-time as a graduate assistant at the University of Dallas, a conservative Catholic school.

In 1999, Sue won a Wagoner Scholarship, a $15,000 grant to be used for research abroad. She decided to go to England to study the writings of G. K. Chesterton, a prolific British author and philosopher in the early part of the twentieth century. It was an interesting choice. Gilbert K. Chesterton, like Bob, had converted from Protestantism to Catholicism after becoming an adult. Besides his philosophical musings, he wrote fifty books featuring a Roman Catholic cleric, Father Brown. Chesterton's priest was a detective who tried to understand the psychology of crime.

This sample of Chesterton's thought, written in 1901, could easily have been written by Bob Hanssen:

> The vast mass of humanity, with their vast mass of idle books and idle words, have never doubted and never will doubt that courage is splendid, that fidelity is noble, that distressed ladies should be rescued, and vanquished enemies spared. There are a large number of cultivated persons who doubt these maxims of daily life, just as there are a large number of persons who believe they are the Prince of Wales; and I am told that both classes of people are entertaining conversationalists.

The two eldest Hanssen males have also made their parents proud. John, better known as Jack, graduated from the College of William and Mary in Virginia and was in the second year of law school at Notre Dame when his father was arrested. He is an editor of its law journal and has interned summers at the Washington conservative think tank, the Heritage Foundation. Mark Hanssen was a political science major at the University of Dallas in 2001, attending the school with the son of Mark Wauck, the other FBI agent in the family. Only the two younger Hanssen children, Greg and Lisa, were still living at home when their father was captured.

Bonnie was no slouch in the Catholic education field despite her many stay-at-home-mom duties. She picked up the Wauck family torch of translating or writing religious tomes. In her case, she recorded a tape on wholesome activities in which Catholics can participate with their family. It is still sold commercially over the Internet and in some Catholic bookstores. She had also begun teaching religion at Oakcrest part-time to defray the children's tuition costs.

On paper, Bob and Bonnie appeared to be struggling. Records show they took out a second mortgage on their house in 1992 and received $156,000. The house was refinanced again a year later, and in 1996, Bob asked for and got a $40,000 secured loan. As late as the year 2000, he borrowed $110,000 on the house and took out a $35,000 line of credit. But when a son's car broke down because the teen had forgotten to put oil in the engine, it would be Roy and Fran Wauck who loaned the youngster $3,000.

All this could be considered a perfect cover. Any financial check by the FBI would have shown the Hanssens to be anything but wealthy. What was the $600,000 in cash that the FBI says Bob received from the Russians between 1985 and his arrest worth anyway? Over fifteen years it averaged a tax-free $40,000 per annum. That may have been enough of a subsidy to pay for the children's education and maybe even a fling at reforming a stripper or two, but it was far from a princely sum.

Bob Hanssen should rightly have been proud of his wife and children. He must also have been pleased with the profuse praise coming his way from the top levels at the KGB. In truth, he was likely tied in knots on the inside. Bob knew more than anyone that arrest and shame were always one wrong move away. Did he eventually come unglued?

He was in an automobile accident on Wisconsin Avenue, near the Russian embassy, in the early 1990s where he fractured an elbow and for a while had to be driven to work by his friend Paul Moore. And a 1993 assault incident where he attacked Kimberly D. Lichtenberg outside his office also seems uncharacteristic. Lichtenberg disagrees. Bob Hanssen was her boss, she says, but also a misogynist of the first rank, out to cop an uninvited feel on the sly. Perhaps the stress of serving two different masters—the opposite of his wish to be master of two worlds—was getting to him.

At 3 P.M. on February 5, 1993, Kimberly Lichtenberg was at her desk in the counterintelligence section at FBI headquarters. Her title was intelligence assistant, and she had been with the FBI since 1987, joining the Bureau just after high school. Bob Hanssen was her immediate superior, or in FBI parlance, her unit chief.

Bob called Kim into his fourth-floor office for a quick meeting that afternoon without any warning. The subject seemed to be petty—office gossip that revolved around a possible termination. Besides Kim, the unit's typist, Nicole Swans, and the unit's secretary, Diane Eckert, were also ordered in. Bob began by asking Lichtenberg if she had told Swans that he was going to fire Swans if her job performance didn't improve. Lichtenberg claimed she had never made such a statement, and Swans backed her up.

Bob seemed perplexed. He turned, looked at Eckert, and said, "But you told me that Kim said that to Nicole."

Eckert denied it: "I never said that to you."

Then in a heated discussion between Bob and Diane Eckert, Bob said to her, "I'm sick of you coming in to me with stories about people in the office."

According to Kim Lichtenberg, bickering continued between Bob and Eckert. Believing she was no longer needed, and knowing her car pool left exactly at 4 P.M., Kim went back to her cubicle to secure her desk as FBI procedures dictated. Waiting for Kim in her space was a young woman from another unit, Candy Curtis. Kim began to say hello to her friend, but suddenly Bob's hand was on Kim's shoulder and he was saying, "I'm your unit chief, and you'll do what I say. I want you back in the meeting."

Then, according to Kim Lichtenberg's sworn testimony, Bob began shaking her back and forth. The slim, five-foot-seven-inch, 120-pound blonde lost her balance and fell to the floor and, as she did, yelled out, "Candy, help me!"

Upon seeing the witness to the violence, Bob's expression changed from anger to surprise, and he commented about Lichtenberg's insubordination. Still, according to witnesses, he did not stop but continued shaking her as she lay on the ground. He then pulled her along the floor back to his office. When he finally let her up, Lichtenberg punched him in the chest to break free and, when she was successful, bolted for the exit with Candy Curtis.

"I told him I had to go home," she said in a written statement. "He twirled me around and I fell to the ground. He just dragged me along the ground back towards his office."

Both Lichtenberg and Curtis went to Bob's boss, Nicholas J. Walsh, and told him of the incident. Walsh went to Bob's office and instructed him to stay inside while Lichtenberg secured her desk and gathered her belongings.

Instead of going home, Lichtenberg went to her parents' house in Glen Burnie, Maryland. When her husband, Michael, arrived and she told him her arm still hurt, he suggested they go to nearby North Arundel Hospital to see if anything was broken. There wasn't, but the doctors treated a bruise on her face and several on her arm.

The next day, she went to the D.C. Police Department and tried to swear out a complaint. Within hours, her FBI supervisors had her in a meeting saying, "We'll handle this. It's an internal matter."

In her sworn statement to Richard Spicer and Garrett Davis, the investigating agents assigned to the case, she complained of several other incidents and named people who she said had observed them. She also stated that she had recently sent a memo to Bob asking for a review for a recent denial that her pay grade be raised from a GS-8 to a GS-9. This implied that Bob might be responsible for blocking it, even though her most recent performance appraisal rating (PAR in government speak) was "exceptional."

She reported that Bob had come up to her before to grab and shake her, with one event occurring just a few days before the incident. When he did these things, she claimed, he would say things like "I'm just trying to shake you up this morning." Lichtenberg told the investigators that Bob had done the "shaking thing" at another time when an FBI agent, Frank Figluisi, was present. She also said that Bob had done the same to another FBI employee, Betsy Carroll, and had "touched her in ways which made her uncomfortable."

"Unit Chief Hanssen also had a habit of walking up to my desk and standing and just staring at me," her affidavit read. "The way he stands and just stares makes me very uncomfortable. When I ask him what he wants or if I can help him, he just says 'No' and walks away. In talking to some other unit members I have found that he does the same thing to them, including Betsy Carroll.

"Betsy and I have talked about what we should do because we don't like it being done to us, but we are also concerned that this man is our Unit Chief and if we complain or make a comment about it, he is in a position to take punitive administrative action against us as revenge."

The FBI suspended Bob Hanssen for five days without salary. Kim Lichtenberg believes Bonnie Hanssen may never have known about the disciplinary action. A year later the FBI reprimanded Kim with a letter of censure. The memo from the Bureau said that although Bob was wrong, she had provoked him by leaving the meeting.

"I never had anyone make me feel like he made me feel," she said after his arrest in February. "He was creepy. He tried to belittle women and would rub up against them just to get cheap thrills."

After the FBI action against Bob, Kim Lichtenberg filed a civil action against him asking for a total of $1,360,000. The suit alleged assault and battery, gross negligence, intentional infliction of emotional distress, false imprisonment, defamation of character, and loss of consortium with her husband, Michael. She claimed that she had undergone psychological counseling in order to recover. Part of her suit charged that "the Defendant grabbed K. Lichtenberg's left arm, wrenching her back and forth, and, while verbally abusing her, continued to wrench her arm until she lost her balance and fell to the floor. The Defendant continued to assault and physically batter K. Lichtenberg about her head, body and limbs, dragging her across the floor for a great distance before the Plaintiff was able to free herself from his grasp and regain her footing. Upon her escape, the Defendant continued to violently and maliciously abuse K. Lichtenberg verbally, in front of her fellow employees, all without due care, or any provocation or action on the part of K. Lichtenberg."

Years later, when she saw Bob Hanssen's grinning face on the evening news, she at first thought that the picture was a fabrication. "All those years, I don't think I ever saw him smile," she said.

The government defended Bob in the action by using U.S. Attorney Eric Holder, who would soon be appointed assistant U.S. attorney general under Janet Reno. That the FBI would use such a high-powered lawyer to defend such a minor infraction offers evidence of what Lichtenberg said was then "a little boy's club."

"Everyone knew that Dr. Death was strange," Kim said, "but nobody ever did anything about him. He was always hacking into someone's computer hard drive and then pointing out how easy it was to get their classified information. I feel badly that nobody figured it out. There was a lot of reasons to look into Bob Hanssen."

According to Kim Litchenberg, her suit was dismissed when her original attorney, who had been hired on a contingency basis, failed to appear in court. She still is not sure why.

"Hanssen thought, how dare I disobey him," she said. "That was the worst thing I could have done in his mind."

On Monday, May 7, 1990, Bob carried out a dead drop exchange at the new DORIS site. B enclosed his nineteenth computer disk and 232 pages of hard copy, which included addenda to the highly classified document he had given them on August 7, 1989. He also disclosed that he would be traveling a lot overseas during the next year and discussed ways for them to stay in touch. The KGB's package contained $35,000 in hundred-dollar bills and a computer disk. The disk identified another new dead drop site they wanted to use, Lewinsville Park in McLean, Virginia, which, audaciously, was about eight blocks from the entrance to CIA headquarters. They named the site FLO and enclosed the usual grocery list of wants and needs. There was also a letter, which read in part:

Dear Friend:
We attach some information requests which we ask your kind assistance for. We are very cautious about using your info and materials so that none of our actions in no way causes *[sic]* no harm to your security. With this on our mind we are asking that sensitive materials and information (especially hot and demanding some action) be accompanied by some sort of your comments or some guidance on how we may or may not use it with regard to your security.
We wish you good luck and enclose $35,000.
Thank you.

Sincerely,
Your friends.

That same May, Bob Hanssen was promoted. He left the Intelligence Division's Soviet Analytical Unit and was assigned to the FBI's Inspection Staff. In his new position he flew to world capitals like Hong Kong and Paris to inspect FBI legal attaché offices that were inside major embassies. On May 21, the KGB loaded the ELLIS dead drop site at Foxstone Park with two computer disks. One of them contained a farewell letter that appeared to be a response to B's written criticism of the decaying Soviet empire:

Dear Friend:
Congratulations on your promotion. We wish you all the very best in your life and career.
We appreciate your sympathy for some difficulties people face—your friendship and understanding are

very important to us. Of course, you are right, no system is perfect and we do understand this.

Speaking about the systems. We don't see any problem for the system of our future communications in regard to this new circumstances of yours. Though we can't but regret that our contacts may be not so regular as before, like you said.

We believe our current commo plan—though neither perfect—covers ruther [sic] flexibly your needs: You may have a contact with us anytime you want after staying away as long as you have to. So, do your new job, make your trips, take your time. The commo plan we have will still be working. We'll keep covering the active call out signal site no matter how long it's needed. And we'll be in a ready-to-go mode to come over to the drop next in turn whenever you are ready: that is when you are back home and decide to communicate. All you'll have to do is to put your call out signal, just as now. And you have two address to use to recontact us only if the signal sites for some reason don't work or can't be used. . . . But in any case be sure: You may have a contact anytime because the active call out site is always covered according to the schedule no matter how long you've been away.
Thank you and good luck.

Sincerely, your friends.

The KGB requested that their spy "give us some good leads to possible recruitments among interesting people in the right places." They also asked B for information about a Soviet embassy employee whom he had previously identified as an FBI recruitment-in-place and who they thought was about to defect.

PART THREE

In Philby's own eyes, he was working for a shape of things to come from which his country would benefit.

Like many Catholics who, in the reign of Elizabeth, worked for the victory of Spain, Philby has a chilling certainty in the correctness of his judgement, the logical fanaticism of a man who, having found a faith, is not going to lose it because of the injustices or cruelties inflicted by erring human instruments. How many a kindly Catholic must have endured the long bad days of the Inquisition with this hope of the future as a riding anchor.

—FROM GRAHAM GREENE'S
INTRODUCTION TO
KIM PHILBY'S
My Silent War

TWELVE

Time Is Flying As a Poet Said

One of the many conundrums surrounding the Robert Hanssen case and debated long after his arrest was the polygraph question. Why hadn't he taken a lie detector test—*ever*—during his twenty-five years with the Bureau? And if he had, would he have been able to beat the exam?

William J. Casey, the controversial, larger-than-life director of the CIA between 1981 and 1987 was fond of saying that anyone could beat a polygraph machine. His method was simple. "Take a Valium and tighten your sphincter," he advised.

Were it so simple. A comprehensive polygraph test in the twenty-first century often begins with a urine sample to detect any drugs that might slow down a body's reactions. A competent licensed polygraph examiner who has the right questions in front of him can administer a test with between 85 and 90 percent accuracy. But that means at least one out of ten who are judged liars may have been telling the truth. This is one reason why the results from polygraph exams are generally not admissible in court.

As expected, proponents of the craft have a different view. In April of 2001, the U.S. Senate Judiciary Committee got an earful from both sides as its members pondered an expanded government use of polygraph tests following Bob's arrest.

"It is my opinion that in a security-screening polygraph, Robert Hanssen would have reacted with greater than ninety-nine percent certainty," Richard Keifer, a past president of the American Polygraph Association told the senators. His statement that Bob Hanssen would have had a less than 1 percent chance of beating the machine was immediately refuted.

"In order to discover if another Robert Philip Hanssen exists among its ranks, the federal government may as well put its faith in Wonder Woman's magic lasso than to rely on the accuracy of the polygraph," said Mark Zaid, an attorney who was in the midst of suing both the FBI and the Secret Service for what he claimed were faulty preemployment polygraph programs.

"The fact of the matter is that the use of polygraphs by the federal government consistently leads to false accusations of wrongdoing against innocent persons. Moreover, the device routinely fails to identify those individuals who truly are committing criminal acts," Zaid testified.

Most experts believe that Bob Hanssen likely knew every trick there was to cheat a polygraph machine and had probably learned them from the FBI itself in one of its counterintelligence classes. A University of Minnesota psychology professor, William Iacono, told the senators that Bob would have had no problem beating a lie detector: "Someone who is clever enough to be a spy should be clever enough to learn the simple techniques that beat a polygraph."

The government uses other methods to measure truthfulness. Other intelligence agencies have forced outside contractors not only to take the so-called truth serum, sodium Pentothal—an anesthetic that puts one into a twilight state—but also after the questioning has informed them that they will be kept under spot surveillance by an outside team during their entire employment. Hypnosis has also been used. But the polygraph—which the late Senator Sam J. Ervin called "twentieth-century witchcraft"—is the instrument of choice in government agencies.

A polygraph exam sounds simple at first. The machine begins by measuring respiration at two points: on the upper chest, and on the abdomen. The movements associated with breathing are recorded so that the rate and depth of inhalation and expiration can be measured. The machine also measures skin conductance or galvanic skin response. Electrodes connected to the fingertips or the palm of the hand indicate changes in sweat-gland activity. The device also measures increases in blood pressure and the heart rate. Some more sophisticated machines have what is known as a plethysmograph, which measures blood-supply changes in the skin that occur as vessels in the fingers constrict because of stimulation. The polygraph expert attempts to interpret all of these readings while asking questions.

The validity of the test depends on the skill of the examiner. In the final analysis, the result of the test is only the opinion of the person giving the exam.

Lie detector tests of varying accuracies date back to before the birth of Christ. In ancient Chinese dynasties, a handful of dry rice would be inserted into a man's mouth. He was then asked to spit it out. If any of the rice stuck to his tongue, he was thought to be lying.

William Marston, a Harvard psychologist, invented the modern lie detector machine in the 1920s. It was at first embraced, then rejected, by the FBI. The genesis for the resistance can be traced to J. Edgar Hoover. In the 1930s, a kidnapping suspect in Florida was misidentified because of a faulty polygraph exam, and Hoover was embarrassed. After that, Hoover all but prohibited the device, using it only on rare occasions. His successors talked about using the machine more widely, particularly William Webster, who advocated using it on employees every five years. But Webster's plan was never implemented. Only in March of

1994, under Louis Freeh, did the Bureau begin to routinely test new applicants, regardless of the sensitivity or the lack of importance in the job description. But that was for new-comers. The Bureau was largely a gentlemen's club and the FBI was not about to humiliate or embarrass its older members by having them submit to anything like a lie detector exam, no matter what the CIA or the Pentagon was doing.

Most estimates placed the failure rate among FBI job seekers taking the polygraph at 20–40 percent. A lot of questions centered around the use of drugs, particularly marijuana. Many applicants denied ever using drugs and thus failed the test. Had they only known. The FBI policy for new applicants was not to disqualify applicants who had smoked marijuana, providing the use had been more than three years ago and not more than fifteen times in total. Even if one had experimented with harder drugs, such as cocaine or heroin, it was still possible to be welcomed into the new "not your FBI, J. Edgar," providing one had quit ten or more years ago and had only used the substance on five or fewer occasions.

Aldrich Ames himself has offered advice on how to pass a polygraph: "Confidence is what does it. Confidence and a friendly relationship with the examiner. You need rapport, where you smile and you make him think that you like him."

Following the arrest of Ames, the CIA beefed up its polygraph examinations. This resulted in some three hundred employees failing the tests although the agency often had no other evidence of wrongdoing. They were said to be in "poly hell," a purgatory from which there was no return—the person's career was effectively over. New CIA policies also dictated that a four-page financial disclosure form be filled out. Perhaps because of the many CIA employees in limbo, and a belief that Bureau men were purer than those of the CIA, Freeh had made only token changes—the testing of raw applicants being the most visible.

Freeh was against polygraph tests. He believed them to be 86 percent accurate. "Removing someone from a position based on a polygraph can ruin a career, even if the test turns out to be a false positive," he told a Chamber of Commerce audience just days after Bob Hanssen was arrested. He reversed that position days later. It was disclosed that Bob had never taken a polygraph exam in twenty-five years with the Bureau, despite the sensitivity of his various counterintelligence positions. Now, all bets were off.

Weeks after Bob was accused of passing at least six thousand pages of classified materials to Moscow, the Bureau began testing five hundred of its own people, largely drawn from the counterintelligence ranks. Freeh had changed his mind—or maybe it was changed for him. He was one of the first to volunteer to take one, saying through a spokesman that he "always included himself in whatever policies applied to FBI employees." His examination was unnecessary. Weeks later he would resign, one of the first domestic casualties in the Robert Hanssen case.

Bob Hanssen may have been buzzing around both the nation and the world inspecting field offices and making sure they were safe and secure, but he couldn't stay away from his KGB handlers. B found time to mail out the twentieth computer disk to them in August 1990 and told them to fill the FLO dead drop site in Lewinsville Park on September 3. The KGB loaded it on that date with $40,000 in cash and a thank-you message that said the information he had provided on "political issues of interest . . . were reported to the very top." B wrote back on his twenty-first computer disk and told them the money was "too generous." He also gave up the identity of a Soviet citizen who was working for the FBI and a dangle operation the FBI was starting against the KGB. (A dangle is a double-agent operation where one spy agency sends one of its own to meet with a rival spy agency under seemingly innocent circumstances in order to gain insight into their inner workings.) B said he would be ready for a new exchange in February of 1991.

On Monday, February 18, the KGB left B $10,000 cash at the CHARLIE dead drop site in Eakin Park. There was also a computer disk that named a new site the Soviets called GRACE—the first one in Washington. The exchange point was under a footbridge in Rock Creek Park, the long, snakelike greenway that separated the rich from the poor in the nation's capital. Besides the usual long list of needs and wants, the Russians scheduled an April exchange at DORIS or the park next to Canterbury Woods in Northern Virginia.

On Monday, April 15, 1991—Bob must had paid his taxes early—the KGB picked up B's twenty-second computer disk, which filled a number of wants the KGB had specified. One prime piece of information was that the NSA was currently reading the entire diplomatic communications of a nation allied with the Soviet Union. B's package contained $10,000 and a melancholy note. The KGB, as clued in on political matters as anyone, doubtlessly knew that Mikhail Gorbachev was about to dissolve the Soviet Union and that their lives could dramatically change.

Dear Friend:
Time is flying. As a poet said:

> What's our life.
> If full of care
> You have no time
> To stop and stare?

You've managed to slow down the speed of your running life to send us a message. And we appreciate it. We hope you're ok and your family is fine too. We are sure you're doing great at your job. As before, we'll keep staying alert to respond to any call from you whenever you need it.

We acknowledge receiving one disk through CHARLIE. One disk of mystery and intrigue. Thank you.

Not much of a business letter this time. Just informalities. We considered site-9 cancelled. And we are sure you remember: our next contact is due at ELLIS.

Frankly we are looking forward to JUNE. Every new season brings new expectations.

Enclosed in our today's package please find $10,000. Thank you for your friendship and help.

We attach some information requests. We hope you'll be able to assist us on them.

Take care and good luck.

Sincerely,
Your friends.

Aware of what was going on in their own disintegrating nation, the KGB included among its usual inventory of wishes a request for U.S. intelligence plans on how America might respond to domestic turmoil in the Soviet Union.

On Monday, July 15, 1991, B and the KGB carried out another exchange at ELLIS, or Foxstone Park. Bob gave them his twenty-third computer disk and 284 pages of material. Bob—who was in the midst of his strange infatuation with Priscilla Sue Galey—seemed almost breathless, as if he were a teenager returning home late from a date. "I returned, grabbed the first thing I could lay my hands on," their double agent wrote, a statement that said volumes about FBI security.

"I was in a hurry so that you would not worry, because June has passed, they held me there longer. I have at least five years until retirement so maybe I will hang in there longer," he reported. B's package contained a thick pile of documents, everything from nuclear and missile proliferation secrets to a joint FBI-CIA operation. Grabbing things off the desk on the fly was profitable. The KGB's package contained $12,000 in hundred-dollar bills and a computer disk with a letter. Their message seemed to imply that Bob thought some of the classified materials he was giving them were too complex. The disc also contained the usual—a roster of wants and needs, and a communication that read in part:

Dear friend:

Acknowledging the disk and materials ... received through DORIS we also acknowledge again your superb sense of humor and your sharp-as-a-razor mind. We highly appreciate both.

Don't worry. We will not steam out incorrect conclusions from your materials. Actually, your information grately *[sic]* assisted us in seeing more clearly many issues and we are not ashamed to correct our notions if we have some. So, thank you for your help. But if some of our requests seem a bit strange to you, please try to believe us there were sufficient reasons to put them and that what we wanted was to sort them out with your help.

In regards to our "memo" on security. Just one more remark. If our natural wish to capitalize on your information confronts in any way your security interests we definitely cut down our thirst for profit and choose your security. The same goes with any other aspect of your case. That's why we say your security goes first.

Sincerely,
your friends.

P.S. Enclosed in the package please find $12,000.

A month later, on Monday, August 19, a FLO exchange in Lewinsville Park was made. B's twenty-fourth computer disk was proffered, on which he furnished a wide variety of intelligence documents. With his eye on the current upheaval in the Soviet Union—the failed coup against Mikhail Gorbachev would take place in just three days—the double agent lectured the Soviets on how they might benefit from studying the history of Chicago under Mayor Richard J. Daley. The tough, sometimes dictatorial Catholic mayor had ruled Chicago all of Bob Hanssen's adult life when he lived there—between 1955 and 1976—and would have continued longer had he not died while serving in office.

In return for this advice on Chicago politics and other national matters, the KGB enclosed $20,000. They scheduled the next drop at GRACE.

Louis Freeh had survived eight years as head of the FBI because he was an astute politician. Turning against both President William Jefferson Clinton and Attorney General Janet Reno on the issue of campaign finance contributions long before Clinton's term was up had made him a darling of the Republican right. He became one of the few conservatives in King William's court. When George W. Bush was elected, Freeh was allowed to stay on, with nearly three years of his ten-year term remaining.

The Clinton years had been tumultuous. They had begun with shoot-outs in rural parts of Texas and Idaho—Waco, Ruby Ridge—that had resulted in deaths of both government men and, in the case of Waco, twenty-four innocent children. The Bureau had covered up its misconduct in the militia standoff and later had to admit to designing the game plan that had led to the immolation of the Branch Davidian families. Those two events served as Gulf War veteran Timothy McVeigh's excuse for the explosive murders of 168 people—ranging from infants to elderly adults—in a federal building in Oklahoma City.

The blame for all of these debacles had largely fallen on Janet Reno's shoulders. Freeh hadn't been aboard during Ruby Ridge or Waco, though he had tried to make the man responsible for them, Larry Potts, his deputy. Freeh was too suave, the Bureau too deified, and Reno too willing to take the blame for any congressional fingers to be wagged in Louis Freeh's direction for anything.

Still, the missteps kept piling up. The bombing at the 1996 Atlanta Olympics found the FBI prematurely pointing at a pudgy security guard named Richard Jewell. He had at first been investigated via a corny con job in which the FBI invited him to help make an FBI training video. Freeh then directly ordered Jewell's interrogators to read him his Miranda rights even though there was as yet no evidence or reason to indict him. Jewell wouldn't speak to the FBI after that. He was eventually cleared and then made millions of dollars suing the media who had implicated him in the crime based on some bad FBI news leaks.

That same year, a TWA passenger jet had seemingly blown up off the coast of Long Island, killing 230 passengers bound for Paris. The Bureau pushed the National Transportation Safety Board out of the way and then botched the investigation. The G-men spread the word that the explosion resulted from a terrorist bomb. It hadn't. In 1997, the much praised FBI lab was accused of sloppiness and the mishandling of evidence. A government report confirmed the charges. Next came the strange case of Wen Ho Lee, a Taiwan-born scientist who had immigrated to the United States in 1965 and had become a naturalized citizen. The FBI filed fifty-nine felony charges against Lee, all related to their belief he had stolen nuclear warhead secrets from the Los Alamos laboratory in New Mexico.

As with Felix Bloch, on its face it appeared the Bureau had a substantial case against Lee. The FBI had investigated him off and on since 1982. As with Bloch, they had been alerted when they had overheard him on a tapped telephone line speaking to another Taiwanese American whom the FBI already suspected of passing neutron bomb secrets to Beijing. Lee at first denied he had ever spoken to the suspect or even knew him. The Bureau had to present him with the recorded evidence before he admitted he had lied to them. He then agreed to cooperate with the Bureau in a sting operation against the suspect. After he did so, the Bureau ended the affair without prosecuting Lee.

During both 1986 and 1988, Lee traveled to mainland China and visited Beijing's nuclear weapons lab, all under U.S. sponsorship. But by 1993, it appeared he was about to be laid off as part of a government reduction-in-force movement in federal offices everywhere that marked the end of the Cold War. Lee began copying classified material from his computer and wound up taking home ten of the tapes. He would later claim he copied them in case the Los Alamos computers failed and they were lost. Another story was that they would be used to bolster his résumé when he looked for a new job. The FBI's belief was that he intended to sell them to the highest bidder. But he wasn't terminated from the Los Alamos lab, and in March of 1999, the FBI accused Lee of giving nuclear secrets to the Chinese.

He took two polygraph tests. When he passed the first, the agents lied to him and said he hadn't. They questioned him again and Lee admitted that maybe he had given Beijing more information than he should have back in 1986 and 1988. He then failed a test. That was when the government fired him.

After searching his home and finding handwritten notes about the tapes, the FBI arrested Lee and kept the $75,129-a-year scientist in virtual isolation for 278 days. The feds did let him out of his cell for an hour daily near midnight and then only while manacled and chained. His family was allowed weekly visits but only under the watchful eye of agents. The government hoped the solitary confinement would make him crack and confess. It didn't. So they continued to interrogate him. At one point, the FBI threatened him with the electric chair.

"Do you know who the Rosenbergs are?" an agent asked him before answering his own question. "The Rosenbergs are the only people that never cooperated with the federal government in an espionage case. And you know what happened to them. We electrocuted them, Wen Ho."

"I heard," Lee answered.

"Wen Ho, you're in trouble. Big trouble."

"I know. But I tell you one thing. I'm a victim. I am innocent."

Lee said he would just retire and collect his pension. The FBI disputed that.

"Do you really think you're going to be able to collect anything? They're going to garnish your wages. They're not going to give you anything but your Advice of Rights and a pair of handcuffs."

Lee never confessed. Perhaps there was nothing to tell. His family loudly suggested he had been singled out because of his race. Lee's lawyer said the security at Los Alamos was so loose, anyone could have given secrets to the Chinese. In the final analysis the FBI was forced to drop fifty-eight of the fifty-nine charges against him. A federal judge apologized and President Clinton publicly said he was "troubled" by the FBI's treatment of the espionage suspect. Lee was allowed to walk out of prison with time served as part of the deal on the single charge. He returned home to a hero's welcome.

Freeh and Reno were hauled before Congress and, in one of the few times they ever presented a united front, tried to defend their heavy-handedness by pointing to a so-called mountain of circumstantial evidence that had been collected by their agents. Reno called Lee "a felon," and Freeh added that Lee's "conduct was not inadvertent, not careless, and not innocent." And though Freeh had said he didn't think much of the polygraph test, more than eight hundred were given at the Los Alamos lab in the months that followed Lee's release.

Freeh admitted that his G-men had bungled their investigation, beginning in 1996 when Lee was identified as a suspect. Among the mistakes: agents for the Bureau had not independently verified the suspicions of the Energy Department, and an FBI agent had given false testimony at a bail hearing for Lee. The senators expressed skepticism at Freeh's and Reno's testimony. Like Felix Bloch, Wen Ho Lee had escaped the FBI's noose, due to the Bureau's incompetence. He has filed a suit against the government for defamation, with the outcome as of yet unresolved.

*   *   *

When Bob Hanssen joined the FBI in 1976, Louis Freeh had just finished an undercover-agent role by playing a stockbroker, assigned to bust a crime ring. He worked out of the New York City office and had already made a name for himself by breaking up the "Pizza Connection," a heroin ring that delivered the drug under the guise of pizza delivery boys.

In the stock jockey caper, Freeh had a recording device taped to his body. But when he walked into a conference room to gather evidence, he was told the meeting had been moved and was going to take place in a steam room. Thinking fast, he went to a men's room and quickly ripped the tape recorder from his body, stuffed it in a briefcase, and nonchalantly strolled naked into the hot, foggy bath, embellishing his growing legend within the Bureau.

Following Bob's arrest, the myth of Louis Freeh was badly tarnished if not gone. Further damage was on the way. It was published that he had been warned in 1999 about a mole in the FBI. At the time Freeh had said the information was flawed, and that if there was a mole, it had to be in the CIA and not at the Bureau.

(In fact, the FBI had suspected a CIA officer who had once lived on Whitecedar Court and who physically resembled Bob Hanssen. The agent was interrogated and passed several polygraph exams, but in the end was put on administrative leave and threatened with arrest. Government officials at one time said they would go to his eighty-four-year-old mother in a nursing home and ask her about his alleged illegal activities. After Bob was apprehended, the CIA refused to apologize to their employee, fearing legal action.)

The newly elected president, George W. Bush, continued to express confidence following Bob's arrest, giving Freeh a "he's doing a good job" pat on the back. Still, most Bureau watchers predicted Freeh would wait until the end of the year to bow out. Sooner than that, they thought, would seem indecent.

Freeh looked as if he were doing the right thing by appointing former FBI and CIA chief William Webster to look into what had gone wrong. But Webster was immediately attacked. Despite his credentials, it was he, critics pointed out, who had been heading the Bureau when Bob crossed the Rubicon. Still, Freeh's announcement that he would resign on May 1, 2001, just ten weeks after Bob's arrest, surprised both Freeh's supporters and detractors. His departure speech let everyone know where his loyalties were. He loudly praised Bush and barely mentioned Clinton, the president who had hired him.

The "Was he pushed or did he jump?" question was at first nearly unanimous. He was leaving voluntarily, his friends said. The reason being whispered was that his father was in ill health or, alternately, that Freeh needed an opportunity to earn more money to be able to pay for the upcoming college costs for one of his six sons. His oldest was sixteen, and the story being passed around was that he had wanted to quit in 1998 when his youngest son was born. But he wouldn't, he had then told his friends, until his work was completed and the Bureau was modernized, made more high-tech, and confidence in the FBI was restored.

Some two weeks later, the Timothy McVeigh bombshell struck and Freeh's reason for resigning was—at least in the minds of some media pundits—revised. Bob Hanssen may have pushed him toward the window, but McVeigh had made him jump from it, were the new whispers.

The thirty-three-year-old McVeigh, who had already been judged to be one of the greatest mass murderers in U.S. history, was scheduled to die by lethal injection on May 16, 2001, and was openly embracing his upcoming demise. But then it came to light that forty-six of the fifty-six FBI field offices had failed to turn over documents on the April 19, 1995, bombing. On the fifth request for the material, 3,135 pages that had never been turned in materialized after his sentencing. McVeigh's lawyers, who were entitled by law to see them before trial, had never been given these papers. An uproar ensued, McVeigh's execution was delayed for almost a month, the victims' families wept anew, and the case appeared to have at least a temporary new life. Freeh had to go before Congress and explain himself just two weeks after he had resigned. On Capitol Hill, Freeh claimed that after the McVeigh fiasco he had ordered a complete shakedown of the Bureau, taken eight management steps, and hired "a world-class records expert." The politicians were not satisfied.

"I think today we have what is close to a failed agency," David Obey, a bearded, bespectacled Wisconsin congressman lectured. "The litany of troubles are astounding and regrettable."

Just one week later, an FBI security expert and a former FBI agent in Las Vegas were both accused of selling classified secrets to the Mafia. That seemed to be the final straw. Attorney General John Ashcroft, a Freeh defender, called for a full review of the Bureau.

The FBI's troubles took the spotlight away from the scandals at the CIA. Following Aldrich Ames's arrest, the spy agency had cleaned up its act by aggressively polygraphing virtually everyone, and looking askance at excessive drinking and womanizing, two habits that had marked Rick Ames's life. (Ames had engaged in desktop sex with women inside CIA headquarters.) But the John M. Deutch affair had again given the Agency another red face.

Deutch was appointed to head the CIA in 1995, but then had quit two years later in a snit when President Clinton wouldn't make him secretary of defense. In February 2000, a report by the CIA revealed Deutch had taken home seventy-four classified files—hundreds of pages—on disks, downloaded them into his computer, then visited hard-core porn Web sites that made him vulnerable to cyber hackers who could have stolen the secrets. After the breach was discovered, the current CIA director, George Tenet, said he couldn't guarantee that the classified material had not been accessed.

The story broke at the same time as the Wen Ho Lee case, prompting embarrassing comparisons. Why was it okay for the CIA chief to take home classified material and not Lee? At least there was no evidence that Lee had down-loaded the material into a computer or visited porno sites. Deutch faced prosecution but was saved in early 2001 when he was absolved by President Clinton in one of several controversial last-minute pardons.

Privately, Freeh blamed the Bureau's computer systems for the McVeigh debacle. He had earlier written a memo re-questing $142 million in computer upgrades, writing that the technology had fallen behind. "To be successful, the FBI must have the capacity for collecting, storing, man-aging, analyzing, and disseminating case and intelligence information on a timely basis, both in-house and throughout the law enforcement system," his request had said.

Louis Freeh, who had followed Bob Hanssen to the altar of Saint Catherine's for Communion on many a Sunday, was gone, and not in glory. He left the Bureau in turmoil, an uncoordinated maze of fiefdoms where half of the agents had fewer than six years of experience and employees were quitting as soon as they could find the exit sign. What was once the nation's most exemplary government organization was now considered a bureaucracy with more holes than the once proud G-men had pumped into John Dillinger's body.

THIRTEEN

A Magical History Tour of Chicago

By the close of the twentieth century, espionage was changing. In 1998, for example, Britain dispatched a gay male couple to spy for the United Kingdom in Eastern Europe. Sir Gerry Warner, a former deputy to "C," the head of the legendary MI6 intelligence service, was not only open about the new policy, but expressed pride in his country's decision. He said his espionage group was dedicated to sexual equality.

"MI6 is the human end of intelligence and operates in a straightforward way," he told a gathering. "It now has a staff of eighteen hundred and has just sent the first homosexual couple abroad. More women have been recruited to the service over the past eighteen months than men, but there are more men in the service. The job requires intelligence and being good at relationships."

He was echoed by a colleague, Sir Colin McColl, who agreed that gay men and women would be welcomed into the British espionage ranks in the new century. "People risk their lives because they believe MI6 is a secret service. I am very anxious that I should be able to send some sort of signal to these people that we're not going to be undressed in public," he said.

Sir Gerry and Sir Colin should have kept quiet. Intelligence services in the Czech Republic were quick to name the two men, one of whom was serving as Britain's spymaster in the country. The opposing espionage agency put both their pictures and residence on the country's evening television news. The reason? The Czech security service (BIS) and MI6 were at odds, and the Czechs wanted to settle a grudge. The spy chief and his partner became easy targets. One diplomat, shrugging off the scandal, spoke for many: "Everything becomes public in the Czech Republic, from the details of President Havel's love life to the cost of the prime minister's new toilet."

Despite having their man revealed as both gay and a spy, the British refused to remove him or his lover from Prague. Christopher Hurran, the gentleman in question, was a much decorated former army officer who had served in hot spots like Kuwait and Venezuela. The Czech intelligence service soon began backpedaling, blaming Russian intelligence for the unwanted outing.

Sex and espionage have long been partners outside America. Bob Hanssen's hero, Kim Philby, had a libido that made room for both genders, a fact he neglected to detail in *My Silent War*. He was married four times and once inscribed a book to the wife of Donald McLean, a member of his Cambridge spy ring, with "An orgasm a day keeps the doctor away."

Certainly nothing that liberating was happening in the American intelligence community. Sex was a hands-off affair—repressed at best—as evidenced by Bob Hanssen's strange encounters with Priscilla Sue Galey and Kimberly Lichtenberg. Watching totally naked strippers at the Good Guys was winked at, but hands-on sex inside FBI headquarters was grounds for dismissal. Watch, but don't touch, was part of the unofficial credo of G-men.

A system was being put into place that would make that a reality. While Bob was slogging around in Virginia's wooded parks, the NSA was busy perfecting an electronic listening network that promised to make espionage—the old-fashioned touchy-feely, people-to-people or spy-vs.-spy kind—superfluous if not extinct.

Called by the code word Echelon, the project had begun in 1971. It was both frightening and awesome. Echelon was an automated global interception system that by the turn of the century was able to listen in on three billion communications per day, worldwide. The capability included E-mails, Internet downloads, and satellite transmissions.

The NSA, with the cooperation of intelligence agencies in four friendly nations—Great Britain, Canada, Australia, and New Zealand—had installed massive processing centers near Denver, Colorado, and overseas in Germany, England, and Australia to catch communications from the air. Surface traffic stations that captured ground transmissions were in the United States, Italy, England, Turkey, New Zealand, Canada, and Australia. Under the ocean, surveillance devices were attached to underwater communication cables.

Supposedly, the main work of Echelon was to apprehend terrorists and drug traffickers. For instance, by using three key words—*bomb*, *fuse*, and *death*—the system can isolate which of the three billion communications contain all three words and then winnow the number down further from there. It is far from perfect. If a budding actor sent an E-mail saying "I bombed" or "I died" about a stage play in which he was appearing, using phrases like "he has a short fuse," his name could wind up on a list of potential subversives.

The NSA and the U.S. government tried for years to shroud the system in secrecy, but in May of 1999, Georgia congressman Bob Barr, a former CIA analyst, proposed that the NSA provide a detailed report to a congressional intelligence committee on Echelon's work. Barr said he was worried that the system could be abused and private conversations could be heard through eavesdropping.

He had good reason to be concerned. One of the more

scandalous charges against Echelon was that the late Princess Diana of Great Britain was being surveilled by the Echelon system just before her death. According to the *Washington Post*, the NSA did admit to having electronic files on Di that were mostly intercepted phone conversations, but wouldn't say why.

Echelon has also been accused of industrial espionage. It is said to have passed along information to American companies so they could win contracts over foreign competitors. For example, critics charge that in 1995, the NSA gave two aircraft manufacturers—Boeing and McDonnell Douglas—intercepted conversations between their European competitor, Airbus, and Saudi Arabian government officials. The two American companies were accused of using the data to win a $6-billion contract with the government-run Saudi airline. Another giant American corporation, Raytheon, is said to have won, using intelligence passed along by Echelon, a $1.3-billion contract for surveilling the Amazon rain forest. When accused of using Echelon to bolster their nations' economies, officials in both the United States and Britain have denied any such misdeeds.

Echelon is also alleged to have surveilled private political groups. Amnesty International and the American Civil Liberties Union are two organizations that the system is accused of targeting.

But Echelon may be just the tip of what is coming during the next decade. A new term, *data-veillance*, is emerging. In 1998, a 112-page paper by the European Parliament, *An Appraisal of Technologies of Political Control*, offered a look at what kind of world is possible in the future.

The report predicts that electronic surveillance will preemptively and secretly track "certain social classes and races of people living in red-lined areas before any crime is committed." There will be DNA data banks that will profile entire countries from birth. Face-recognition systems that can identify people by name from a distance using a camera are only a few years away. Laser microphones will detect distant conversations from behind closed windows. New stroboscopic cameras can group-photograph an entire political demonstration, then separate the images to instantly make mug shots of each participant. Miniature recording devices can now be made so small, the document warns, that an electronic bug can literally be inserted into a real bug—like a cockroach—and let loose inside a home to listen until it meets with an angry heel or a dose of insecticide.

According to the report, Echelon has "been designed for nonmilitary targets: governments, organizations, and businesses in virtually every country." The NSA can decide—with a keystroke—to listen to any person or group by issuing an interception order.

The GRACE exchange was made on Monday, October 7, 1991, in Rock Creek Park. B enclosed his twenty-fifth computer disk and a classified document dated September 10—the ink again was barely dry. The tome was titled *The U.S. Double-Agent Program Management Review and Policy Recommendations*. B also suggested to the Soviets that they attempt to hire "an old friend." He said the man was a military officer who had just been passed over for promotion. Sources in the Bureau would later identify B's pal to be his old school chum Jack Hoschouer.

The KGB package contained $12,000 in cash and a letter on a computer disk, full of broken English and complimentary platitudes. Moscow felt the need to reassure B that the historic changes in the Soviet Union would have no effect on their relationship. Whoever was in charge, they seemed to be saying, intelligence data would always be needed.

Dear friend:
Thanks for the package of 02.13. The materials are very promising, we intend to work on the scenario so wisely

suggested by you. And the magical history tour to Chicago was mysteriously well timed. Have you ever thought of foretelling the things? After your retirement for instance in some sort of your own Cristall *[sic]* Ball and Intelligence Agency? (CBIA)? There are always so many people in this world eager to get a glimpse of the future.

But now back to where we belong. There have been many important developments in our country lately. So many that we'd like to reassure you once again. Like we said: we've done all in order that none of those events ever affects your security and our ability to maintain the operation with you. And of course there can be no doubt of our commitment to your friendship and cooperation which are too important to us to loose *[sic]* . . .

Please note: our next contact is due at HELEN.

Enclosed in the package please find $12,000 and attached are some information requests which we'd ask your kind attention to.

Thank you and good luck.

Sincerely, your friends.

In addition to the usual wish list, the KGB asked specifically for the current 1991 issue of a document that reported on the Soviet Union's satellite reconnaissance systems. "It's fun to read about life in the Universe to understand better what's going on our own planet," the KGB wrote of the request.

They also asked B about several pages that were missing from the document that their agent had hastily grabbed off a desk in mid-July. Not that they were terribly upset, for as they said, "Sometimes it happens, we understand. Life is becoming too fast."

Less than two weeks before Mikhail Gorbachev dissolved the Soviet Union and it became Russia once more, the KGB received an envelope from B bearing the "J. Baker, Houston" return address and postmarked from

Washington. Inside the envelope was a note that read, "BOB on 6/22. T. DEVICE APPROVED 6/16, COMING SOON." Translated, using the 6 coefficient, it meant a dead drop at BOB or Idylwood Park on December 16. The T. DEVICE referred to information about a classified technical operation Bob had previously passed along.

The exchange was made, as always, on a Monday—December 16, 1991—with B giving the KGB his twenty-sixth and final computer disk. He also provided them with a highly classified CIA research document that had been written in November of 1990, titled *The KGB's First Chief Directorate: Structure, Functions, and Methods*. The papers had the caveats SECRET NOFORN NOCONTRACT and ORCON on the cover as well as:

WARNING NOTICE

This document should be disseminated only to persons having both the requisite clearances and a need to have access to its contents for performance of their duties. No further distribution or reproduction is authorized without the approval of the Associate Deputy Director for Operations for Counterintelligence, CIA, and National Security Information.
Unauthorized Disclosure Subject to Criminal Sanctions

B enclosed the most recent volume of a congressional budget justification detailing the needs of the FBI's foreign counterintelligence program. All of the classified caveats were on the documents. Bob also apologized for the missing pages for which he had been gently chided by Moscow.

Since his return from inspecting FBI field offices, Bob Hanssen had been working as a program manager in the Soviet Operations Section, which countered Soviet spying efforts. He had just been informed that beginning in January of 1992 he would be the new chief of the National Security Threat List Unit in the FBI's intelligence division. He was supposed to be working on economic espionage, though he told the KGB the actual mission had yet to be defined. He proposed that they communicate in the future by using a new method, which he did not directly define, but was actually E-mail as it existed in the early 1990s.

B quoted the salty exhortation that General George S. Patton made in Europe in the last months of World War II. The saying, one that some Bureau employees would later remember him as using to prod them into working extra hours, was "Let's get this over with so we can go kick the shit out of the fucking Japanese!"

In 1996, the FBI laboratory in Quantico, Virginia, had developed its own system that at first seemed to be similar to Echelon but, since it only intercepted E-mails sent through Internet service providers (ISP), was narrower in scope. The software/hardware technology was said to be the equivalent of a telephone tap, but in reality was much different and ripe for abuse.

Given the unfortunate name of Carnivore because, as an FBI agent said, "it cuts through to the meat of criminal activity conducted through E-mail," the black box had to be attached to an ISP to work, but unlike a single phone tap, Carnivore looked through every subscriber in search of a crime.

Carnivore did not use key words like the Echelon system but rather scanned E-mail addresses. Critics immediately likened it to reading every letter at the post office to find one with a misdeed. They claimed it violated the Fourth Amendment to the U.S. Constitution, which had been adopted to prevent general searches such as were conducted by British colonial troops prior to American independence. FBI proponents responded with a strange explanation. They cited pagers and cellular phones that aided drug dealers, saying that those devices shouldn't be banned simply because narcotics traffickers used them.

"Congress never contemplated or authorized a wiretapping scheme that accesses everyone's communications, only a small fraction of which involves criminal activities," the ACLU's Barry Steinhardt told the Congressional Judiciary Committee on July 24, 2000. Unlike Echelon, Carnivore was an entirely domestic operation that had been exposed by the *Wall Street Journal*. After that, it was impossible to keep secret.

"The FBI insists it will only record the communications to which it is entitled," Steinhardt said. "The FBI asks you to take an enormous leap of faith that they will strictly stay within the confines of the law. They ask to you to trust them with unsupervised access to the entire stream of communications over an ISP's network, which can amount to literally millions of innocent communications of nontargets of any interception order.

"If you accept this premise, you reject the Fourth Amendment. It is built on the opposite premise: that the executive cannot be trusted with carte blanche authority when it conducts a search," he concluded.

At the turn of the century, 1.4 billion E-mails were being sent a day on eight thousand different domestic ISPs (fifteen thousand worldwide). By the year 2000, Carnivore had been used sparingly, in just twenty-five criminal cases. The Clinton White House wanted approval for the FBI to use the controversial program to come from the highest levels of the Justice Department—and on a case-by-case basis rather than by a simple court order. But electronic privacy was a complex issue; the FBI was already using cell phones to track suspects without court orders, and the Congress had been unable to regulate Carnivore by the time of Bob Hanssen's arrest.

FOURTEEN

The Line Goes Dead, or Does It?

There is no record of any communication between B and his Russian handlers after December 16, 1991 until October 6, 1999, a period of nearly eight years. The question begs itself: Why stop now?

One school of thought says the records are simply incomplete. Some FBI sources claim Bob Hanssen did continue working for Moscow and Russian incompetency left these years blank. Moscow simply misplaced or lost the records. After all, when the correspondence was interrupted in 1991, the last dead drop named was GRACE. But when it resumed in 1999, the first one named is LEWIS. If the Russians were proceeding alphabetically—AN, BOB, CHARLIE, DORIS, ELLIS, FLO, GRACE—as it appeared, then what happened to *H* through *K*? And if you add up the funds put in the Moscow bank between 1985 and 1991, the total is $300,000. But when B's paper trail is picked up in 1999, his handlers informed him the amount had risen to $800,000. Did he get a $500,000 bonus?

That thinking is refuted by Moscow's effusive welcome-back letter in October of 1999. The KGB—now SVR—appears so enthusiastic one has to conclude that B had been away from them for many years. That the Russians felt compelled to update their agent about the extra money in his account—money he was unlikely to ever see—confirms this.

Mikhail Gorbachev dissolved the Soviet Union on December 25, 1991, less than two weeks after Bob went on hiatus. In the first flush of friendship that ensued, KGB teams were touring FBI headquarters. Was their double agent fearful that this new capitalist Russia would betray him, selling his file to the highest bidder? That is what did happen, but not until nine years later. Still, Bob had every reason to be concerned and, from his viewpoint, was wise to go to ground and let his trail go cold. He was a spy who had thought to take every precaution—never showing his face or giving his name—and he wasn't about to get caught by an unexpected change in government. Besides, he had now received $470,000 in tax-free dollars over six years. It was enough for his children's schooling and even extra-curricular pursuits such as Priscilla Sue Galey.

There is also a third speculation. In Bob's disturbed mind he might have easily thought that God's will was finally being done. Perhaps, as the Virgin Mary had prophesied at Fátima, Russia *was* becoming a consecrated nation, and therefore it was time for him to step aside and let God do his work.

This might also explain why he returned to betraying his country. Under the Russian form of capitalism, it can easily be argued that the country was soon debauched, its people's morals becoming even more lax. Certainly, with its casinos, gaudy nightclubs, and a newly organized Moscow Mafia, it was far from a consecrated country.

One could even suppose—though it is highly unlikely—that Bob received a personal entreaty from Vladimir Putin, a career KGB man who was about to assume control of Russia and take it to a harder, near–Cold War edge. Finally, there is a more pedestrian explanation. Bob Hanssen had a hidden type-T disposition and again needed both the thrill of the game and the SVR's money.

Psychologist Frank Farley of Temple University has helped to define type-T personalities. While type T's are always risk takers, there are several kinds. A type-T physical is someone like a bungee jumper or rock climber; a type-T intellectual is an Albert Einstein or Galileo, who risks ridicule by coming up with new thinking. Einstein got his thrills from mental exercise, says Farley, just as the bungee jumper is thrilled from free-falling attached to an elasticized cord.

But there is a darker side to type T that can be classified as type-T negative. These are the people who commit crimes, experiment with drugs, or have questionable, unprotected sex just for the thrill of it. Bob Hanssen fell into that category.

Between February of 1995 and January 12, 2001, Bob was assigned to the U.S. State Department in Washington. His new duties had him serving part of the time as the liaison to the Office of Foreign Missions (OFM), whose responsibilities included monitoring foreign diplomats and intelligence agents, particularly on their travel within U.S. boundaries. Another of his duties was to carry highly classified intelligence documents between the State Department and FBI headquarters—a distance of about three miles—daily. As one State Department official later said, "It was like being in a candy store with no one else around. You can take all the candy you want."

Certainly, it would have been easy for Bob to have stopped off at a copying center on the way and make duplicates of everything, but for what purpose? In four of those five years he may have been inactive, according to the FBI. But was he? During those years, several significant incidents also occurred that could well have involved Bob Hanssen.

If not for the Pentagon, the Department of State would be the largest building in the Washington area. There are 2.6 million square feet of space in the eight-story building that is spread out over two city blocks. The DS houses eighty-five hundred employees. Each year it gets more than two hundred thousand visitors. There are five pedestrian entrances and three accesses to its nine-hundred-car garage. There are also forty-three elevators. Among government buildings in Washington, it is one of the easiest to penetrate.

Few people know that the State Department dining room alone houses paintings and art objects valued at more than $100 million. Controversial world leaders who have lunched there range from Yasir Arafat to the Dalai Lama. Yet in the mid-1990s, security at the State Department was reduced. The DS's own Office of Counterintelligence slimmed its staff from forty-one to twenty-six. Monetary budgets for security were cut by at least 50 percent. The feeling in the State Department was that with the dissolution of the Soviet Union, the Cold War was over and it was time to spend "the peace dividend." Security measures could be relaxed, it was thought. Disaster struck quickly.

In February of 1998, a man described only as "someone in a brown tweed coat" stole some Top Secret documents out of an unlocked briefcase in Secretary of State Madeleine Albright's suite of offices and literally walked out of the building with them. The case was investigated by the FBI but went unsolved.

In early 1999, the FBI's SSG unit began shadowing Stanislav Gusev, a known SVR intelligence officer. (Bob mentioned Gusev in one of his letters: see page 14.) Gusev, security guards had noticed, would arrive early each day to grab a special parking spot in front of the State Department building. Then he would plop down on a bus stop bench and put his hands in his pockets, only getting up to feed the parking meter. Concealed inside his trousers was a high-tech radio signal detector that picked up a radio signal from inside the huge State Department building. The Russians, or someone working for them, had hidden a battery-powered bug inside a length of chair-rail molding that had been blended and placed into the antique woodwork of a conference room on the seventh floor, within steps of Albright's office suite.

Former KGB general Oleg Kalugin explained how it was done: "The design, the camouflage, are all manufactured in Moscow. In my own experience we would send them a description of a specific place. We would then give the details—the size, the measurements, and everything. The color is very important. If it's mahogany, it has to look like mahogany. If it's oak, then it has to be oak. Moscow would simply reproduce a piece of the specified color and then you would have to install it."

The SSG didn't yet know about the bug, but thought that Gusev was behaving suspiciously. To get close to him, they dressed as homeless men or impersonated college students from nearby George Washington University. It appeared to them that Gusev had an antenna hidden inside a Kleenex box on the dashboard of his car. A tape recorder inside the vehicle stored the transmissions. Gusev would position the Kleenex box, then get out and fool around inside his clothing until he found the frequency.

At first the G's thought Gusev was doing a technical survey of the State Department—planning the best way to do an electronic penetration of the building. They decided to sweep the huge building room by room with electronic debugging devices, which resemble the metal detectors beachcombers use to hunt coins at the ocean's edge. The search for the bug was done at night in order not to alert DS employees, and because of the limited time they had, it took weeks to find the tiny transmitter.

Neil Gallagher, the head of the team assigned to the case, admired the Russians' handiwork. "Someone had to go in and take a survey, go back and have a particular device designed, and then somehow get back into the State Department with the device and install it."

Gusev was arrested just before noon on December 8, 1999, caught red-handed with the equipment on him and in his car. But he had diplomatic immunity and nothing could be done of a real punitive nature. The government declared Gusev persona non grata and asked him to leave the country.

Was Bob Hanssen involved? His own office was on the second floor, and as a high-ranking FBI officer with the run of the building, he could have easily penetrated a seventh-floor conference room. Still, in his 1999 letter to the SVR, B complained about not being let in on the operation and said that if he had, he would have warned Gusev that the FBI was on to him. It's more reasonable to accuse him of stealing a Dell laptop computer that disappeared from the State Department on January 31, 2000, a period when Bob was active again.

Part of Bob's work involved the DS's Bureau of Intelligence and Research, known as DOS/INR, and indeed that was where the laptop was last seen. The laptop had been purchased in 1996 for the use of agents temporarily working in counterproliferation assignments who didn't have their own workstations. It was full of, as one official said in government speak, "highly classified information bearing on the proliferation of both weapons and technologies of mass destruction and related delivery systems." In actuality, it was even worse. The computer contained "code-word" information—the highest level of classification the government places on data—available only on a need-to-know basis. Further, the laptop held U.S. secrets on nuclear, chemical, and biological weapons systems—the crown jewels of the American military.

When the laptop was reported missing, the DS's own intelligence division interviewed every employee in the division but came up blank. Like Carnivore, the laptop scandal was kept quiet until revealed by the news media—in this case the *Washington Post*. Within weeks, rumors spread that not only did the Dell computer have top secret information on the hard drive, but that it had the latest in infrared capabilities and was literally able to somehow pull data out of other computers through the air if programmed correctly.

In August 2000, Madeleine Albright directed that the

State Department offer a $25,000 reward for its return. DS spokesman Richard Boucher didn't seem to hold much hope for its retrieval, though he did reveal its five-digit serial number, ending with the letter *Q*. He was hoping pawnshops would check their shelves. "If people with nefarious goals took it, they probably know what they've got already. But if it doesn't really matter to them what's on it, this reward might induce them to look at the laptops and turn it over to us," Boucher said.

The Dell laptop was never found, and the DS took out its frustration on six of the employees in the DOS/INR section. They were either fired or disciplined. The senior member of the section, J. Stapleton Roy, fell on his sword. Roy, a former ambassador to both China and Indonesia, took early retirement when he learned his deputy, Donald Keyser, would be both disciplined and transferred to a non-policy-making position.

In May of 2000 the FBI had revealed there was evidence that several of the fifty-six members of the foreign press corps covering the State Department were actually intelligence officers working on behalf of their respective countries. The Bureau implied that security was lax and security breakdowns were common. Secretary of State Madeleine Albright joked about it while conducting a joint press conference with the French foreign minister.

"Obviously we don't want spies posing as journalists," she said to reporters. "If any of you are spies, please identify yourselves." A few weeks later the DS began restricting access to unescorted visitors.

Ironically, when Bob Hanssen's car was searched the day after he was arrested, the FBI found two envelopes in his silver Taurus. They were both marked SECRET and addressed to J. Stapleton Roy.

"Bob was present for monthly meetings where every counterintelligence and counterterrorist case was discussed," a senior State Department official said. "He knew everything."

Among the meetings he attended: several on the mistaken U.S. bombing of the Chinese embassy in Belgrade, Yugoslavia, during the 1999 Balkans war; discussions of terrorism by foreign nationals from problem nations such as North Korea, Sudan, Cuba, Libya, Iraq, and Iran; a discussion on whether the United States should give permission to Israeli air marshals to carry weapons in U.S. commercial airports; and finally a conference on whether the United States should reduce the number of Russian diplomats allowed into the United States. The FBI wanted fewer of the envoys in the country because it believed that 128 of the visitors from Moscow were espionage agents. The number had been rising each year since hitting a post–Cold War low in 1995 of less than a hundred.

On January 13, 2001, Bob Hanssen was transferred back to FBI headquarters so the Bureau could monitor him. The day before, some of the employees at DOS/INR gave Bob a going-away luncheon at the China Garden restaurant in Rosslyn, Virginia, just across the Potomac River from the State Department, complete with gifts and a certificate of service.

"They take you to a place like that when they're not crazy about you," said a former ambassador, Dennis Hays. "If they're really sad to see you go, then you're invited up to Pennsylvania Avenue or K Street to a good place like the Prime Rib or Mr. K's."

Bob may have been reassigned to FBI headquarters, but he continued to show up at the State Department, wandering around and visiting people in his old office. His last recorded visit was February 9, nine days before his arrest.*

---

* Early in 2001, the new secretary of state, General Colin L. Powell, again relaxed the restrictions imposed by Madeleine Albright. Some ten thousand DS retirees had complained about Albright's post-laptop rule that all visitors must be escorted in the building and claimed they couldn't even use the rest room without someone with them. Powell's new policy allowed the retirees to roam the first two floors without security guards.

During his years at the State Department, Bob Hanssen must have studied the case of a fellow FBI counterintelligence agent, Earl Edwin Pitts. For a time their stories ran parallel. Pitts and Bob had worked side by side in the New York office in 1986 when both were double agents and each had found it tough making ends meet. Two months before Bob had been transferred back to Washington, Pitts had begun working for the KGB, meeting his handlers at the main branch of the New York Public Library. Though not in tandem, Bob and Pitts very likely handed over duplicate documents for a short time. This had to have added to the merriment of the KGB, who couldn't believe their good fortune. Two spies with great access to documents were working for them out of the same FBI office—both for money. God bless capitalism!

Pitts had three children and made even less than Bob Hanssen. He received $129,000 from the KGB and went to ground a year after Bob, in 1992. In 1995, a Russian defector who had once been a handler for Pitts fingered him. The FBI checked Pitts's bank statements, found some extra deposits that shouldn't have been there, and began investigating. The Russian contact soon showed up on his doorstep and offered $65,000 for some classified information. The proposed payment was large enough to make Pitts bite. Of course, it was a sting operation and he was caught red-handed, at that time only the second FBI man—after the aforementioned Richard W. Miller—to be charged with espionage.

Facing a sentence of life without parole, the forty-three-year-old Pitts cut a deal and agreed to tell all in exchange for a lighter sentence. His lawyer, Nina Ginsberg, told everyone after the plea that his sentence would likely be between fifteen and twenty years. The prosecutors asked for twenty-four. Both numbers were wrong. On June 23, 1997, the judge, T. S. Ellis, gave Pitts twenty-seven years after hearing a long, rambling apology.

"You have much more reflection to do," Ellis said. "You didn't make a single reference to the money you took or your lack of regard for your country and the principles for which it stands. Every time you go by Arlington Cemetery, every name you see on the Vietnam Memorial, or the Korean War Memorial, of people who have made the ultimate sacrifice, you have betrayed them especially."

As part of a guilty plea that avoided the death penalty, Pitts was debriefed for seventy hours in 1997, telling the Bureau everything he knew about his Russian handlers and what he had given them. Toward the end of the questioning, he was asked if he knew of anyone at FBI headquarters who was working for the Russians. Pitts said he didn't, but he did know of a few odd incidents involving Bob Hanssen and talked about him hacking into other employees' computers. The Bureau said they already knew about that and ignored the information.

According to the *New York Times,* when Bob Hanssen was arrested, Pitts wrote Nina Ginsberg and reminded her he had warned his interrogators about Bob and asked for a reduction in sentence because of it. Ginsberg made that request to the Justice Department, which ignored her letter.

In 1997, B had to have felt pretty good about the Pitts matter. Unlike Pitts, he had been careful not to make unexplained bank deposits, and his handlers—he thought—didn't even know his name. Best of all, much of the damage he had done would now be blamed on his fellow double agent.

Certainly, the admonition to Pitts by Judge Ellis, so widely quoted in newspapers and on television, made little impression on Bob Hanssen. He resumed working for his Russian handlers two years later.

On October 6, 1999, B received this letter from the recently named SVR, warmly welcoming him home. The message contained a new location for dead drops in Washington, D.C., near the new Russian embassy. Their English hadn't improved, nor had their old-fashioned spy-vs.-spy instructions:

Dear friend: welcome!
It's good to know you are here. Acknowledging your letter to V.K. *[V.K. is believed to be the initials of a senior SVR foreign counterintelligence officer in the Russian embassy at that time.]* we express our sincere joy on the occasion of resumption of contact with you. We firmly guarantee you for a necessary financial help. Note, please, that since our last contact a sum set aside for you has risen and presents now about 800,000 dollars. This time you will find in a package 50,000 dollars. Now it is up to you to give a secure explanation of it.

As to communication plan, we may have need of some time to work out a secure and reliable one. This why we suggest to carry on the 13th of November at the same drop which you have proposed in your letter to V.K. We shall be ready to retrieve your package from DD since 20.00 to 21.00 hours on the 12th of November after we would read you *[sic]* signal (a vertical mark of white adhesive tape of 6–8 cm length on the post closest to Wolftrap Creek of the Foxstone Park sign). We shall fill our package in and make up our signal (a horizontal mark of white adhesive tape).

After you will clear the drop don't forget to remove our tape that will mean for us—exchange is over.

We propose a new place where you can put a signal for us when in need of an urgent DD operation. LO-CATION: the closest to Whithaven *[sic]* Parkway wooden electricity pole at the south-west corner of T-shaped intersection of Foxhall Road and Whitehaven Parkway (map of Washington, D.C., page 9, grid B 11). At any working day put a white thumb tack (1 cm in diameter, colored sets are sold at CVS *[drugstores]* into the northern side of the pole at the height of about 1.2

yards. The tack must be seen from a car going down Foxhall Road. This will mean for us that we shall retrieve your package from the DD Foxstone Park at the evening of the nex *[sic]* week's Tuesday (when it's getting dark).

In case of a threatening situation of any kind put a yellow tack at the same place. This will mean that we shall refrain from any communication with you until further notice from your side (the white tack).

We also propose for your consideration a new DD site "Lewis." DD LOCATION: wooden podium in the amphitheatre of Longbranch Nature Center (map of N. Virginia, page 16, grid G8). The package should be put under the FAR-LEFT corner of the podium (when facing the podium). Entter *[sic]* Longbranch Nature Center at the sign from Carlin Springs Road (near 6th Road south) and after parking your car in the lot follow the sign "To Amphitheatre." LOCATION OF THE DD SIGNAL: a wooden electricity utility pole at the northwest corner of the intersection of 3d Street and Carlin Springs Road neaqr *[sic]* the Metrobus stop (the same map, grid F-7). The signals are the same as in Foxstone Park DD. The white adhesive tape should be placed on the NORTHERN side of the pole, so that it could be noticed fro *[sic]* a car moving along Carlin Springs Road in the southern direction from Route 50.

Please, let us know during the November operation of your opinion on the proposed places (the new signal and DD Lewis).

We are intending to pass you a permanent communications plan using drops you know as well a new portion of money, for our part we are very interested to get from you any information about possible actions which may threaten us.

Thank you. Good luck to you. Sincerely,

Your friends.

On March 14, 2000, Bob answered the SVR's letter. He was despondent. Less than a year later, he would be manacled and put into a ten-by-twelve-foot cell, his life, for all purposes, over. That he had a premonition his long career as a spy for the KGB/SVR was about to end comes through in his writing. The note, released in part by the FBI, has a fatalistic ring.

I have come about as close as I ever want to come to sacrificing myself to help you, and I get silence. I hate silence.

Conclusion: One might propose that I am either insanely brave or quite insane. I'd answer neither. I'd say, insanely loyal. Take your pick. There is insanity in all the answers.

I have, however, come as close to the edge as I can without being truly insane. My security concerns have proven reality-based. I'd say, pin your hopes on insanely loyal. Only I can lose.

I decided on this course when I was 14 years old. I'd read Philby's book. *[Discussion on this matter can be found on page 38.]* Now that is insane, eh! My only hesitations were my security concerns under uncertainty. I hate uncertainty. So far I have just the edge correctly. Give me credit for that.

Set the signal at my site any Tuesday evening. I will read your answer. Please, at least say goodbye. It's been a long time my dear friends, a long and lonely time.

Ramon Garcia

Ten months later and just weeks before he was arrested, Bob Hanssen applied for a position with Invicta Networks, a computer security firm in Herndon, Virginia, seven miles from Talisman Drive, and headed by his old friend Victor Sheymov. As the reader will recall, the former KGB major had defected in 1980, and Bob, who had for a time been Sheymov's FBI contact, had offered his handlers the file

on the defector in 1988. If politics makes for strange bed-
fellows, espionage makes for even stranger companions.
One of the members of the board of directors at Invicta was
R. James Woolsey, the former director of the CIA.

In 1980, Sheymov had been in charge of all codes and
ciphers for the KGB's Eighth Directorate, Moscow's version of the NSA. For a time his job was to read every
incoming and outgoing cipher cable to the Soviet Union.
Earlier, he had begun to develop the Soviet's own fledgling
"Star Wars" missile defense program. He was considered
such a valuable asset that he was constantly surveilled by
a team from his own KGB, who required him to stay on
Soviet embassy grounds whenever he visited a world capital. One day in Warsaw, Poland, he was able to shake his
minders long enough to contact the CIA, which soon spirited his entire family out of the country.

The Russian was seen as a prize defector, so much so
that the CIA had pledged to give him a million dollars when
he defected in 1980 and $27,000 a year—plus health in-
surance—for life. Sheymov began working as a consultant
to the NSA almost immediately, helping to break the
KGB's codes. At the same time he became involved in
what would be a protracted dispute over the defection cash
he had been promised. Sheymov began to say publicly that
the CIA had cheated him and not paid what it had promised
when he defected. In 1991 he sued the Agency for reneging
on the agreement. The spy organization in turn spread stories in the press that no amount of cash could ever have
satisfied him and that he was greedy. Sheymov eventually
hired Woolsey, who had joined the Washington law firm
of Shea and Gardner after his CIA stint, to sue the Agency
which he had recently headed. Woolsey got Sheymov an
out-of-court settlement in 1999. According to the terms of
the deal, the amount Sheymov received was kept confidential. Sheymov, though, wasn't in a mood to bury the
hatchet. "The CIA cheated me in a major way," he told the
New York Times in 2000.

With Woolsey and Sheymov now partners, Bob Hanssen attempted to make it a troika. Sheymov had developed a new algorithm and was patenting a new computer programming system. The algorithm was the heart of a high-tech security system that made computer networks invulnerable to outside hackers. He was already expecting a contract from the NSA, and in December of 2000 Bob Hanssen hinted that he might be able to help Sheymov get the FBI's business as well.

Bob and Bonnie had not seen the Sheymovs socially for two years, but in December Sheymov ran into Bob at the State Department. Sheymov told Bob a little about his algorithm and Invicta. In return, Bob told Sheymov that the Bureau was always interested in new computer security technology and perhaps Bob could grease the wheels for him and help him get a deal there.

Making good on his promise, Bob arranged for Sheymov and the Invicta group to make a presentation to the FBI on January 30, 2001. While Bob sat in rapt attention listening to Sheymov make his pitch, an FBI team was quietly searching Bob's Taurus in the parking garage beneath FBI headquarters. Sheymov sensed something different in his old friend when Bob telephoned him after the meeting and asked him to lunch.

"It seemed like he was rushing, like he was trying to accelerate things," Sheymov told the *Times*. "He was always the kind of guy who seemed laid-back before. But now, he was pushing the timetable."

Bob had lunch with Sheymov and an Invicta officer at a Hilton hotel near Dulles Airport on February 5, 2001, two weeks before Bob's arrest. While he was eating, the FBI was again looking for evidence against him—this time his office was being searched. Sheymov thought the lunch was going to be about how they could secure the FBI contract, but Bob surprised him by saying he wanted to work for his company.

"Our jaws dropped," Sheymov recalled. "He said he wanted some kind of executive job and he wanted to know what kind of salary he could expect on an executive level."

Sheymov had a fledgling company and no room for Bob Hanssen. Sheymov tried to stall: "What kind of a time frame do you have in mind?"

"Right now," Bob answered.

"That put me in a bind," Sheymov said.

On Friday, February 16, two days before he was arrested, Bob showed up at Invicta's offices and tried to impress Sheymov in an effort to get the former KGB man to hire him.

"He got up and drew on my blackboard, describing our technology," Sheymov remembered admiringly. "He did it as well as I could have."

Sheymov wondered out loud whether Bob would have sold his company's secrets to the SVR: "The Russians are always interested in breakthrough technologies. They would definitely be after this."

FIFTEEN

Spy Tunnel, What Spy Tunnel?

One of the first things the public wanted to know when Bob Hanssen's arrest made headlines was this: How did he get caught? The spy had taken so many precautions by never revealing his name or meeting with the KGB/SVR that he seemed to be committing the perfect crime. Few thought the collar had happened through good gumshoe work by the FBI, though Director Louis Freeh implied as much. In a press conference two days after Bob was arrested, he claimed, "We didn't stumble into this investigation. This was very carefully planned and deliberately investigated. It really testifies to the extraordinary work and talent of the people involved and the cooperation between the CIA and the FBI."

In fact, the FBI clearly did stumble into the investigation. Though it has yet to be revealed who was responsible for giving or selling B's Moscow file to the FBI, or if more than one person was involved, most experts have pointed in the direction of longtime Russian diplomat Sergey Tretyakov.

Tretyakov, Moscow's former ambassador to Iran, had earned the enmity of the United States in 1995 by pushing for Russia to supply nearly $800 million in financing and technical help to the Iranians. The purpose of the cash: to build a nuclear power plant in the oil-rich country, the first of three. For the United States, plutonium-powered nuclear power plants built by the people who gave the world Chernobyl were one step removed from nuclear warheads or, equally bad, a meltdown.

In 1996, the tall, bulky Tretyakov became a first secretary at the Russian mission to the United Nations and simultaneously, according to reports, an SVR intelligence officer. His salary was small, despite his lofty title, forcing him to live in the Russian-owned apartment complex in Riverdale, New York. The housing had been built in the section of the Bronx borough by the former Soviet Union in 1974. In October of 2000, Tretyakov, who was nearing his fiftieth birthday—along with his wife, Elena, and their teenage daughter—quietly defected to the United States. Since Russia was now technically a friendly nation, defections had decreased, and because of Tretyakov's actions in Iran, he would not normally have been welcomed with such open arms by U.S. government officials. On the other hand, if he had come with a gift—the file of an American double agent who had gone undetected for fifteen years—he would not only have been gladly received, but paid handsomely for his efforts.

Tretyakov and his family were accepted into a special U.S. government "valuable defectors" program immediately, and when Russia asked for a conference with him to confirm he had voluntarily defected, Washington refused. That was a first—a chaperoned good-bye meeting had been considered standard procedure for defectors. When asked at the Bob Hanssen postarrest press conference if Tretyakov was the informant, Freeh tersely dismissed the questioner with a quick denial and went back to his claim of the Bureau's "counterintelligence coup."

The last letter recorded in B's FBI file is dated November 17, part of a supplement given to the FBI. Thus there were two separate deliveries of Bob's file, the large first one and then the last loose ends. The Bureau's SSG had begun to surveil him in early December. The first B or Ramon Garcia file would have had to have been received by the United States in either late November or early December. If Tretyakov had surrendered the file, there could have been a week or two devoted to price haggling plus the time needed to ship the B package out of Moscow.

When the FBI agents first got the documents, they thought they had a puzzler. Just a series of letters and papers and disks without the author's identity. None were originals. Everything had been photocopied. The Russian agent working for the United States had left the originals in place so as not to alert B's handlers. The SVR would surely have warned him.

It would have taken months to zero in on all the agents who had access to the documents—there would have been dozens—and then it would have taken as much as a year or more to investigate every suspect. The process could have been so unwieldy as to have been impossible. But the KGB had kept everything, including the plastic trash bags used to protect the shipments from the elements. When the trash bags used to package the documents were sent to the FBI's lab, the G-men got an unexpected break. Bob had made an error. His fingerprints were all over the black plastic sacks.

Within days after putting him under surveillance, the SSG team believed that Bob was its man. Driving slowly four times by the Foxstone Park sign on December 12 gave him away; a surreptitious search of his offices at FBI headquarters and at the State Department produced more evidence; and a check of their own computer network confirmed the rest of their suspicions. Bob had hacked into the Bureau's system every few weeks to see if his name or the word Vienna or any of the drop sites had shown up. When the searches came up blank, he had thought he was still clean. The investigative team also checked through fifteen years of covertly made audiotapes featuring known

KGB agents speaking with Americans. Bob's voice was identified twice and the conversation wasn't innocent—he was discussing a document drop-off. Others recalled the colorful quote by General Patton that B had used in two letters and said the phrase was identical to one Bob often used at the FBI. As far as the Bureau was concerned, their suspect was a dead man walking.

The Bureau spared little expense in shadowing Bob Hanssen. At the end of Carrhill Road in Vienna, an FBI unit set up cameras on a house that overlooked a soccer field within walking distance of the double agent's house. Small planes with silencers on their engines flew over his home, and the nearby dead-drop sites were checked several times each day. But by far the best move the Bureau made was in finding a house available for sale almost directly across the street from the Hanssen family.

The five-bedroom, three-bath house, on a slight incline at 9419 Talisman Drive and fifty yards down and near where Talisman came to a dead end, looked down into Bob and Bonnie's living room window. Frank Hood and his wife, Laura, had bought it back in 1987, moving in at almost the same time as the Hanssens. They were building their dream home on the ocean coast of Delaware, and it was a bad time of the year to be listing real estate. Still, they decided to go ahead and test the waters.

On November 19, 2000, they did so, asking an inflated price of $375,000. They got one offer for $315,000, and then on December 1, they received an all-cash offer of $362,500, with the mysterious buyer, Ann Manning, ignoring the loose bathroom tiles and the fogged-up windows. She had but one condition. The Hoods had to move out by December 21. The Hoods, pinching themselves at their good fortune, scampered.

When the Hoods were out, a telephone crew arrived. Bob didn't notice the complicated installation, but a neighbor did. "They were out there putting in eight new lines," Henry Franklin, who lived next door, told the *Washington*

Post. "I know because they cut our cable in the process of digging the ditch, and I went out to see what they were doing."

Things seemed quiet after that. All the window shades were drawn, an old quilt covered the sliding glass doors, and the neighbors say they never saw anyone going in or out. After Bob was arrested, Frank Hood put it all together. He called his real estate agent, Claudia Callis, saying, "You know what? I think the FBI bought our house."

Hood based his theory on pictures he had just seen in a newspaper. In one of them, their house purchaser, Ann Manning, could be seen searching the yellow-taped perimeter of Bob and Bonnie's front yard. She had the initials FBI printed on the back of her navy windbreaker.

With Bob Hanssen locked away in a cell at a Northern Virginia detention center, the FBI began analyzing the damage. Perhaps the juiciest piece of news was that one of the first secrets he revealed to the KGB was the existence of a tunnel the United States had built to eavesdrop on the Soviet Union. The underground passage was constructed under Moscow's new embassy as it was being constructed during the 1970s and 1980s.

The cost of the tunnel was considerable—informed estimates put it at around $200 million—almost as much as the embassy complex itself. The plan was so audacious that anyone who really studied the project might well have wondered how the United States could pull it off secretly. It couldn't, and Bob Hanssen may not have been the first to tell the Russians of its existence.

It was an interesting tale, though, something that could have been inserted into a Bond movie. But it wasn't anything new. In the 1950s the CIA had dug a tunnel into East Berlin to tap Soviet telephone lines. A British double agent had betrayed the operation. In the early 1970s, the FBI had listened to conversations in the seven-story Soviet consulate in San Francisco from a tunnel that ran under the building.

An FBI agent who was suing the Bureau for firing him blurted out the story in a letter that was released in court. When the Soviets found out, they dug a deep trench around the building to check for spies. After a soaking rain, it looked more like a moat. In the 1980s, an NSA double agent, Ronald Pelton, told the KGB that Washington was eavesdropping on a Soviet navy underseas cable on the bottom of the Pacific Ocean.

Neither were the Russians innocent when it came to spy tunnels. In 1978, the NSA had found one under the former American embassy in Moscow that was loaded with electronic eavesdropping equipment and complete with a KGB agent wearing headphones. But despite the lack of success by both sides, that didn't stop the FBI and the NSA from launching their most ambitious spy tunnel project yet.

The history of the embassy and the tunnel that followed dated back to Bob Hanssen's college days at Northwestern. In 1969 the Soviets had decided to expand from their distinguished, but small, Sixteenth Street NW mansion. They chose a 12.5-acre promontory on a hill called Mount Alto after being rejected at locations they had wanted more— one in midtown Washington and the other in Chevy Chase, Maryland. In 1975, the United States gave permission to begin construction of five separate buildings on the land, including one of nine stories and one of eight. In hindsight, it proved to be colossal bad judgment on the part of the United States.

Mount Alto, at 350 feet above sea level, was the third-highest point in Washington and had direct visual sight lines to the Capitol, the White House, the Pentagon, and the State Department. In the early 1970s, direct-line surveillance was not fully understood in the United States. It was in the Soviet Union. The Russians couldn't believe their good luck when the United States independently suggested the location that fronted on Wisconsin Avenue.

By the time America realized its mistake, construction

had begun. The only deal the United States could cut was to force the Soviet Union to give it a reciprocal site in Moscow and a permit to construct a new high-rise embassy complex of its own. The Soviets did so, but wisely offered acreage next to the Moskva River on one of the lowest points in the Russian capital. U.S. government officials accepted the offer. The KGB then added injury to the unspoken insult by riddling nearly every piece of construction material with electronic listening devices. When the United States found the bugs in 1985, it halted construction and made the find a propaganda coup, complaining loudly. In 1987, a State Department study concluded that America had underestimated the intelligence capabilities of the Soviet Union and had been wrong in assuming that American technology would repulse any efforts the KGB made to electronically eavesdrop on the new buildings.

America's complaints were part of a tit-for-tat spy game. In 1980, Moscow charged that the United States had planted bugs in the high-rise apartment that was to house five hundred Soviets inside their new compound. FBI agents had been part of the construction crew that had built the residence. The Moscow newspaper *Izvestia* called it a scandal and said Washington wanted to listen to both "whispers in the bedroom and conversations in the drawing room."

It was spy-vs.-spy posturing, with the drawn-out contest paid for by the taxpayers. The U.S. tunnel was planned in the late 1970s, and in 1981 while the FBI was still helping to build the embassy complex above ground, they were building the tunnel underground with technical help from the NSA. To aid in the multimillion-dollar undertaking, the Bureau sent a memo to all undercover agents asking anyone who had a background in construction, engineering, or architecture to step forward. The hierarchy of the FBI began verbally telling those who did, "This is top secret, codeword, cut-off-your-balls-with-a-rusty-hatchet Classified, with a capital *C*!"

The Bureau and the NSA started the tunnel endeavor by purchasing a town house near the compound and began digging using equipment that had special silencers covering the drills. When they got under the embassy, they learned the Russians had their own maze of tunnels, and the U.S.'s tunnel had to weave around them. They would implant listening devices every few feet. They also tapped into the building's underground metal pilings, which had copper wiring embedded in them, and used lasers that captured sound waves as they beamed up. The project took years.

Yet in spite of the FBI's rusty-hatchet threats, it may have been the worst-kept secret in Washington. When it was finished, the FBI gave tours of the new toy to politicians and cabinet officials who had classified clearances. The news media knew about it as well. Jim Risen of the *New York Times*, Lowell Bergman of PBS's *Frontline*, and author Ron Kessler—who said he learned about it in 1985—were some of the more prominent members of the press who had knowledge of the tunnel long before Bob Hanssen's arrest and the stories about it that followed.

"I had information about this for quite a while," Bergman told National Public Radio's Robert Siegel. "I was unsure, without exposing my sources, how to proceed."

Those who lived around the Soviet embassy's perimeter appeared to have known about the tunnel for years. One of the entrances had been through the city's sewer system, and the neighbors were well aware of it. "Every day for about ten years, a van from the telephone company would arrive and these men would get out, open a manhole cover, climb down, and spend the day there," one resident said. "I could see them from my front porch and then look up and see the Soviet embassy. But this was what happened during the Cold War and I supported what they were doing."

The home purchased by the FBI was one of many "watch houses." Another, right on Wisconsin Avenue, was directly opposite the entrance. The curtains stayed permanently drawn and no mail was ever delivered. The "residents" came and went in eight-hour shifts through the rear of the three-story building. A black sedan was always parked in front. Sometimes a man with a crew cut sat in it, writing down the license plates of cars driving through the embassy gates.

Another residence, on Fulton Street, backed up to the embassy. Some of its windows had been painted black, and from time to time men huddled around telescopes would be spotted by dog walkers. When the men noticed they were being watched, the blinds would quickly shut.

"Once I came back from a party and I could see a telephoto lens sticking out of the upper window," a resident of the neighborhood, Beth Spatz, told the London *Independent* after revelations of the tunnel broke.

But the tunnel was a dud despite all the cost and planning that had gone into its construction. At first the G-men could hear conversations above them. But they had no way of telling whose voice they were hearing, and the Soviets were so guarded in their speech the FBI got little intelligence for its investment. In 1985, when the Russians were alerted to the tunnel, they began jamming the transmissions with their own equipment and sometimes had discussions designed to mislead the FBI. Whether Bob Hanssen was the first to tip the Russians to the tunnel's existence may not really matter. In this case, he may even have saved his country time and money by indirectly helping them to abandon a project that was going nowhere.

Moscow tried to turn the tunnel revelations into a public relations victory. They appeared to be shocked that America would do such a deed against an ally and made sure to mention the past tunnels that the United States had built to spy against them.

"If this report is true," a press release from the Russian Foreign Ministry thundered, "it will be a flagrant violation of the recognized norms of international laws that throughout the world govern relations with foreign diplomatic missions."

Tatyana Samolis, an intelligence spokesperson, took to NTV, the Russian television channel, and reminded Russians of America's past sins. "Digging tunnels is a favorite pursuit of Americans," she said. "The U.S. intelligence services harbor a passion for tunneling. Take, for instance, the Berlin tunnel in the 1950s."

On March 8, 2001, Moscow appeared to change tactics. News agencies began quoting Russian intelligence services as saying that the tunnel never existed. Rather, they claimed, it was just a U.S. invention aimed at discrediting poor Bob Hanssen. "America has little concrete evidence against Hanssen, especially that he is a double agent," a Russian counterintelligence source told the press corps. "The FBI dug a tunnel under him."

The source went on to claim that the United States had spied on the new embassy but only by tapping into underground telephone lines, and using existing sewage pipes to get under the compound and tap into the central pillars of the embassy. The source was careful to stay close to his country's party line, charging that the United States was perpetrating a "blatant violation of all recognized norms of international law," repeating almost verbatim the "flagrant violation," quote that had come two days earlier from the Russian Foreign Ministry.

Whenever a spy is caught, the other side, in standard operating procedure, retaliates by arresting one or more of the other's citizens visiting its country and charging them with espionage. Another tactic is for both sides to begin expelling diplomats, who have immunity, while pointing the finger at them. The magnitude of the Robert Hanssen case was so great, both avenues were taken. John "Jack" Tobin, a twenty-four-year-old American Fulbright scholar studying at Voronezh State University in western Russia, 350 miles south of Moscow, was the fall guy.

Tobin, who spoke fluent Russian, was studying the nation's politics at the school. Reportedly, he also had a wild side that liked parties, dancing, drinking vodka, women, and sometimes even a good brawl. On January 26, 2001, the risky lifestyle caught up with him. He had gone to a casino and dance club called Night Flight. There, the waitresses wore special brassieres that glowed in the dark when the black lights illuminating the club shone upon them. That night, according to Tobin, he met two women who suggested they buy some drugs. Soon after, the local police arrested him and accused him of drug possession. The charge: possession of a matchbox containing a plastic bag with 0.15 ounces of marijuana inside, hidden in a pocket of his shirt. Searching his apartment, the cops claimed to find more—1.5 ounces—and, upon learning Tobin had thrown parties there for his Russian friends, said he was "operating a drug den."

Normally, such charges against a young American college student would be dropped, and after a scare of a couple of days in jail the youth would be sent home. But in a reestablished Cold War, with a former KGB colonel, Vladimir Putin, running Russia and the Bob Hanssen case dominating the news broadcasts, the charges against Tobin instead seemed to magnify. A few weeks after Tobin was arrested the Russian security service began to say that he had ties to American intelligence, upping the ante by using the word *hashish* instead of *marijuana*.

On the surface, there was some circumstantial evidence. Tobin had been in the army, studied languages at the Defense Language Institute in Monterey, California, and gone to Intelligence School at Fort Huachuca, Arizona. What didn't make sense was this: Why would a U.S. spy agency choose to hire a youth with such a loose lifestyle?

Russia kept piling on accusations, saying Tobin had been spotted near the local power plant—a location forbidden to foreigners—and that he was using a tape recorder. The city's main park was also near the power plant, and the tape recorder was used to record interviews for his paper on politics, his Russian attorney, Maxim Bayev, pointed out.

Tobin became one of the pawns taken off the board following the Bob Hanssen arrest. After a short trial in April, he received thirty-seven months in a penal colony that was famed only for its recurring tuberculosis epidemics. In the summer of 2001, he was appealing the conviction on the grounds the sentence was too harsh for the crime.*

Even before Tobin was convicted or, for that matter, Bob Hanssen indicted, America had taken a measure of revenge. On the morning of March 22, Secretary of State Colin L. Powell told Russian ambassador Yuri V. Ushakov that four suspected SVR agents had to be out of the country within ten days, and forty-six others had until July 1 to get out. It was the biggest expulsion since 1986. The State Department tried to whisper that the thinning of the Russian spy corps had been contemplated for months, meetings had taken place (ironically many attended by Bob Hanssen), and the reduction in size had been a foregone conclusion. Others blamed it on the new Bush administration and its harder edge. Few bought the stories. All of those expelled were said to have had ties to the accused FBI spy, and the four who were to immediately leave were the handlers who had made the dead drops. Vladimir Frolov, an SVR intelligence officer who supervised the B operation, had flown home two weeks earlier, almost immediately after Bob's arrest.

Bob Hanssen, it appeared, was a much bigger fish than Rick Ames. When Ames had been arrested, only the local spymaster had been sent packing. Moscow had in turn put a U.S. diplomat on a plane headed west, and that had been the end of it.

But now it was Moscow's turn. First there was the bluster. "This is an unfriendly act, aimed at worsening Russian-

---

* In Early August, after intensive lobbying by U.S. officials, Tobin was released and returned to the United Sates.

American relations. It follows that this will not remain without consequences and will receive an adequate answer," said Russian foreign minister Georgy Mamedov. He rambled on about the uprooting of embassy families and how it would affect them, sounding a bit like Dr. Laura on a rant. The head of Russia's tax police protested by canceling his tour of the FBI and several planned meetings with Director Louis Freeh where they were to have exchanged information.

The next day Russia bounced four Americans in Moscow and promised that forty-six others would be asked to leave by summer as soon as they could come up with the names. "We have time to think, to carefully pick from among more than a thousand U.S. diplomats in Russia, and choose those who are most precious to the Americans," said Sergei Ivanov, who headed Russia's Security Council.

Three days later the Russians produced a grainy videotape and some phone taps that they said showed an American spy operation in action. They also identified Paul A. Hollingsworth as one of the four and claimed he was the CIA station chief in Moscow. Their tape showed Anatoly Popov, reputed by the Russians to be a convicted airline hijacker who had served his term, in a restaurant with Robert Brannon, the U.S. naval attaché in Moscow. Brannon was described as paying Popov $400 for some maps of a minefield in Serbia. Brannon denied everything and said the SVR had "pulled it from the clouds. These fellows are capable of fabricating the most extraordinary pieces. We're all quite open people, trying to do a tough job in a tough country. We're victims of circumstance."

America's ambassador to Russia, James Collins, thought the brouhaha would soon blow over: "There will be no confrontation. No one wants this."

SIXTEEN

The Road to Oblivion

When Bob didn't return home after taking Jack Hoschouer to Dulles Airport, Bonnie became worried. Several hours went by and he didn't call. She thought it was strange and got it into her head that maybe Hoschouer's flight had been delayed and the two men were still at the airport together. She drove out to the airport, tailed by FBI agents who wanted to make sure she wasn't meeting with a Russian herself.

When it appeared she wasn't, she was surrounded by SSG men, who took her to a hotel where she was questioned for six hours. The Bureau wanted to be sure that the Hanssens were not the Walker family redux. The interrogation went on longer than the Bureau had anticipated when Bonnie shocked her interrogators by telling them about Bob's dealings with Moscow while they were living in Scarsdale. Finally satisfied, the G's let her two children living at home join her. They spent the night in the hotel while the FBI secured the family's Talisman Drive home and its so-suburban basketball hoop in the driveway, surrounding the property lines with yellow police tape. It gave the neighbors quite a start when they headed off to work on Monday morning.

Of course, Bonnie didn't at first believe what the FBI said about her husband. If he had done it, she told everyone who would listen, he had to have been blackmailed or framed or worse. She was allowed to see Bob in prison for two minutes the day after he was arrested.

Bonnie appeared to be in shock and at times couldn't speak. Richard McPherson, the headmaster at the Opus Dei–affiliated school, the Heights, where their son Greg was a junior, attempted to speak for her:

"She is obviously devastated. Her voice was very weak. She could barely get the words out. She has known this man for thirty-five years. It is a struggle for her to enunciate words and she can't finish a sentence. She is praying that it turns out to be blackmail, because if it turns out he got himself into a bind and couldn't get out of it, then that would be some comfort."

Jack, Sue, and Mark rushed home from their respective universities, and Jack, the law student at Notre Dame, sat his mother down and read her the FBI's 103-page affidavit. Only then did she begin to realize that the charges had validity. She hadn't ever really known her husband and, for that matter, neither had their children.

Bonnie and her family were allowed to leave the hotel, but the FBI wasn't ready to let them back in the house. They were still searching it. The Hanssens went to a friend's house to stay, and all promptly came down with the flu. The Heights headmaster urged Bonnie to keep Greg and Lisa in school.

"Let's get Greg back into a routine," he advised her. "He's got to do it sometime."

Unsure of what to do, Bonnie hired a lawyer, Janine Brookner, to represent her. Brookner, a former CIA agent, had sued the spy agency in 1994, winning $410,000 after she charged the Agency with trying to destroy her reputation. She wasted no time telling the press that Bonnie and the children were innocent of any espionage.

"My understanding is that they know she wasn't involved," Brookner said. "I don't think the government is blaming the family at all."

Bob also needed an attorney, and Bonnie, no fool, called one of the best, though she told him she had no idea where the money would come from to pay him. Plato Cacheris, a former Korean War–era U.S. marine who had gone to law school under the G.I. Bill, was reputed to be a brilliant trial lawyer and negotiator. His roster of former clients was a disparate list. Cacheris had represented Aldrich Ames and Monica Lewinsky, Washington Redskins owner Jack Kent Cooke, and former attorney general John Mitchell during the Watergate investigation. "He helped build my tennis court," he quipped after seeing his client off at a minimum security prison.

Oliver North's assistant Fawn Hall was Cacheris's client during the Iran-contra scandal. In that matter, Cacheris visited prosecutor Lawrence Walsh's office and reportedly made this speech: "Look, Fawn Hall is a secretary. Yes, perhaps she did something wrong by removing documents and shredding documents. But you were not appointed to prosecute secretaries. Give her immunity. She'll be a good witness for you." Walsh agreed and Hall stayed free.

When Cacheris was appointed to represent Ames, the double agent was said to have smiled for the first time since being arrested. "I was wondering what I would do for a lawyer, and I get Plato Cacheris," he said, beaming. Cacheris advised Ames to plead not guilty and go to trial. But Ames thought that a long struggle in court would make the federal government furious. The Justice Department, in turn, would then take their anger out on his wife, Rosario, he thought. They would give her a harsher sentence. So he refused and pled guilty.

The seventy-one-year-old Cacheris could be a bit of a dandy. He liked to wear $1,500, London-tailored, Tasmanian-wool suits to court, dine at the best restaurants, and make regular visits back to his Greek roots in Athens. These luxuries compensated for humble beginnings. His immigrant father, Christos, had once owned a series of diners and Plato had bused tables at them. Now, he had few financial burdens. At his regular billing rate the British suits were paid for in less than three hours. He gave a quick press conference at Bob's first arraignment on February 20, 2001.

"He is an FBI agent. For twenty-five years. As far as I know, he has got a good character," Cacheris said to the press mob surrounding him. When asked to evaluate what he had been told about the case, he seemed to bristle: "They always talk like they've got a great case. But we'll see."

Bonnie went without the children to the first hearing, held at a newly built Alexandria, Virginia, federal courthouse. Bob hadn't been issued a prison uniform yet and was still wearing the same black shirt layered over his black turtleneck that he had had on when he'd left the house with Jack Hoschouer. As Cacheris and the federal prosecutor, Randy I. Bellows, went through the preliminary motions in front of Judge Theresa Carroll Buchanan, Bob kept turning his head to look back at Bonnie. She appeared stricken, as if she were watching him die before her eyes. When it was over and the correctional officers were walking him out the side door to a holding cell, he kept his head turned toward her. He disappeared into the void, manacled and guided by a marshal. There was little doubt that Bob knew he was entering—to use the word diplomat Felix Bloch liked to utter—oblivion.

Bob was a pack rat. Armed with search warrants, the FBI went through his office, house, cars, and yard, looking in and under everything, even raking the grass and looking into a tool shed, where they removed mundane items such as bicycles and a manure spreader. Amid some leaves, they solemnly picked up a matchbox and a shotgun shell. In the house there were twelve handguns, which included the two Walther PPKs, a shotgun, and a Russian-made AK-47 automatic weapon. They also confiscated a set of lock-picking tools and a bottle of Stolichnaya vodka. There were marked-up maps of Hong Kong, Rome, the island of Oahu, and Tokyo; and several books on how to catch spies. In his car, besides a radio scanner, there were two photos of the film actress Catherine Zeta-Jones.

Within a week, the supermarket tabloid *Star* would run a story entitled "The Spy Who Loved Catherine Zeta-Jones," which speculated that Bob had fallen in love with her while watching *Entrapment*, a 1999 caper film about an art thief and a stolen Rembrandt featuring his favorite James Bond, Sean Connery. The scandal sheet was, in fact, right on target. Bob had let slip to his FBI coworkers that he did indeed have a bit of a middle-aged crush on the Welsh beauty, an admission that was remembered as it seemed so out of character for him.

In his computer room there were several diaries and ledgers, meticulously kept. There were thumbtacks and a twelve-piece box of chalk. And there was a book by his former supervisor David Major, titled *U.S. Counterintelligence, Ethics, and Conflict.* "Obviously, he didn't read my book," Major told the magazine *U.S. News and World Report.*

There were statements from two Swiss banks—Credit Suisse and Bank Leu—and several American banks. There was an unsigned letter that was apparently written by Bob to a Marxist magazine, *Proletarian Revolution*, and two envelopes addressed to J. Stapleton Roy. In the car there was also a rosary, Bob's passport, a photo of the grave of one of Bob's heroes, General George Patton, a manual entitled *Soviet Active Measures in the Post Cold War*, and a counterintelligence poster.

The FBI froze Bob's bank accounts and stopped his salary, but gave Bonnie a small allowance. The stipend was helped by donations from Opus Dei and Saint Catherine's Church members who slipped her cash and checks. Even the public-school crossing guards at the end of her street pitched in and gave her $100.

Richard McPherson speculated that she might leave town: "Bonnie's wondering what to do now, whether she should move out of the area. Her world is shattered."

The Bureau notified the rest of Bob and Bonnie's family one at a time. Vivian Hanssen was alone in Venice, Florida, with a newly framed photo of Bob on the end table beside her when she got the news. Howard had passed away on July 22, 1993, and was buried in a Chicago cemetery. His will had left everything to his wife.

The picture of Bob was a Christmas gift he had given to his mother. It was the same photo that was flashed in newspapers around the world when he was arrested. The FBI had taken it for his twenty-fifth anniversary with the Bureau, and when he was arrested, his congratulatory photo was looking out from the *Investigator*, the FBI's employee magazine, and gracing many a G-man's coffee table. Soon, it seemed, every reporter in the country was calling or knocking on Vivian's door—from *Dateline* to Connie Chung—and when she wouldn't talk, they would go to the neighbors next door and speak to them instead.

"I have no statement. I'm in a state of shock," Vivian told Matthew Henry of the *Sarasota Herald-Tribune*. Then she added, her voice breaking, "I just love him, that's all." Later she added, "I can't believe it. I can't believe he would lead two lives."

Her next-door neighbors Truman and Betty Reed said that Bob had visited his mother each summer with the children and that Howard and Vivian had been enthralled with their son's success at the FBI. Mrs. Reed thought the allegations weren't true: "It's too hard to believe. You can't believe what's in the paper."

Truman Reed's reaction differed. "Well, they ought to give it to him, right out in the street," he said, running a fingernail across his throat. "Anybody that does that, I don't care if I knew them."

A week later, after Vivian Hanssen had composed herself, she was asked the big question: Did he do it? "In the beginning, I thought he might have been pretending to be a double agent," she said. "But it doesn't look that way now. What a shame."

Just outside Chicago, Roy and Fran Wauck, semiretired and living in a third-story condominium unit, fielded calls. Roy Wauck worried about what Bonnie and the children were going to do for health insurance and how they were going to make the mortgage payments on the house. When Bob was arrested, the FBI had simultaneously fired him. "Thirty-five years and I never knew this man," Roy Wauck said. "The big thing now is to get the children settled down. It's been the hardest on the two youngest."

At the FBI field office in Chicago, Bonnie's brother Special Agent Mark Wauck was taken aside and debriefed. The Bureau had not told him in advance that they were surveilling his brother-in-law. There was always the chance he might have been involved.

On Talisman Drive, neighbors were unanimous in describing Bob Hanssen's taciturn mannerisms. "The thing that stuck out about him was that he was arrogant when he dealt with people," said neighbor Robert Snyder. Others said that when they said hello, he would never answer. On the other hand, everyone had good words for Bonnie and her sunny personality.

A teenager, Ryan Bennett, said he had been in the off-limits basement throne room and remembered several computers and a sink. "I called him Bob once, and he let me know I wasn't to do it again," Ryan said.

On March 5, 2001, Bob was given a bond hearing inside the same fourth-floor Alexandria federal courtroom of Judge Theresa Buchanan. Plato Cacheris was flanked by two partners with his firm, Preston Burton and John S. Hundley. The tone had changed. This time the room was so full of news reporters that the press was allowed to sit in chairs normally reserved for members of a jury. No members of the Hanssen family were present. Bob wore a dark green prison jumpsuit with PRISONER printed on the back and government-issue black tennis shoes. Patches of his hair had gone white, and there were enough dark black circles under his eyes to give him the appearance of a large owl.

Randy Bellows adjusted his glasses and began by asking that no bail should be considered for the accused, saying that "Robert Hanssen possesses in his head alone enough secrets to cause significant damage to the United States. Given the sentence he faces, he poses a severe risk of flight."

Cacheris didn't fight it: "We don't object to the detention, nor do we subscribe to the facts Mr. Bellows has presented." Later Cacheris explained, "That's not a finding of guilt, it's just detention. There are a lot of gaps in that affidavit if you look at it. We're not discussing a deal. There's no pressure."

He also claimed that the story of the tunnel under Mount Alto could be a sham, cautioning reporters, "This defunct tunnel under the Russian embassy that some unnamed officials are now disclosing, I think it is abominable and you should be skeptical about that. Nobody's ever heard about it before. Why would they be telling that story now?"

Would Hanssen then plead not guilty? Cacheris was asked. "That's absolutely right," he answered.

Judge Buchanan denied bail, as expected. "The government has an extraordinarily strong case and he presents a severe risk of flight," she said. "I am in favor of detainment. He had access to top-secret information and could pose damage to the American people."

After Aldrich Ames had been convicted, new laws had been passed that made giving up the identity of a U.S. agent that caused the agent's death a capital punishment case. Few believed it would come to the death penalty. It was a bargaining chip, was the conventional thinking. But the new Bush administration—headed by the man the Hanssens had so much wanted to be president—did seem to want death. *U.S. News and World Report* buttressed the rumor in its "Whispers" column:

MACHO MAN

Attorney General John Ashcroft is at loggerheads with Helen Fahey, the federal prosecutor in charge of the Robert Hanssen spy case. Fahey wants a life sentence for the FBI agent and alleged Russian spy. The administration wants death. Fahey reasons that it will be tough to get a death penalty in the post–Cold War world. But Bushies, says a Justice source, have a case of the "machos."

Ashcroft couldn't wait for Bob Hanssen's next hearing to begin lobbying for Hanssen's execution. As attorney general he had to approve the seeking of the death penalty in a federal case, and on March 27, he stated that he would consider capital punishment for Bob Hanssen. He elaborated in a news conference. "The laws provide for, in some cases, the death penalty, and I would not hesitate to include the death penalty among the options that are to be considered, based on making sure that we pursue the national interest at the highest level. I take the death penalty seriously because I think that it is, obviously, the ultimate sanction."

Later in the day he seemed to amend his words. Reading between the lines, one could gather that the threat of execution would more than likely be used to extract information from Bob Hanssen. "There is a national interest in making sure that we send a signal that we take seriously any compromises of national security. But, we would also take very seriously the need or opportunity to ascertain things important for us to know about the nature of what had happened that might be available to us in the context of a plea bargain," he said in government-speak.

Rather than take his hat in hand to Ashcroft's office and attempt to make a deal, Cacheris pounced. He wrote a letter to Ashcroft lecturing him that his remarks were not appropriate and cited the Attorney General's own manual: "The death penalty may not be sought, and no attorney for the Government may threaten to seek it, for the purpose of obtaining a more desirable negotiating position," he said. Several legal experts agreed that Ashcroft's words were a violation of the U.S. Department of Justice rules, and federal guidelines did prohibit using the death penalty as a threat.

If the chastisement by Cacheris was intended to caution Ashcroft, it had little effect. The government refused to negotiate with Bob's attorneys. On May 15, the government indicted Bob Hanssen on twenty-one counts of espionage, conspiracy to commit espionage, or attempted espionage. Fourteen of the counts provided for the death penalty as the maximum if convicted. The others called for life in prison.

"We felt they had more than enough time to resolve the issue of the death penalty," Cacheris said. "We do not think the death penalty is justified."

The parties were unable to reach an agreement. A protracted trial appeared to loom ahead that seemed certain not only to reveal secrets the U.S. government would like to keep hidden, but to prolong the anguish of Bonnie Hanssen and the six children she had produced with Bob.

On May 31, 2001, Robert Philip Hanssen was driven to the same federal courthouse escorted by guards with automatic weapons. Plato Cacheris and his two associates waited for him there. Except for the same lawyers and press corps, everything appeared to be different. There was a new judge, Claude Hilton, an eighth-floor courtroom, and there also appeared to be a new Bob Hanssen.

He had lost nearly forty pounds in the three and a half

months he had been in prison. His hair had become grayer and the bald spot at the back of his head was larger. Still, Bob appeared confident, almost jocular. He smiled virtually the entire time before the proceeding began, trading quips with Cacheris, leaning back in his chair, and at times craning his neck to see who was present. He was not disappointed. David Major, his old FBI boss was there, as was his eldest daughter Jane's husband, Richard.

When Judge Hilton asked how he would plead, Bob stood and leaned into the microphone, clearly saying "not guilty" and requesting a jury trial. The trial was set for October 29, 2001.

Plato Cacheris was asked why Bonnie wasn't present. "She is seeking anonymity but is here in spirit," he said. David Major told everyone he was shocked by the amount of weight Bob had lost.

After the plea, Cacheris hired a psychiatrist, Alen J. Salerian, to examine Bob and evaluate his sanity. Salerian had been a psychiatric consultant to the FBI during the Branch Davidian crisis in Waco, Texas, and frequently authored articles on espionage and intelligence matters. Not surprisingly, he had already written an article analyzing Bob Hanssen even before he met him, writing that "Hanssen appears to fit the classic profile. Spies and undercover agents have certain common denominators, most particularly courage, low anxiety levels, and high intelligence. They must also be tremendously self-satisfied because spying is a lonely business."

But after Salerian spoke to Bob for forty hours, he began leaking to the press that Bob was "tortured by psychological demons" and suffered from "factor x—a psychological wound." He claimed that Bob was secretly obsessed with pornography and had been beaten and abused by his father. He also said that when Bob confessed these sins to Opus Dei priests, he was simply told to pray more. "He is not mad, but thinks he's going mad because of the contents of his thoughts," Salerian said. "He snaps, and the snapping is in the form of spying."

Cacheris quickly fired Salerian and accused him of breaking his confidentiality agreement. Family members also began to get into the act, leaking Bob's earlier Scarsdale activities with the Russians—information that had at first been kept quiet by both the FBI and the Hanssen family.

Bonnie Hanssen's biggest concern was money. She didn't know when the allowance the FBI was giving her would stop or when the money Opus Dei members were slipping her would dry up. She wondered whether or not she was entitled to any part of Bob's FBI pension or if she should try to sell the house and move away. Her future was as uncertain as her husband's.

Bonnie knew some facts were carved in stone, dictated by her faith. She repeated the answer every time the question came up, which was often.

"I'll never divorce him. I love him and I'll pray for the salvation of his soul every day for the rest of my life."

EPILOGUE

During May of 2001, Plato Cacheris and the government hammered out an agreement that saved Robert Hanssen's life. He would plead guilty and tell the government everything he could remember about his two decades of espionage. In return, the traitor would be given a life sentence without parole and his wife would receive the equivalent of an FBI widow's pension—$37,648 a year—for the rest of her life.

Many in the Bureau grumbled about the payments to his wife, pointing out that at the very least Bonnie Hanssen was guilty of obstructing justice. After all, she did not report her husband to legal authorities when she first noticed he was selling secrets to the Soviets in 1979. In a defense, Bonnie told the *New York Times* that she had passed a polygraph test which proved she had no further knowledge of her husband's activities.

Others later lamented the timing of his capture. "If Hanssen had been arrested after September 11, 2001, there would have been no deal or pension and he would be on death row by now," one official told me.

The solution appeared orchestrated. The understanding was first announced the day before the American Independence celebration—July 4th, 2001. Then, 24 hours later, President Bush announced a new head of the FBI, Robert S. Mueller III.* (In talks, Mueller had argued for the death penalty.) Next, Bob Hanssen appeared in a hushed Alexandria, Virginia, courtroom on July 6th to verbally admit he was guilty of fifteen of the charges against him.

After entering the chambers that Friday, he scanned the room looking for friends or family. There were none, but many in the first two rows were FBI employees and some were his former colleagues. They got a smirky sort of grin as he recognized them. They grimaced back as if smelling a foul odor. Plato Cacheris tried to explain why the Hanssen family was absent.

"They visit him each week," he said, "but they value their privacy."

In the months that followed Bob Hanssen was interviewed for 200 hours over seventy-five different days and polygraphed twice. In spite of the exhaustive interrogations the government was largely unsatisfied with his answers.

"I have a poor memory," he told them by way of explanation. When a polygraph examiner told him he was being evasive, a physical altercation ensued between the two men. The interrogation team became angry.

"His claim of a poor memory was an excuse for not engaging fully in the debriefing or was a means to hide facets of his activity," a government assessment concluded. "Hanssen's answers were often contradictory, inconsistent, or illogical. His cooperation concerning his finances, the significance of his espionage and his motives were problematic."

Many government officials wanted to renege on the

*Following Mueller's appointment, the disgraced Louis Freeh joined a Delaware credit card company, MBNA. Many of the firm's executives are former FBI employees.

agreement, but Plato Cacheris's skills ultimately carried the day and the deal remained in place. With so many fingers pointed at the Bureau after the terrorist attacks of 9-11-01, the FBI was so distracted it was unable to change the understanding. Still, many agents believed satisfaction was just ahead.

"Hanssen won't adjust well to life in prison," an FBI official predicted. "His arrogance will have to be knocked out of him—either by correctional officers or the other prisoners."

At his sentencing on May 10th, Bob appeared to have aged ten years. Gaunt, pale, slender, and stooped over, he said he regretted committing his crimes. He also apologized to his absent wife and children who he said were innocent and had been slandered in the press. He seemed to be responding to reports that he had photographed himself having sex with Bonnie and then had allowed his pal, Jack Hoschouer, to view the results.

Another "revelation," which claimed that Bonnie's brother, Mark Wauck, told FBI headquarters in 1990 that $5,000 was lying around the Hanssen household and that the Bureau failed to act may be incorrect. In her lie detector test, Mrs. Hanssen both denied the story and passed the polygraph question.

Despite the personal sexual reports, Bonnie and the children continued their visits on a weekly basis. In an act of solidarity, his mother, Vivian Hanssen, moved from Florida to Talisman Drive to live with the family.

Robert Hanssen's new home is Allenwood, a federal institution near Lewisburg, Pennsylvania, a three-and-a-half hour drive from his home in Virginia. Called a country club prison during the 1970s when it was home to several Watergate figures, the new, improved Allenwood is high-security and not immune to violence.

*   *   *

In what appeared to be a cryptic warning, Plato Cacheris assessed the espionage skills of Robert Hanssen following his client's sentence: "He was as artful a spy as we've ever seen. Except for the one who's out there now and hasn't been caught."

APPENDIX

On March 2, 2001, in his column for the *Washington Post*, Al Kamen described what life is like for other members of the elite club of convicted U.S. spies and gunrunners at Allenwood Federal Penitentiary. Kamen reported that Edwin Wilson, a former CIA agent, who is in his nineteenth year of a fifty-two-year sentence for gun and bomb smuggling to Libya, had spoken to Aldrich Ames, the CIA turncoat, about their soon-to-be prisonmate, Robert Hanssen.

Kamen wrote that Wilson told Ames he did not know Hanssen, although he "thought he had met him in New York." Wilson talked to Ames in the law library at Allenwood, where Wilson is assigned and where "they both hang out." According to Wilson, it was dangerous for him to speak to Ames in public places. Many inmates, unschooled in the gray areas of counterintelligence, did not take kindly to traitors, and anyone seen speaking to Ames might find themselves on the wrong side of the more common class of inmates, Kamen wrote.

Ditto for John Walker, the former navy communications officer who recruited his family to spy for the Soviets. Kamen reported that Wilson's and Walker's paths cross three

times a day because Walker teaches a course in business
that is held near the library. Wilson said Walker also did
not know Robert Hanssen but he did have an educated
opinion about Hanssen:

"He don't talk much," Wilson said of Walker. But Walker did discuss with Wilson "what a professional operation
[Hanssen's] was, and the fact that [the government] hadn't
picked it up." Kamen wrote that Wilson avoided public
conversations with Walker, although one time they did chat
in the mess hall. "Boy, I caught a lot of shit about it. All
those Mafia guys, they're all anti-communist, and they were
real upset about it," Wilson said.

Wilson and his two prisonmates said they were monitoring the Hanssen case with great interest on TV and in
the newspapers. (Wilson subscribed to *USA Today*, Ames
to the *International Herald Tribune*, reported Kamen.) As
Kamen observed, "Maybe [the trio will] finally get their
fourth for bridge."

Dear Mr. Ames:
I received your letter regarding Bob Hanssen saying you
"are in no position to comment" on his personality, but
I'm not sure by that statement if you are prevented from
commenting or that you don't have enough information
to comment. As the saying goes, "persistence is omnipotent" so forgive me if I try again.

As I am writing a book about Mr. Hanssen and have
so far interviewed more than 100 people in both his past
and present, I believe I have information that not only
has never been printed, but offers surprising revelations
as to his motivations. My ultimate plan is to visit you
in person, share this information, and then get your observations.

                                        Adrian Havill
                                        April 21, 2001

Dear Mr. Havill:

I don't know about persistence being omnipotent, but it certainly is a virtue without which very little of value would get done in this world.

And serious titillation as well! It is a great temptation to sit down with you and be one of the first to learn interesting and startling things. But I must control myself, for reasons I'll explain.

I feel strongly—as do most prisoners, I think—that one prisoner ought not to talk publicly about another. For all practical purposes, Mr. Hanssen is now one of us, though I'll be pleased to see him extract a better plea bargain and sentence than I managed. So far as I know, the government has no hostages to blackmail him with.

This particular reason was brought home to me a month or so ago, when a convict here was so careless as to discuss me with a *Washington Post* columnist— and so mendacious as to suggest I'm in danger from other prisoners. The Bureau of Prisons reaction was not so extreme as to lock me up in solitary—which was considered—but did result in loss of telephone privileges and disapproval of two interview requests of great interest and value to me (not about Hanssen of course).

Now, I doubt I would have anything particularly bad or prejudicial to say about Hanssen, but that's not really the point. There's not much ethics in prison, but what I can hold to, I will.

And it appears to me that a request to interview me, especially about Mr. Hanssen would be turned down. I think that the recent policy of no Ames interview does not come from the warden here, but from Washington. We'll have to wait until post-Hanssen to see.

I should reassure you though, that I am not being prevented from commenting on the Hanssen case at all. It is quite true, too, that I have little or nothing of my own to say. At the same time I regret that we can't sit down for a talk, you telling me new and interesting things, and me regaling you with my own fascinating reactions. But, I'll have to wait, regretfully.

A word of advice, based on my own experience. Whatever the truth of Mr. Hanssen's relationship and activities with the Russians, it will be a requirement of whatever plea agreement is settled on that he subscribe to what the government wants him to say about it.

Good fortune with the book.

Regards,
Rick Ames
April 30, 2001

BIBLIOGRAPHY

Though all the books that are relevant to *The Spy Who Stayed Out in the Cold* are listed, all newspaper and magazine articles, columns, radio and television programs, etc., are not. This is because thousands were consulted. Only primary sources are named here.

BOOKS

Adams, James. *Sellout*. New York: Viking Penguin, 1995.

Allen, Thomas B., and Norman Polmar. *Merchants of Treason*. New York: Delacorte, 1998.

Barker, Rodney. *Dancing with the Devil*. New York: Simon & Schuster, 1996.

Chesterton, G. K. *The Wisdom of Father Brown*. London: John Lane, 1915.

Crosby, Travis L. *The Two Mr. Gladstones*. New Haven: Yale University Press, 1997.

Currey, Cecil B. *Code Number 72/Ben Franklin: Patriot or Spy?* New Jersey: Prentice Hall Press, 1972.

Earley, Pete. *Confessions of a Spy*. New York: G. P. Putnam's Sons, 1997.

———. *Family of Spies*. New York: Bantam, 1988.

Escriva, The Blessed Josemaria. *The Way*. Princeton: Scepter Publishers, 1985.

Havill, Adrian. *Deep Truth*. New York: Birch Lane Press, 1993.

Kessler, Ronald. *The FBI*. New York: Pocket Books, 1993.

———. *The Spy in the Russian Club*. New York: Charles Scribner's Sons, 1990.

Knight, Amy. *Spies Without Cloaks*. Princeton: Princeton University Press, 1996.

Knott, Stephen F. *Secret and Sanctioned*. New York: Oxford University Press, 1996.

Leen, The Reverend Edward. *The Holy Spirit*. Princeton: Scepter Publishers, 1954.

Lloyd, Mark. *The Guinness Book of Espionage*. New York: Da Capo, 1994.

Lunev, Stanislav. *Through the Eyes of the Enemy*. Washington: Regnery, 1998.

Maas, Peter. *Killer Spy*. New York: Warner Books, 1995.

Mankiewicz, Frank. *Perfectly Clear*. New York: Quadrangle, 1973.

Martin, David C. *Wilderness of Mirrors*. New York: Harper & Row, 1980.

Miller, Nathan. *Spying for America*. New York: Marlowe, 1997.

Newton, Verne W. *The Cambridge Spies*. London: The McDonald Group, 1991.

Persico, Joseph E. *Casey*. New York: Viking, 1990.

Philby, Kim. *My Silent War*. London: MacGibbon & Kee Ltd, 1968.

Shvets, Yuri B. *Washington Station*. New York: Simon & Schuster, 1994.

Sontag, Sherry, and Christopher Drew, with Annette Lawrence Drew. *Blind Man's Bluff*. New York: PublicAffairs, 1998.

Stoll, Clifford. *The Cuckoo's Egg*. New York: Doubleday, 1989.

Tapia, Maria del Carmen. *Beyond the Threshold*. London: Continuum Publishing Group, 1998.

Tolstoy, Leo. *War and Peace*. New York: Modern Library Edition, 1994.

Weiner, Tim, David Johnston, and Neil A. Lewis. *Betrayal*. New York: Random House, 1995.

West, Nigel. *Games of Intelligence*. New York: Crown, 1989.

Winks, Robin W. *Cloak and Gown*. New York: William Morrow and Company, 1987.

Wise, David. *Nightmover*. New York: HarperCollins Publishers, 1995.

PERIODICALS AND NEWSPAPERS

"Accused Spy an NU Graduate." *Daily Northwestern*, 21 February 2001.

"Alleged Spy Feared End Was Near." ABC News.com, 1 March 2001.

"Alleged Spy Got His Start in Chicago." Associated Press, 21 March 2001.

"Alleged Spy Lawyers Accuse Ashcroft." Associated Press, 29 March 2001.

"Baker Fires Spy Suspect, State Dept. Contends Bloch Lied." *Raleigh News & Observer*, 6 November 1990.

"Bloch Case: Shnook or Spy?" *U.S. News & World Report*, 5 March 2001.

"Bring 'em in from the Cold." *New York Daily News*, 28 February 2001.

"Bush 'Extensively Involved' in Spy Case." UPI, 22 February 2001.

"Bush Voices Confidence in FBI Chief." Associated Press, 22 February 2001.

"Chile: Ricardo Lagos Elected President." *NotiSur*, 21 January 2000.

"CIA Became More Secure than FBI." Associated Press, 24 February 2001.

"Congress Grills Security Chiefs on Spy Case." UPI, 28 February 2001.

"Counterspy Training Helped Hanssen Lay Low." MSNBC.com, 21 February 2001.

"Ex-Diplomat Works at Grocery Store." Associated Press, 31 August 1992.

"FBI Agent Trained Too Well." Associated Press, 21 February 2001.

"FBI Official Urges Swap of Spy Tips, Soviet Aid." *Los Angeles Times,* 11 September 1991.

"FBI Spy Was in Pope Task Force." UPI, 26 February 2001.

"Flores to Help Peru with Tax Cuts." Reuters, 4 April 2001.

"Former CIA Head Careless with Sensitive Information." CBS.com, 2 February 2000.

"Freeh Is Free to Earn." *U.S. News & World Report,* 14 May 2001.

"Fun and Games with the KGB." *Time,* 30 August 1993.

"Hanssen Arrest May Clear CIA Officer." Reuters, 23 February 2001.

"Hanssen Describes 'Career' Choices." *Edison-Norwood Times Review,* 1 March 2001.

"Hanssen Lawyer Familiar with Spies." Associated Press, 21 March 2001.

"Hanssen's Access Brings Systems Probe." UPI, 5 March 2001.

"Hanssen to Remain Jailed until Trial." MSNBC.com, 5 March 2001.

"The Long Betrayal." *The Times of London,* 22 February 2001.

"MI6 Posts Gay Agents Abroad." *London Telegraph,* 2 February 1998.

"Operation Damage Control." *Time,* 24 June 1985.

"Palm Pilot Helped Send Secrets to Russians." *London Telegraph,* 23 February 2001.

"Peru's 'Girl Power' Aims for Presidency." Reuters, 26 April 2001.

"President Calls Lee Case 'Troubling.' " CNN.com, 14 September 2000.

"Project Echelon: We're All at Risk." ACLU Web site, 16 May 2001.

"Putin's Mask Slips to Show Face of Committed KGB Fan." *London Telegraph,* 18 March 2000.

"Recalled Russian Diplomat Said to Be Hanssen Handler." CNN.com, 19 March 2001.

"Robert Hanssen: Spy or Geek?" *The Industry Standard,* 23 February 2001.

"Russian Tip Set the Trap." *USA Today,* 17 March 2001.

"Spy Games: How FBI Tracked Hanssen." ABC News.com, 22 February 2001.

"Spy Suspect Wife Hopes Blackmail Involved." UPI, 7 March 2001.

"To Catch a Spy." CBS News.com, 28 February 2001.

"Two Sides to Alleged Spy, Neighbors, Classmates Shocked." *Chicago Sun-Times,* 22 February 2001.

"U.S. Considers Execution in Spy Case." Reuters, 27 March 2001.

"U.S. Spy Suspect Seemed Fervent Catholic." Reuters, 24 February 2001.

"Woman Vies to Lead Peru." Associated Press, 2 March 2001.

Bamford, James. "My Friend, the Spy." *New York Times,* 18 March 2001.

Belluck, Pam. "The Chicago Years: Time in Elite Police Force." *New York Times,* 21 February 2001.

Broadway, Bill, and David Cho. "FBI Spy Case Arrest Blows Parish's Cover." *Washington Post,* 3 March 2001.

Caryl, Christian. "From Russia with Indifference." *Newsweek International,* 21 February 2001.

Cha, Ariana Eunjung. "Carnivore Debate Centers on FBI Trustworthiness." *Washington Post,* 7 September 2000.

Cloud, John. "Plato Cacheris, Courtroom Impresario." *Time,* 15 June 1998.

Coco, Marie. "Can You Believe the FBI?" *Newsday,* 13 May 2001.

Cooper, Richard T., and Megan Garvey. "In the End, a Soul Lost and Lonely." *Los Angeles Times,* 25 February 2001.

Curnutte, Mark. "From Envoy to Bag Boy." *Raleigh News & Observer,* 18 September 1992.

Daley, Suzanne. "An Electronic Spy Scare Is Alarming Europe." *New York Times,* 24 February 2000.

Davies, Hugh. "KGB 'Infiltrated the White House.' " *London Telegraph,* 1 November 1995.

Drummond, Daniel, and Larry Witham. "Hanssen Belonged to Catholic Group That Proselytized Elites." *Washington Times,* 22 February 2001.

Earley, Pete. "Hanssen Holds Some Cards in His Favor." *USA Today,* 26 February 2001.

Eggen, Dan, and Brooke A. Masters. "U.S. Drops Demands for Hanssen's Execution." *Washington Post,* 15 June 2001.

Faiola, Anthony. "Peruvians, Shocked by Scandal, Turn to Female Candidate." *Washington Post,* 8 March 2001.

Fenton, Ben. "World of Secrets Has Long Been a Gay Affair." *London Telegraph,* 4 February 1999.

Flach, Michael F. "Opus Dei Members 'Shocked, Saddened' by Hanssen's Arrest." *Arlington Catholic Herald,* 1 March 2001.

Gertz, Bill. "Freeh Picks FBI Veteran as Counterintelligence 'Czar.' " *Washington Times,* 15 March 2001.

Grier, Chris. "A Unique Burden." *Sarasota Herald-Tribune,* 9 March 2001.

Heimberger, Ann. "Former Spying Suspect Accused of Food Theft." *Raleigh News & Observer,* 12 January 1993.

———. "Shoplifting Charge Resolved, Bloch to Pay Fine." *Raleigh News & Observer,* 30 January 1993.

Henry, Matthew. "Venice Mother Shocked over Son's Spy Arrest." *Sarasota Herald-Tribune,* 22 February 2001.

Jackman, Tom, and Brooke A. Masters. "For Hanssens,

Survival Needs Surpass Shock, Family Returns Home, Finances Shaky." *Washington Post,* 3 March 2001.

Jehl, Douglas. "Senators Criticize FBI on McVeigh Papers." *New York Times,* 14 May 2001.

Johnston, David. "Ashcroft Delays Death of McVeigh." *New York Times,* 12 May 2001.

———. "Lawyer Says Ashcroft Spoke Inappropriately in Spy Case." *New York Times,* 29 March 2001.

Kappstatter, Bob. "From Russia with Shove." *New York Daily News,* 23 March 2001.

Karon, Tony. "Wen Ho Lee Case: More like Dreyfus than Rosenbergs." *Time,* 11 September 2000.

Kessler, Ron. "Fire Freeh." *Washington Post,* 27 February 2001.

Kilian, Michael. "Cold War Legacy: Spying Never Stopped." *Chicago Tribune,* 25 February 2001.

Klein, Edward. "The Hunting of Wen Ho Lee." *Vanity Fair,* December 2000.

Lathem, Niles, and Andy Geller. "Accused Spy Won Trust by Playing the Patriot's Role." *New York Post,* 22 February 2001.

———. "FBI 'Spy' Contact Left KGB Bozo in the Dark." *New York Post,* 23 February 2001.

Leavitt, Linda. "Accused FBI Spy Lived Here—Briefly." *Scarsdale Inquirer,* 23 February 2001.

Lewis, Neil A. "Zigs and Zags of Spy Cases Put a Damper on Predicting." *New York Times,* 22 February 2001.

Lichtblau, Eric. "Bush Voices Confidence in FBI." *Los Angeles Times,* 23 February 2001.

———. "U.S. Bugging Program Feared Breached." *Los Angeles Times,* 28 February 2001.

Loeb, Vernon. "Defectors Say CIA Reneges on Promises." *Washington Post,* 11 July 2000.

———. "Spy Case Prompts Computer Search." *Washington Post,* 5 March 2001.

MacDonnell, Clare. "Bishop Blesses Padre Pio Shrine in Clifton." *Arlington Catholic Herald,* 1 June 1998.

————. "Santorums Receive Service Award." *Arlington Catholic Herald*, 13 May 1999.

Miller, Bill, and Walter Pincus. "Plea Deal in Ames Case Said to Hinge on Wife's Sentence." *Washington Post*, 23 April 1994.

————. "Rosario Ames Gets 5-Year Term." *Washington Post*, 22 October 1994.

Morello, Carol, and William Clairborne. "A Question of Why." *Washington Post*, 25 February 2001.

O'Brien, Chris. "Former Spy Suspect Charged with Shoplifting." *Raleigh News & Observer*, 21 December 1994.

————. "Former U.S. Diplomat Seeking Counseling." *Raleigh News & Observer*, 6 January 1995.

Ohu, Eugene Agboifo. "Escriva as Man of the Century." *Africa News Service*, 28 March 2001.

Philips, Alan. "KGB Regains Lost Power." *London Telegraph*, 27 January 1998.

Pincus, Walter. "Ames Pleads Guilty to Spying, Gets Life Term." *Washington Post*, 29 April 1994.

————. "Ames Turned Over Secrets from the Start Soviet Says." *Washington Post*, 11 February 1997.

————. "Documents Fuel Suspicions Ames Had CIA Accomplices." *Washington Post*, 26 February 2001.

————. "Hanssen Attorneys Plan to Fight Death Penalty." *Washington Post*, 25 May 2001.

————. "Hanssen Lawyer Says Ashcroft May Have Broken Justice Rules." *Washington Post*, 29 March 2001.

————. "Lee: Tapes Went in Trash." *Washington Post*, 1 December 2000.

Pound, Edward T., and Kevin Johnson. "Hanssen Had No Role in Hunt for Ames." *USA Today*, 13 April 2001.

Quindlen, Anna. "Lu Bloch Wants Her Reputation Back." *New York Times*, 2 February 1994.

Risen, James. "Days before Arrest, Suspected Spy Sought Job outside FBI." *New York Times*, 20 April 2001.

————. "FBI Agent Accused as Spy Had Active Swiss Bank Account." *New York Times*, 2 March 2001.

————. "Gaps in Ames Case May Be Filled by FBI's Own Spy Case." *New York Times,* 21 February 2001.

————. "Rules of Espionage—Get Caught? Lose Players." *New York Times,* 23 March 2001.

————. "Spy Handler Bedeviled U.S. in Earlier Case." *New York Times,* 22 February 2001.

Risen, James, and David Johnston. "Wife Says Suspect Told a Priest 20 Years Ago of Aiding Soviets." *New York Times,* 16 June 2001.

Rodriguez, Alex. "Chicago Native Quickly Made Mark." *Chicago Tribune,* 21 February 2001.

————. "U.S. Says FBI Agent Spied for Russia." *Chicago Tribune,* 21 February 2001.

Rogers, Dennis. "The Nostalgia of Spy Stalking." *Raleigh News & Observer,* 8 September 1992.

Roth, Soban. "Spy Prosecution: A High-Wire Act." *Legal Times,* 26 February 2001.

Safire, William. "The Molehill Mountain." *New York Times,* 22 February 2001.

Savino, Lenny. "Family of Accused Spy Could Get His $36,000 Annual Pension." Knight-Ridder, 5 April 2001.

Schmidt, Alan. "Remembering Hanssen's Norwood Years." *Edison-Norwood Times Review,* 1 March 2001.

Shenon, Philip. "Paradox of Pious Spy for Godless Foe." *New York Times,* 25 February 2001.

Sisk, Richard. "Spy Suspect Eyed Hack-Bust Job." *New York Daily News,* 23 February 2001.

Sneed, Michael. "Two Sides to Alleged Spy." *Chicago Sun-Times,* 22 February 2001.

Thomas, Evan. "Prayers to Save a Spy's Soul." *Newsweek,* 12 March 2001.

————. "Spy's Secret World." *Newsweek,* 5 March 2001.

————. "Washington's Quiet Club." *Newsweek,* 9 March 2001.

Torkelson, Jean. "Opus Dei: Sect or Sacrament?" *Rocky Mountain News,* 25 March 2001.

Walsh, Edward. "FBI Found Papers During Fifth Search." *Washington Post,* 12 May 2001.

Warren, James. "Alleged Spy Thought the Boss Could Teach Kremlin." *Chicago Tribune,* 25 February 2001.

White, Josh, and Brooke A. Masters. "Stripper Says Hanssen Tried to Rescue Her." *Washington Post,* 29 April 2001.

Willing, Richard. "Charge: Hanssen Foiled '89 Spy Pursuit, Felix Bloch." *USA Today,* 26 February 2001.

Willing, Richard, and Traci Watson. "FBI Portrays Robert Hanssen's Double Life." *USA Today,* 21 February 2001.

Zakaria, Tabassum. "Ashcroft Orders FBI Review." Reuters, 20 June 2001.

RADIO AND TELEVISION

"Accoutrements of Espionage." *Weekend Edition,* NPR, 9 June 1996.

"Aspects of Internet Privacy." *Talk of the Nation,* NPR, 20 July 2000.

"Espionage in the 21st Century." *Talk of the Nation,* NPR, 21 February 2001.

"Ex-Snoop Confirms Echelon." *60 Minutes,* 1 March 2000.

"Ex-Stripper Discusses Relationship with Robert Hanssen." *Larry King Live,* CNN, 21 May 2001.

"FBI Agent Is Espionage Suspect." MSNBC, 21 February 2001.

"Federal Judge to Decide Whether to Release Robert Hanssen on Bail." *All Things Considered,* NPR, 2 March 2001.

"Former Diplomat Working in Chapel Hill Targeted by FBI Affidavit." MSNBC, 22 February 2001.

"Friends of Robert Philip Hanssen." MSNBC, 24 February 2001.

"Hanssen's Early Start." CBS News, 15 June 2001.

"Lewinsky's New Legal Team." *Good Morning America,*
3 June 1998.
"Opus Dei." *Weekend Edition,* NPR, 25 July 1998.
"Rationalizing Treason (Aldrich Ames)." CNN, 12 March
1998.
"Russia Furious over Expulsions." MSNBC, 22 March
2001.
"To Catch a Spy." *Nightline,* ABC, 20 February 2001.
"Wen Ho Lee Investigation Opens Up Further Scrutiny of
John Deutch's Mishandling of Classified Materials."
NPR, 17 September 2000.

TESTIMONY AND DOCUMENTS

Affidavit in Support of Criminal Complaint. *United States
of America v. Robert Philip Hanssen,* 16 February 2001.
Affidavit in Support of Search Warrants. *United States of
America v. Robert Philip Hanssen,* 19 February 2001.
Criminal Indictment. *United States of America v. Robert
Philip Hanssen,* 16 May 2001.
Government's Motion for Protective Order. *United States
of America v. Robert Philip Hanssen,* 5 March 2001.
Superior Court of the District of Columbia. *Kimberly Lich-
tenberg v. Robert P. Hanssen,* 24 May 1994.
Testimony of David G. Carpenter before the House Inter-
national Relations Committee, 11 May 2000.
Testimony of J. Stapleton Roy before the House Interna-
tional Relations Committee, 11 May 2000.

INDEX